Financial Reporting Standards

Financial Reporting Standards

A Decision-Making Perspective for Non-Accountants

David T. Doran

business expert Press

Financial Reporting Standards A Decision-Making Perspective for Non-Accountants

First published in 2012 by
Business Expert Press, LLC
222 East 46th Street, New York, NY 10017
www.businessexpertpress.com

ISBN-13: 978-1-6064-9387-8 (paperback)

ISBN-13: 978-1-60649-388-5 (e-book)

DOI 10.4128/9781606493885

A publication in the Business Expert Press Financial Accounting and Auditing collection

Collection ISSN: 2151-2795 (print)
Collection ISSN: 2151-2817 (electronic)

Cover design by Jonathan Pennell
Interior design by Exeter Premedia Services Private Ltd., Chennai, India

First edition: 2012

10 9 8 7 6 5 4 3 2 1

Printed in the United States of America.

To my lovely, patient and understanding wife Mary Anne,
and our three children Patrick, Caley, and Matthew.

Abstract

Accounting is the score keeping system in the "game" of business—you can't do well in any "game" if you don't understand how the score is kept. This book is intended to benefit practicing managers, MBA students, and nonaccounting business majors. United States financial reporting standards are compared and contrasted with international financial reporting standards where appropriate. The book emphasizes how management's choice of accounting methods and their required estimates in reporting transactions and events impact financial statements, both immediately and in the future. Unlike typical accounting books, journal entries are not used to illustrate topical coverage.

This unique book exclusively provides a user's decision-making perspective by using the accounting equation format to directly illustrate financial statement effects of transactions and events. Most of the topics addressed in this book are typically studied by accounting majors in the two course "intermediate" accounting sequence, but the text also includes discussion of consolidations—a topic generally covered in the "advanced" accounting course. Intermediate accounting textbooks alone typically exceed well over 1,500 pages. By exclusively applying a user's perspective, and limiting topical content to areas relevant for decision making, this book allows nonaccountants to acquire the requisite underlying knowledge in a concise, easy to understand text.

Keywords

Financial Statements, GAAP, Cash Flow vs. Earnings, Accounting Equation Format, Accounting Method Choice, Accounting Estimates, Off-Balance-Sheet Financing, Economic Consequences of Accounting, Earnings Management, Substance Over Form, IFRS.

Contents

CHAPTER 1

Overview of Financial Accounting

Introduction

The objective of accounting is to provide information useful for users' decision making. Two primary areas of accounting are financial accounting and managerial accounting.[1] Financial accounting is intended to provide information to "external" users in meeting their decision making needs and is the exclusive topic of this text. Unlike managers, external users are not involved in the day-to-day decision making within the firm, but need information in making decisions. The two key external user groups with the greatest financial interest targeted to benefit from financial accounting information are current and potential creditors and investors. Since this text assumes the corporate form of business throughout, investors are stockholders. Creditors need to decide whether or not to lend money to the corporation and if so what interest rate should be charged to compensate for the level of risk. Stockholders need information to accommodate buy, hold, or sell decisions. Management has a vested interest in understanding financial accounting information because it impacts the corporation's stock price, and the corporation's ability to obtain loans and the related borrowing rates.

[1] Managerial accounting is intended to help "internal" users (management) in making decisions. Since management is in the best position to determine what specific information optimally suits their particular decision making needs, there are no rules or guidelines regarding what information is provided for managerial accounting purposes. As such, the study of managerial accounting involves examination of common conventions and practices, for example, cost-volume-profit analysis, budgeting and variance analysis, differential analysis, etc.

Both creditors and stockholders provide resources to the corporation in order to receive future cash flows; creditors in the form of principal and interest payments and stockholders in the form of dividends and proceeds from sale of the stock. Since the corporation has numerous creditors and stockholders, it cannot conceivably provide information to each on an individual user basis. Therefore, financial accounting information is intended to be useful in assessing the future cash flows of the firm. Three things are important regarding the firm's future cash flows for valuation purposes, their amounts, timing, and uncertainty. Considering each individually, the greater the amounts, the sooner they occur, and the lesser their uncertainty, the more valuable is the debt or stock investment. By meeting the information needs of investors and creditors, financial accounting information is useful in meeting the decision making needs of other external user groups. For example, customers look to financial accounting information in order to assess a firm's ability to continue providing goods and services in the future; and employees are interested in financial accounting information as it relates to the firm's ability to pay them salaries and wages in the future.

The financial statements (including disclosure notes) are the primary product of financial accounting and the information provided therein is the exclusive topic of this book. The three primary financial statements include a balance sheet, an income statement, and a statement of cash flows. Most firms also provide a statement of stockholders' equity. The financial statements of Behrend Corp. are illustrated in Exhibits 1.2–1.5. These financial statements are intended to be useful to external users in assessing the amounts, timing, and uncertainty of Behrend's future cash flows. These users compare Behrend Corp. with other corporations and over time in making their decisions. This is why the information provided in the financial statements needs to comply with certain rules and guidelines—so that it is comparable across firms and within the firm over time. The rules and guidelines that the financial statement information must comply with are referred to as generally accepted accounting principles (GAAP). GAAP information must be both "relevant" (make a difference) **and** provide "faithful representation"[2] (actually represent what is supposed to be represented) in order to be useful for decision making. An important part of the financial reporting process is the audit opinion, where independent Certified Public Accountants attest to the fairness of the information provided in the financial statements in conformity with GAAP.

The organization with legal authority to establish GAAP for publicly traded firms in the United States is the Securities and Exchange Commission (SEC). The SEC has primarily delegated the responsibility for setting U.S. GAAP to nongovernmental organizations. The current private sector organization with the responsibility to determine U.S. GAAP is the Financial Accounting Standards Board (FASB).[3] Although U.S. firms comply with FASB GAAP, most non-U.S. corporations report financial statements based upon a similar but not identical set of GAAP that is formulated by the International Accounting Standards Board (IASB). This IASB set of GAAP is commonly referred to as International Financial Reporting Standards (IFRS).[4] At the time of writing this text, the SEC has indicated it may in the future require U.S. firms to comply with IFRS. Financial accounting topics are addressed in

[2] Previously, the two primary qualities considered necessary for information to be useful for decision making were "relevance" and "reliability." In a September 2010 revision, the FASB changed the primary quality of "reliability" to "faithful representation." In doing so, the FASB pronouncement regarding the two primary qualities information must have to be useful for decision making is now consistent with those identified by the IASB relevance and faithful representation. Both of these organizations are discussed below.

[3] The FASB replaced the Accounting Principles Board that presided from 1959 to 1973. The original private sector organization that formulated U.S. GAAP was the Committee on Accounting Procedure that was formed in 1939. Pronouncements of these predecessor bodies that have not been superseded by the FASB remain part of U.S. GAAP. U.S. GAAP is contained in the "Accounting Standards Codification" ASC. The FASB's website is at www.fasb.org.

[4] The IASB was formed in 2000 and was preceded by the International Accounting Standards Committee IASC. Pronouncements of the IASC that have not been superseded by the IASB remain as part of IFRS.

this text primarily from a U.S. GAAP perspective, but highlight significant differences between GAAP and IFRS when appropriate.

Financial Statements

The balance sheet depicts a corporation's financial position at a **point** in time. All the other financial statements are for a **period** of time and explain changes that occur in certain balance sheet items during the period. It is important to note that these "change" statements are for the same period of time, beginning and ending at the comparative balance sheet dates. For Behrend Corp. the change statements are consistently for the year ended 12/31/12. The ending balance sheet of the previous period is the current period's beginning balance sheet. Comparing Behrend's year-end 12/31/12 balance sheet (Exhibit 1.5) with its beginning balance sheet at 12/31/11 (Exhibit 1.1) indicates that cash has decreased by $80,000 during the year. This change in cash is illustrated in detail in the statement of cash flows for the period 2012 (see Exhibit 1.4). Likewise, changes in retained earnings and other components of stockholders' equity that occurred during 2012 are depicted in the income statement and the statement of stockholders' equity (see Exhibits 1.2 and 1.3). The FASB has defined the basic elements contained in the financial statements. These elements are next discussed as they relate to the particular financial statement.

Balance Sheet

The balance sheet presents a corporation's financial position at a point in time by reporting its assets (things of worth) versus its liabilities plus stockholders' equity (claims to the assets). The balance sheet accounting equation is expressed as: ASSETS = LIABILITIES + OWNERS' EQUITY (A = L + OE). The financial statements result from the accumulation, classification, and summarization of numerous individual transactions and events. Each transaction or event that impacts the financial statements is termed to be "recognized." The accounting equation is always in balance. As discussed later, each transaction or event recognizes its dual (at a minimum) effects, which in turn maintains the equality of the accounting equation. This is referred to as "double entry" accounting.

Exhibit 1.1. Behrend Corp. Balance Sheet at 12/31/2011

Assets:			**Liabilities:**		
Current Assets:			Current Liabilities:		
Cash and Cash Equivalents	$150,000		Accounts Payable	$100,000	
Accounts Receivable (net)	140,000		Debt Currently Due	100,000	
Inventory	250,000	$540,000	Salaries & Wages Payable	50,000	
			Interest Payable	25,000	$275,000
Long-Term Assets:			Long-Term Liabilities:		
PP&E (net)		400,000	Long-Term Debt		400,000
			Total Liabilities		$675,000
			Stockholders' Equity:		
			Paid In Capital	$100,000	
			Retained Earnings	165,000	265,000
Total Assets		$940,000	Total Liabilities & Stockholders' Equity		$940,000

Exhibit 1.2. Behrend Corp. Income Statement for the Year Ended 12/31/2012

Net Sales Revenue		$1,900,000
Cost of Goods Sold		1,000,000
Gross Profit		$900,000
Operating Expenses:		
Selling & General Administrative Expenses:		
Salary and Wage Expense	$610,000	
Research and Development Expense	55,000	
Depreciation Expense	40,000	705,000
Operating Income:		$195,000
Other Revenue, Expense, Gain and Loss:		
Interest Expense		45,000
Income From Continuing Operations Before Tax		$150,000
Income Tax Expense		30,000
Income From Continuing Operations		$120,000
Extraordinary Loss	$50,000	
Less Tax Benefit	10,000	40,000
Net Income		$80,000
Earnings Per Share assume 100,000 shares of stock outstanding:		
Income From Continuing Operations		$1.20
Extraordinary Loss		$.40
Net Income		$.80

Exhibit 1.3. Behrend Corp. Statement of Stockholders' Equity for the Year Ended 12/31/2012

	Paid-in capital	Retained earnings	Total stockholders' equity
Beginning of Year 12/31/2011	$100,000	$165,000	$265,000
Issued Stock	50,000		50,000
Net Income 2012		80,000	80,000
Dividends		<25,000>	<25,000>
End of Year 12/31/2012	$150,000	$220,000	$370,000

Exhibit 1.4. Behrend Corp. Statement of Cash Flows for the Year Ended 12/31/2012

Cash Flow from Operating Activities:			
Collected from Customers		$1,890,000	
Paid to Suppliers for Inventory	$1,120,000		
Paid to Employees for Salary and Wage	600,000		
Paid for Research and Development	55,000		
Interest Paid	50,000		
Income Tax Paid	20,000	<1,845,000>	$45,000
Cash Flow from Investing Activities:			
Cash Paid for Truck			<50,000>
Cash Flow from Financing Activities:			
Stock Issuance		$50,000	
Payment of Principal on Debt	$100,000		
Payment of Dividends	25,000	<125,000>	<75,000>
Change in Cash During 2012			$<80,000>
Cash at 1/01/2012			150,000
Cash at 12/31/2012			$70,000

Assets are defined as "probable future economic benefits as a result of past transactions or events." **Liabilities** are the opposite of assets and are defined as "probable future economic sacrifices as a result of past transactions or events." These are the most important definitions of financial statement elements because all other elements are defined in terms of assets and liabilities. For example, the remaining balance sheet element is **equity**, which is defined as "the residual interest in the assets that remains after deducting its liabilities." A classified balance sheet separates "current" from "long-term" assets and liabilities. A current asset is one that will be realized in cash or used up within the next year or the "operating cycle"—whichever is longer. A current liability is one that will be satisfied by using current assets. The operating cycle is the period that begins with the corporation's acquisition of goods held out for sale or the providing of services and ends with the collection of cash from customers in the normal course of business. Although there are exceptions, current liabilities are generally those that will be satisfied within one year or the "operating

Exhibit 1.5. Behrend Corp. Balance Sheet at 12/31/2012

Assets:			**Liabilities:**		
Current Assets:			Current Liabilities:		
Cash and Cash Equivalents	$70,000		Accounts Payable	$80,000	
Accounts Receivable net	150,000		Salaries & Wages Payable	60,000	
Inventory	350,000	$570,000	Interest Payable	20,000	$160,000
			Long-Term Liabilities:		
Long-Term Assets:			Long-Term Debt		400,000
PP&E net		360,000	Total Liabilities		$560,000
			Stockholders' Equity:		
			Paid In Capital	$150,000	
			Retained Earnings	220,000	370,000
Total Assets		$930,000	Total Liabilities & Stockholders' Equity		$930,000

cycle"—whichever is longer. Since most businesses have an operating cycle of less than one year, unless indicated otherwise, this book assumes classification of assets and liabilities as current or long-term based upon the one-year period.

The balance sheet is used to gauge a firm's debt paying ability. The term "liquidity" is used in two ways. The liquidity of individual assets is determined by their nearness to cash—therefore, cash is deemed to be the most liquid of all assets. Investments in marketable debt and equity securities can be easily and quickly converted to cash and are considered highly liquid. Comparing inventory with accounts receivable, inventory is deemed less liquid because, relative to accounts receivable, it is one step removed from cash receipt—the sale has not yet occurred. Liquidity is also used to describe a firm's short-term debt paying ability. Current assets (CA) must be considered relative to current liabilities (CL) in making this liquidity assessment. Frequently used liquidity measures are working capital, the current ratio, and the quick ratio. Working capital is calculated as: CA – CL. Although working capital provides an important numeric measure of a firm's short-term debt paying ability, it is difficult to compare the amount of working capital across firms of different size. Ratios provide relative measures that accommodate comparison across firms. Both the current ratio and the quick ratio use CL as the denominator but their numerators are different. The current ratio is computed as CA/CL, whereas the quick ratio's numerator includes only the most liquid of current assets, called quick assets. Quick assets (QA) are CA excluding inventory and prepaid expenses and typically include cash, short-term investments, and accounts receivable. The quick ratio is computed as QA/CL.

A common measure of a firm's capital structure is the debt-to-equity ratio. The debt-to-equity ratio includes all debt (D) or total liabilities in the numerator and total stockholders' equity (E) in the denominator. The debt-to-equity ratio is calculated as D/E. The D/E ratio generally influences a firm's long-term debt paying ability (solvency). Although a numeric measure of a firm's solvency can be considered its net assets, or stockholders' equity A – L = OE, the debt-to-equity ratio provides a more comparable measure across firms. The D/E ratio can be used to gauge a firm's "leverage" or degree to which assets are financed through debt versus equity. The degree of leverage can also be used to assess the firm's "financial flexibility." Financial flexibility is the firm's ability to respond to unexpected needs and opportunities. Generally, the higher the D/E ratio, the more difficult it is for the firm to make interest and principal payments on its debt, particularly during bad times, or to quickly borrow funds in order to take advantage of business opportunities when they arise.

Income Statement

Comprehensive income is defined as all changes in net assets (equity) during the period except those resulting from contributions by owners and distributions to owners. Comprehensive income has two components, "net income" and "other comprehensive income." The income statement[5] of Behrend Corp. for the year ended 12/31/2012 is illustrated in Exhibit 1.2. Net income or loss is the difference between the sum totals of revenues plus gains versus expenses plus losses. **Revenues** are defined as "increases in net assets from providing goods or services that constitute the firm's ongoing central operations." **Expenses** are "decreases in net assets from providing goods or services that constitute the firm's ongoing central operations." Like revenues and expenses, **gains** and **losses** also respectively provide increases and decreases in equity, but they result from nonowner "peripheral or incidental" transactions rather than "ongoing central operations."

Net income and net cash flows over the entire life of the firm are equal after excluding cash flows that result from contributions by and distributions to owners, but on a period by period basis, may differ in terms of timing. Revenue and gain may be included in the income statement (recognized) concurrent with, before, or after the related net cash inflow occurs. This timing issue is likewise the case for income statement recognition of expenses and losses relative to the related

[5] Technically the correct title should be the "Statement of Net Income" however, because it is commonly used in practice, the text also refers to such as the "Income Statement."

net cash outflow. This timing difference is caused by GAAP's requirement to apply the "accrual" basis of accounting. The accrual basis of accounting is based upon two underlying principles—the "revenue (recognition) principle," and the "expense recognition principle." The revenue principle requires that revenue be included in the income statement (recognized) in the period "earned" whether or not the cash is received in that period. Normally, revenue is deemed to be earned in the period the goods or services are provided to the customer. The expense recognition principle attempts to assure that expenses follow revenues in order to provide a meaningful measure of income. Income is sometimes termed the "change in well-offness" that occurs during the period. The expense recognition principle requires that expenses be recognized with revenue of particular periods, whether or not the cash is paid in that period.

When a firm incurs costs that provide probable future economic benefit, they are presented as assets in the balance sheet. When these economic benefits are realized, the asset must be recognized as expense in the income statement. The expense recognition principle considers four different classifications of costs for purposes of determining the period(s) in which the related expense should be recognized. These cost classifications are:

1) directly related to revenue with a cause and effect relationship—examples include cost of goods sold and sales commissions;
2) directly related to particular income statement time periods—examples include rent, interest, and sales salaries;
3) systematically and rationally allocated to income statement periods estimated to be benefited—examples include depreciation and amortization; and
4) immediately recognized as expense due to a high degree of uncertainty that future benefit will result—examples include research and development or R&D.

The FASB contends that the accrual basis of accounting provides users with information more useful in assessing the firm's future cash flows than a cash basis income statement would provide. It is ironic that income reported under GAAP is based upon **past** transactions and events, but is primarily beneficial to creditors and stockholders only to the extent that it is useful in predicting future income (and cash flows). The degree to which a firm's reported income is useful in predicting its future income and cash flow performance is termed the "Quality of Earnings." The FASB's requirement to use the accrual basis is predicated upon their contention that reporting income under the accrual basis results in higher quality of earnings than would result if the cash basis of accounting was applied. Higher quality earnings should occur with full disclosure and transparency in the financial reporting process where managements' requisite accounting method choices and estimates regarding future events are made with neutrality—with freedom from bias. Of all the financial statements, many users place primary emphasis on the income statement in making decisions. Therefore, the concept of **Quality of Earnings** is of utmost importance and will be revisited in future chapters.

Although the accrual basis is usually considered an income concept, there are directly related implications for assets and liabilities in the balance sheet. As discussed previously, the accrual basis requires revenue to be recognized in the period earned—whether or not the cash is received in that period, and expenses follow revenues and are recognized in particular periods—whether or not the cash is paid in that period. When the income statement recognition of revenue or expense precedes the cash flow, it is termed an "accrual." When the cash flow precedes the revenue or expense recognition in the income statement, it is termed a "deferral." Accruals include revenue recognition with related asset recognition, for example, interest revenue and interest receivable, and expense recognition with related liability recognition, for example, interest expense and interest payable. Deferrals include increases and decreases in cash with the related recognition respectively of liabilities, for example, unearned rent revenue, or recognition of an asset, for example, prepaid rent.

Those income statement items that are considered more recurring or "permanent" in nature are more important to the user than those items that are nonrecurring or "temporary" in nature. The income statement for Behrend Corp. in Exhibit 1.2 is in "multiple-step" form. The items that are given prominence by appearing first are generally deemed to be more important because they are more permanent in nature. The first step in the income statement deducts cost of goods sold from sales revenue to present gross profit of $900,000. The normal recurring operating costs for selling and general administrative expense are deducted to yield $195,000 for operating income. Next, the more peripheral or incidental "other revenues, expenses, gains, and losses" category is added or deducted to determine income from continuing operations before tax. This example assumes only interest expense of $45,000 is reported in this "other" category. A tax rate of 20% is assumed which reduces income from continuing operations to $120,000 after income tax. This is commonly referred to as "the line" for purposes of presenting two potential "below the line items" under U.S. GAAP. The first is "discontinued operations" followed by "extraordinary items." Each is presented separately net of tax effect because there is little if any implication concerning future cash flows.

Discontinued operations involve component operations of a business that will not be continued in the future. There are two elements of this first below the line item: 1) revenues versus expenses from the component's operation during the period, and 2) gain or loss on disposal. Although Behrend has no discontinued operations to report during 2012, it does report an extraordinary loss. The gross amount of the loss is $50,000, but with a 20% tax rate, results in a tax savings of $10,000, that reduces the reported loss net of tax to $40,000. For an item to be considered "extraordinary," it must be: 1) infrequent in occurrence, and 2) unusual in nature. According to U.S. GAAP, very few items should meet both criteria and be presented as extraordinary. Presentation of extraordinary items differs under U.S. GAAP and IFRS. Differences between U.S. GAAP and IFRS will be indicated throughout the text by highlighting. Although IFRS in accounting for discontinued operations is similar to U.S. GAAP, IFRS does not permit separate reporting of extraordinary items in the income statement. Behrend reports net income of $80,000 for 2012.

Earnings per share is a standardized measure of earnings performance that can be compared over time. The Behrend Corp. example assumes 100,000 shares of stock outstanding during the period. The amounts of income from continuing operations, extraordinary loss, and net income are each divided by the 100,000 shares resulting in the earnings per share amounts reported in Exhibit 1.2.

Comprehensive Income

As mentioned previously, comprehensive income has two components. In addition to net income discussed above, it also includes "other comprehensive income" (OCI). The FASB has identified four areas where changes in equity from nonowner exchanges elude inclusion in the income statement and are instead included in OCI net of tax effects. Each exception involves the application of fair value accounting with resulting recognition of "unrealized" gain or loss. These four areas are: 1) translation of foreign subsidiaries' financial statements into U.S. dollars, 2) certain hedging activities using derivative securities, 3) funded status of pension and other postretirement plans, and 4) accounting for certain investments in marketable securities. Although OCI items are discussed later in the text, it is worth noting here that a significant difference between "below the line" and OCI items is that OCI items do not affect reported earnings per share.

Presentation of comprehensive income is consistent across U.S. GAAP and IFRS. Comprehensive income must be presented in one of two ways: 1) two separate statements (NI and OCI), or 2) one single combined statement of comprehensive income.[6] In our illustrations, Behrend does not report OCI in its financial statements because we assume none of the four OCI items occurred during 2012.

Statement of Stockholders' Equity

The statement of stockholders' equity is a detailed reconciliation of beginning to ending balances in the individual components of stockholders' equity in the balance sheet. Behrend's statement of stockholders' equity for the year ended 12/31/2012 is illustrated in Exhibit 1.3. Each income

---

[6] Prior to 2012, U.S. GAAP allowed a third presentation format—including OCI in the statement of stockholders' equity. This was the primary choice by firms prior to 2012. *Accounting Trends & Techniques-2010 New York: AICPA* p. 425, indicates 492 of 500 surveyed firms reported comprehensive income in their financial statements with 408 of them doing so within the statement of stockholders' equity. IFRS never allowed the U.S. GAAP alternative of presenting OCI within the statement of stockholders' equity.

statement account is "closed" to the permanent balance sheet account—retained earnings at the end of the period. Net income of the period increases retained earnings whereas a net loss would decrease retained earnings. The closing process accomplishes two things: 1) the income statement accounts are brought to a zero balance to accommodate the next period, and 2) retained earnings is adjusted to the correct end of period balance. Although **distributions to owners** (dividends) do not affect income in any way, dividends of the period do reduce the amount of retained earnings. Unlike net income that is closed to retained earnings, OCI is closed to "accumulated other comprehensive income" (AOCI), which is another permanent component of equity. The 12/31/11 balance sheet (Exhibit 1.1) does not include AOCI, which indicates Behrend has no unrealized gain or loss from the four items included in OCI under GAAP at the beginning of the year. Since Behrend has no OCI during 2012, net income and comprehensive income are one and the same, and no AOCI is reported at 12/31/12. Consistent with dividends, **contributions by owners** do not affect income. Contributions by owners increase "paid in capital." The statement of stockholders' equity is generally considered to be of least importance to users.

Statement of Cash Flows

Like the income statement and the statement of stockholders' equity, the statement of cash flows is for a period of time—the year ended 12/31/2012. The statement of cash flows shows the change in cash that occurred during the period in three categories: 1) operating, 2) investing, and 3) financing. Users place primary emphasis on the net cash flow from operating activity because a firm's long-term viability is dependent upon its ability to generate sufficient positive net cash flow from its ongoing central operations. Ironically, GAAP does not provide an all-inclusive list of cash flows that are classified as operating activities. Instead, GAAP specifically identifies cash flows that constitute investing or financing activities, and any remaining cash flows not specifically identified as investing or financing are to be classified as operating activities. There are two formats used in presenting operating cash flow—the "direct" method, and the "indirect" method. Behrend Corp. is using the direct presentation format in Exhibit 1.4.

Investing activities include cash flow from purchase or sale of PP&E and securities of other entities, making loans to other entities, and the collection of principal on those loans. Financing activities include issuance and reacquisition of stock, issuance of debt, repayment of debt principal, and payment of dividends. Although an all-inclusive list is not provided for operating activities, its main cash flow components generally include: collections from customers, payments to suppliers, payments to employees and others for expenses, payments of interest, and receipts of interest or dividends from investment securities. Theoretically, dividends and interest received on investment securities are considered investing activities, while interest paid on debt is considered a financing activity. However, since GAAP does not specifically identify them as such, they are classified as operating activities.

Review of the Accounting Process

The accounting process is the underlying system that accumulates the requisite information presented in the financial statements. Using Behrend Corp. as our example we will review the accounting process under the accounting equation framework. We start with Behrend's beginning balance sheet (Exhibit 1.1). Note that total assets ($940,000) are equal to the sum of liabilities ($675,000) and stockholders' equity ($265,000). This 12/31/2011 balance sheet information is transferred to Exhibit 1.6 where we next illustrate the impact that various transactions and events have on the accounting equation.

Summary Entries

Each transaction or event is individually entered into the accounting system. "Summary entries" are used here to illustrate the impact that numerous similar individual transactions have on the accounting equation as a whole. For example, transaction b. involves sales to customers on account. This likely involves thousands of sales transactions throughout 2012, each of which needs to be recorded. All of the sales for the entire year are summarized, and the effects on the accounts analyzed as if there was only one transaction recorded.

Exhibit 1.6. Financial Statement Effects of Transactions and Events Using the Accounting Equation Format

	Cash	SCF class	Accounts receivable (net)	Inventory	PP&E (net)	=	Accounts payable	Debt currently due	Salaries & wages payable	Interest payable	Long term debt	+	Paid in capital	Retained earnings	Explanation of change in retained earnings
Beginning balances (Balance Sheet 12/31/11)															
	150,000		140,000	250,000	400,000	=	100,000	100,000	50,000	25,000	400,000		100,000	165,000	
SUMMARY ENTRIES:															
a Pur. Inv. from suppliers all on account				1,100,000			1,100,000								
b. Sales to customers all on account, and			1,900,000											1,900,000	Revenue earned
Record cost of sales and reduce inventory				<1,000,000>										<1,000,000>	Cost of goods sold
c. Collections from customers	1,890,000	O	<1,890,000>												
d. Payments to inventory suppliers	<1,120,000>	O					<1,120,000>								

(Continued)

Exhibit 1.6. Financial Statement Effects of Transactions and Events Using the Accounting Equation Format—(Continued)

	Cash	SCF class	Accounts receivable (net)	Inventory	PP&E (net)	=	Accounts payable	Debt currently due	Salaries & wages payable	Interest payable	Long term debt	+	Paid in capital	Retained earnings	Explanation of change in retained earnings
e. Payment to employees	<600,000>	O							<50,000>					<550,000>	salary & wage exp.
f. Pay estimated income tax for 2012	<20,000>	O												<20,000>	Income taxes
SPECIFIC ENTRIES:															
g. Purchase new vehicle for cash 1/26/12	<50,000>	I			50,000										
h. Pay for market research project 3/12/12	<55,000>	O												<55,000>	R&D exp.
i. Pay annual interest on debt 6/30/12	<50,000>	O								<25,000>				<25,000>	Interest exp.
j. Principal payment on debt 6/30/12	<100,000>	F						<100,000>							

k. Declare and pay dividend 9/30/12	<25,000>	F												<25,000>	Not on income state.
l. Meteor loss to build. 10/19/12					<50,000>									<50,000>	Extra. loss bef. tax
m. Issue stock for cash 12/30/12	50,000	F											50,000		
ADJUSTING ENTRIES each dated 12/31/12:															
n. Depreciation and amortization for year					<40,000>									<40,000>	Depreciation exp.
o. Interest on debt 7/01/12–12/31/12										20,000				<20,000>	Interest exp.
p. Wages and salaries owed at 12/31/12									60,000					<60,000>	Salary & wage exp.
ending balances Balance Sheet 12/31/12	70,000		150,000	350,000	360,000	=	80,000	0	60,000	20,000	400,000	+	150,000	220,000	

Transaction a.—Purchase inventory on account from suppliers for $1,100,000. The effects on the accounting equation are that the asset (inventory) and the liability (accounts payable) are both increased by $1,100,000.

Transaction b.—Goods (inventory) is provided to customers on account for an aggregate selling price of $1,900,000. Also, assume that Behrend's cost of the inventory transferred to customers is $1,000,000. Because the goods are transferred to the customers in 2012, revenue should be recognized in the 2012 income statement whether or not the cash is received in 2012. In terms of the accounting equation, the asset accounts receivable is increased $1,900,000 as will be retained earnings when the income statement account sales revenue is closed. The expense recognition principle requires that $1,000,000 cost of goods sold be recognized in 2012 because the expense is directly related to the $1,900,000 in sales revenue recognized. The asset inventory is reduced by $1,000,000, as will be retained earnings when the income statement account cost of goods sold is closed.

Transaction c.—Cash of $1,890,000 is collected from customers on account. There is no effect on the right side of the accounting equation. The asset cash is increased while the asset accounts receivable is decreased, each for $1,890,000. This cash inflow is classified as "operating" in the statement of cash flows.

Transaction d.—Cash of $1,120,000 is paid to suppliers on accounts payable. Both the asset cash and the liability accounts payable are reduced by $1,120,000. This cash outflow is classified as "operating" in the statement of cash flows.

Transaction e.—Employees are paid monthly in the month following the month of service. There is a one-month time lag between employees providing services and Behrend paying them for those services. For example, employees are paid for work performed in December 2011 in January 2012, work performed in January 2012 is paid in February 2012, ... and work performed in December 2012 will not be paid by Behrend until January 2013. Under the expense recognition principle, this is an example of an expense that is directly related to periods of time. The expense must be recognized in the period the employee provides the service, whether or not the cash is paid in that period. Behrend pays salaries and wages during 2012 in the amount of $600,000. A portion of this payment ($50,000) relates to employee services that were provided in December 2011 (see salaries and wages payable in the 12/31/11 balance sheet Exhibit 1.1), and the remainder ($550,000) is recognized as a 2012 expense because it relates to services provided by employees from January through November 2012. Note that an "adjusting entry" will be needed to recognize salaries and wages expense for December 2012 that will not be paid until January 2013 (see adjustment p. below). The effects on the accounting equation are: a reduction in the asset cash for $600,000, the liability salaries and wages payable is decreased by $50,000, and retained earnings will be decreased by $550,000 when the income statement account salaries and wages expense is closed. This cash outflow is classified as "operating" in the statement of cash flows.

Transaction f.—Paid $20,000 in income taxes based upon estimated 2012 taxable income of $100,000 and tax rate of 20%. Estimated tax payments are due periodically during the year. Actual taxable income is equal to the $100,000 estimated, and the actual income tax due for the year was $20,000.[7] Note from the income statement (Exhibit 1.2) that income tax expense on the income statement is $30,000. This is based upon the 20% rate applied to income from continuing operations before tax ($150,000). Behrend experienced an extraordinary loss (event l.) below) of $50,000 before considering its tax benefit of $10,000 ($50,000 loss deduction @ 20% = $10,000 tax savings). These two net out to the correct total tax provision, $20,000. The effects on the accounting equation are a decrease in cash of $20,000 and an eventual decrease in retained earnings when the income statement accounts are closed. This cash outflow is classified as "operating" in the statement of cash flows.

Specific Transactions and Events

Transaction g.—Purchased a new delivery truck for $50,000 cash on 1/26/12. The effects on the accounting equation are strictly within

[7] Later in the text we discuss differences between GAAP-based income before tax and taxable income per the return, but until then will assume there are no differences.

assets with cash decreased and "property plant and equipment" (PP&E) increased by $50,000. This cash outflow is classified as "investing" in the statement of cash flows.

Transaction h.—On 3/12/12 Behrend received the results of a marketing research project and immediately paid the research firm for its service, $55,000. Under the expense recognition principle, this is considered R&D and must be immediately recognized as an expense because there is a high degree of uncertainty regarding whether or not a future benefit will result. The accounting equation is affected by a reduction in the asset cash, and decrease in retained earnings when the income statement accounts are closed. This cash outflow is classified as "operating" in the statement of cash flows.

Transaction i.—Interest on outstanding debt is payable annually on 6/30 at a 10% rate. Interest is calculated as: PRINCIPAL × INTEREST RATE × PORTION OF YEAR. Interest for the one year period ending 6/30/12 is $50,000 ($500,000 × 10% × 12/12), half of which is for the period 7/1/11–12/31/11, and the other half is for the period 1/1/12–6/30/12. This is the interest payable liability from the 12/31/11 balance sheet (Exhibit 1.1). Consistent with transaction e. above, this is an expense directly associated with specific income statement time periods and must be recognized in the period incurred regardless of when the cash is paid. The effects on the accounting equation are cash is decreased $50,000, interest payable is decreased $25,000, and retained earnings is decreased by $25,000 after closing the interest expense account. Note that an adjustment will be needed at 12/31/12 to accrue interest expense for the period 7/01/12–12/31/12. This cash outflow is classified as "operating" in the statement of cash flows.

Transaction j.— Record the $100,000 debt principal payment made on 6/30/12. This payment reduces cash and eliminates the $100,000 of "debt currently due" liability that appeared on the 12/31/11 balance sheet. Note that the amount of debt principal is reduced to $400,000. This cash outflow is classified as "financing" in the statement of cash flows.

Transaction k.—On 9/30/12 Behrend declared and paid a cash dividend to shareholders at the rate of $.25/share × 100,000 shares = $25,000. The effects on the accounting equation are cash and retained earnings are each decreased by $25,000. **There is no income statement effect**. This cash outflow is classified as "financing" in the statement of cash flows.

Event l.—On 10/19/12 a meteor fell from outer space and unfortunately destroyed an empty storage building with a book value of $50,000. The loss was uninsured. This hopefully meets the criteria for classification as an extraordinary item—both infrequent in occurrence and unusual in nature. The effects on the accounting equation are a decrease of $50,000 in PP&E and an equal reduction in retained earnings to recognize the gross loss. Although the gross loss was $50,000, the associated tax deduction with a 20% tax rate, results in a $10,000 tax benefit that reduces the extraordinary loss reported in the income statement to $40,000 (net of the $10,000 tax benefit). Recall that transaction f. discussed the 2012 $20,000 overall tax burden's presentation in the income statement. The amount of tax burden that would have been incurred if there were no below the line items is reported as tax expense ($150,000 @ 20% = $30,000), above the line; and the tax benefit resulting from the tax deductibility of the meteor damage reduces the reported extraordinary loss, below the line.

Transaction m.—Behrend issues an additional 50,000 shares of stock for $1/share on 12/30/12. The effects of this transaction on the accounting equation are an increase in cash of $50,000 and an increase in paid in capital for an equal amount. **There is no income statement effect**. This cash inflow is classified as "financing" in the statement of cash flows.

Adjusting Entries

Adjusting entries are necessary for the financial statements to be presented under the accrual basis of accounting, which is required under GAAP. Adjusting entries are generally needed in the case of "accruals" and "deferrals" discussed previously, and therefore should affect at least one income statement account and at least one balance sheet account.

Adjustment n.—Recognize depreciation expense. The expense recognition principle requires that when costs are incurred that benefit multiple periods they be systematically and rationally recognized as expense over the estimated periods benefited. Depreciation is an example of such a cost under the accrual basis of accounting. You may be familiar with the "straight line" depreciation method. Under the straight line method periodic depreciation is computed as: (ASSET COST-ESTIMATED RESIDUAL VALUE)/ESTIMATED SERVICE LIFE. For purposes of this example assume PP&E has an aggregate cost of $600,000, zero estimated residual value, and an average estimated service life of 15 years. Assuming Behrend uses the straight line method, annual depreciation is computed as: ($600,000 – $0)/15 years = $40,000 per year. The effects of this adjustment on the accounting equation are PP&E (net) is reduced by $40,000 and retained earnings is reduced by $40,000 when the income statement account depreciation expense is closed. Note that PP&E (net) represents the "book value" of the assets. Book value is equal to cost minus accumulated depreciation. At 12/31/11 Behrend had PP&E with a cost of $600,000 and a book value of $400,000, which indicates that "accumulated depreciation" at the beginning of the year was $200,000.

Adjustment o.—Recognize interest expense incurred but not paid on outstanding debt. Recall from transaction j. that interest cost incurred for the period 7/1/12–12/31/12 must be recognized as expense on the 2012 income statement even though it will not be paid until 6/30/13. Interest expense for this period is computed as: $400,000 × 10% × 6/12 = $20,000. The effects of the adjustment on the accounting equation are to increase the liability account interest payable by $20,000 and to reduce retained earnings by $20,000 when the income statement account interest expense is closed. Note that the income statement now includes interest expense for the full calendar year 2012 of $45,000, $25,000 for the first six months, plus $20,000 for the last six months. The $20,000 interest expense that will be paid on 6/30/13 is presented in the 12/31/12 balance sheet as a current liability.

Adjustment p.—Recognize salaries and wages expense for employee services provided in December 2012 that will be paid in January 2013. As discussed in transaction e. under the accrual basis salaries and wages must be recognized as expense in the period the employee provides the services, whether or not paid in that period. In order to recognize expense for the full calendar year, an adjustment is necessary to recognize the expense for December employee services. Assume that the

December payroll is $60,000. The necessary adjustment increases the liability salaries and wages payable by $60,000 and also reduces retained earnings by $60,000 when the income statement account salaries and wages expense is closed to retained earnings. Note that this adjustment combined with transaction e. provides that the income statement include salaries and wages expense for the full year 2012 of $610,000, $550,000 of which was paid in 2012 and the $60,000 accrual that will be paid in 2013. Note also that the 12/31/12 balance sheet reflects the current liability "salaries and wages payable" for $60,000.

In summary, we started the accounting process using the beginning of the period balance sheet at 12/31/11. Pertinent transactions and adjustments recorded during the year using the accounting equation format were used to develop the change statements for the year ended 12/31/12 (income statement, statement of stockholders' equity, and statement of cash flows). After closing, the effects of all changes are reflected in the year-end balance sheet at 12/31/12. We will continue to use the accounting equation format to illustrate the effects of particular transactions and events upon the financial statements in all future chapters.

CHAPTER 2

Cash, Receivables, and Revenue Recognition

Cash and Cash Equivalents

Cash is the most liquid of all assets. Cash includes currency on hand and unrestricted funds deposited with banks. Also included in cash are instruments that can be immediately deposited in bank accounts for credit at face value (e.g., negotiable customer checks, money orders, and travelers' checks). Since postdated checks cannot be immediately deposited, they are classified as receivables. Although some companies report "cash" on the balance sheet, about 95%[1] report "cash and cash equivalents" or "cash and equivalents." The FASB defines cash equivalents as highly liquid, short-term investments that are readily convertible into known amounts of cash, and are so near to maturity that there is inconsequential risk of change in value caused by interest rate shifts. Usually only debt instruments purchased within three months of maturity qualify as cash equivalents.

Restricted Cash

The current asset classification cash and cash equivalents should only include funds available to satisfy current liabilities. If there is any restriction of cash, it must be disclosed in the notes to the financial statements. If the restriction dictates that the cash be used to satisfy long-term debt or to acquire long-term assets, the related cash should be classified as long term. An example of restricted cash involves compensating balances associated with financing arrangements. Compensating balance restrictions dictate

---

[1] Accounting Trends & Techniques—2010 (New York: AICPA 2010), p. 148.

that the borrowing firm maintains minimum (compensating) balances in zero or low return accounts at the lending institution. The compensating balance reduces the actual amount borrowed, which increases the effective interest rate incurred. These compensating balance restrictions must be disclosed in the financial statement notes, and if they relate to long-term borrowings, the restricted cash must be excluded from current assets and instead included in long-term investments or "other assets."

Bank Overdrafts

In the case of payment by check, cash is considered to be decreased at the time of check issuance, not when the bank reduces the account balance. This time period is commonly referred to as "float." Although this float period has been significantly reduced with electronic funds transfers, accounts receivable conversions, Check 21, etc. there remains the possibility of being in an overdraft (negative cash) position. Under U.S. GAAP, overdraft positions are reported as current liabilities. An exception applies in situations where the firm has sufficient positive cash balances in other accounts with the same institution to offset the overdraft; in which case, netting to the overall positive cash balance is permitted. IFRS allows overdrawn accounts to be netted with positive account balances within cash and cash equivalents for particular bank balances that often fluctuate from positive to overdrawn amounts as an integral part of an entity's cash management.[2]

Internal Control

Internal control is the system of policies and procedures that a firm develops and applies with the following objectives: 1) provide fair representation in the financial statements, 2) assure effectiveness and efficiency of operations (including safeguarding firm assets), and 3) comply with all relevant laws and regulations. Since cash is the medium of exchange, easily concealed and difficult to trace, it is the asset most susceptible to theft. Therefore, internal control of cash receipts and disbursements is

[2] International Accounting Standard No. 8, "Statement of Cash Flows," IASB.

of critical importance. In response to fraudulent financial reporting by Enron, WorldCom, etc., the Sarbanes-Oxley Act of 2002 was passed that now requires increased scrutiny of publicly held firms' systems of internal control in an attempt to improve the financial reporting process.

Revenue Recognition and Receivables

GAAP requires that two criteria be met in order to recognize revenue: 1) it is realized or realizable and 2) it is earned. Revenue is realized or realizable when there is reasonable certainty as to the ultimate increase in net assets to be derived (usually from collection of cash), and is earned when the earnings process (what the company provides to the customer in order to generate revenue) is virtually complete. Recall from chapter 1 that the revenue principle generally requires revenue to be included in the income statement of the period the goods or services are provided to the customer. This is usually considered the "critical point" at which both criteria are met.

Most receivables are considered "trade receivables" which result from providing goods or services to customers. Although there are other types of receivables for utility deposits, employee loans, travel advances, etc. that may be classified as long term, trade receivables being part of the operating cycle are almost always considered current assets. Terms of sales on account generally require customer payment within 30 to 60 days. Since the cash receipt may occur in a period following that of revenue recognition, sales on account may be considered a type of "accrual." Most trade receivables are on "open account" where there is documentation supporting the indebtedness (customer purchase order and sales invoice), but no formal instrument evidencing the debt. Notes receivable are formal written promises to pay certain amounts at certain future dates and unlike accounts receivable usually include an interest element. A formal note receivable may be requested in the case of sales to customers when extended payment is requested or ultimate collection is deemed high risk. Specific issues related to accounting for notes receivable will be discussed in a future chapter.

At the time of sale, sales revenue and the receivable are both recognized at the invoiced price agreed to by the buyer and the seller. Theoretically, any time cash payment or receipt is delayed to the future, the amount of cash ultimately paid or received includes an interest component. In the case of sales on account, true sales and receivables recognized should be the present value of the future customer payment. However, GAAP excludes "receivables arising from transactions with customers in the normal course of business that are due in customary trade terms not exceeding approximately one year" from presentation in the financial statements at present value.[3] Even though sales and accounts receivable are initially recognized at the gross invoiced amount, they are presented in the financial statements at "net" amounts. Accounts receivable is presented as the amount of cash expected to eventually be collected or "net realizable value" and sales is reported net of sales discounts, and sales returns and allowances. Presenting items "net" in the financial statements is accommodated by subtracting related offsetting account balances that are referred to as "contra" accounts.

Uncollectible Accounts

Whenever a firm provides goods or services on account, inevitably some customers will not pay the amounts they owe. This gives rise to "uncollectible accounts." There are two methods of accounting for uncollectible accounts: 1) the direct write-off method, and 2) the allowance method. Each method recognizes uncollectible accounts as an operating expense in the income statement; the difference is a matter of when. The direct write-off method recognizes uncollectible accounts expense when a particular customer's account is deemed uncollectible and is written off. The allowance method recognizes uncollectible accounts expense earlier, based upon accounts receivable estimated to become uncollectible in the future. The allowance method offsets uncollectible accounts expense recognition in the accounting equation by adjusting a contra asset account—"allowance for uncollectible accounts" (AFUA). The AFUA account only exists under the allowance method. AFUA reduces accounts receivable to their estimated net realizable value in the balance sheet. Unlike the direct

[3] FASB ASC 835-30-15-3; Original Pronouncement: Accounting Principles Board Opinion No. 21, "Interest on Receivables and Payables," (New York: AICPA 1971).

write-off method, when a specific customer's account is deemed uncollectible under the allowance method, it is written off to the AFUA account. Specific customer account write-offs under the allowance method reduce accounts receivable and its contra account (AFUA) equally, and have no impact upon accounts receivable (net) or net income.

Although the direct write-off method is the only method allowed for tax purposes, it is not permitted under GAAP—the allowance method must be used for financial reporting.[4] The direct write-off method violates the expense recognition principle because customer accounts may be written off (and uncollectible accounts expense recognized) in periods following the period of revenue recognition. Also, failure to recognize an AFUA overstates accounts receivable relative to their probable future economic benefit (net realizable value) in the balance sheet. For these reasons, unless uncollectible accounts are considered to be "immaterial" in amount, the direct write-off method is disallowed under GAAP. The concept of materiality is important to financial reporting because only items that are considered to be "material" need to comply with GAAP. Per the FASB: "Information is material if omitting it or misstating it could influence decisions that users make on the basis of the financial information of a specific entity."[5] Materiality is a matter of judgment and not quantitatively defined within GAAP.

Allowance Method

The effects of the end-of-period adjusting entry required under the allowance method on the accounting equation are:

1) Retained earnings is reduced through recognition of the **income statement** account uncollectible accounts expense, and
2) Accounts receivable is reduced to net realizable value on the **balance sheet** through recognition of the contra asset account—AFUA.

---

[4] This is the first example of GAAP rules differing from tax accounting laws and regulations. Uncollectible accounts accounting is a "temporary" difference between GAAP and tax recognition. The financial reporting implications of these temporary differences are discussed in a future chapter.

[5] Statement of Financial Accounting Concepts No. 8, "Qualitative Characteristics of Useful Financial Information," FASB 2010, p. 17.

There are two adaptations of the allowance method. The "income statement method" stresses the importance of presenting estimated uncollectible accounts expense on the income statement, whereas the "balance sheet method" stresses the importance of presenting accounts receivable at estimated net realizable value on the balance sheet. In discussing the differences in these adaptations of the allowance method we will consider the following example: Behrend Corp. has been in existence for many years and has consistently sold to customers exclusively on account. At the beginning of 2012, Behrend had a balance of $100,000 in accounts receivable and $2,000 in its contra asset account AFUA. Although all income statement accounts have beginning balances of zero, the beginning balances in balance sheet accounts are the same as their ending balances from the preceding period (the 12/31/2011 balance sheet). The following is a presentation of Behrend's accounts receivable from the current asset section of its 12/31/2011 balance sheet:

Accounts Receivable	$100,000
Less AFUA	2,000
Accounts Receivable (net)	$98,000

During 2012, Behrend had $1,000,000 in sales (all on account), collected $950,000 from customers, and wrote off $1,000 in customers' accounts that were deemed uncollectible. Ignoring cost of goods sold, the effects upon the accounting equation are:

ASSETS		=	LIABILITIES	+	SE	
Record sales (all sales are assumed to be on account)						
+ Accts Rec.	+1,000,000				+ Sales	+1,000,000
Record collection of cash from customers on account						
+ Cash	+950,000					
– Accts Rec.	–950,000					
Write off specific customers' accounts that are deemed to be uncollectible						
– AFUA	+1,000					
– Accts Rec.	–1,000					

Based upon this information Behrend has 12/31/2012 account balances before the end-of-period adjustment as follows: sales = $1,000,000, accounts receivable = \$149,000 (100,000 + 1,000,000 − 950,000 − 1,000), AFUA = \$1,000 (2,000 − 1,000),[6] and uncollectible accounts expense = \$0. It is important to note that either adaptation of the allowance method involves an end-of-period adjustment that requires **estimates** of what will happen in the future. Required estimates are usually based upon past experience but can be affected by changes in credit granting policy, economic conditions, etc.

The balance sheet adaptation of the allowance method concentrates on presenting accounts receivable at net realizable value on the balance sheet by adjusting the AFUA account to the estimated amount that will be uncollectible. Although application of one single rate to the entire balance of accounts receivable may suffice, usually firms develop an aging schedule based upon the logic that the older a receivable is, the more likely it will become uncollectible. Assume that based upon past experience and current conditions Behrend develops the following aging schedule for its accounts receivable at 12/31/12:

Age Category	Amount	Est. % Uncollect.	Est. \$ Uncollect.
1–30 days	60,000	.5%	300
31–60 days	40,000	1%	400
61–90 days	30,000	2%	600
Over 90 days	19,000	5%	950
Totals	149,000		2,250

Based upon the aging schedule, Behrend estimates that \$2,250 of its \$149,000 year-end accounts receivable will be uncollectible. In order to present accounts receivable at their estimated net realizable value of \$146,750 in the balance sheet, the after adjustment balance in the contra asset account AFUA should be \$2,250. Recall that in our example the balance in AFUA before adjustment is \$1,000. The adjusting entry that Behrend will make under the balance sheet method increases the contra asset account AFUA by \$1,250 and recognizes uncollectible accounts

[6] If the amount of accounts receivable written off during a period exceeds the beginning balance in allowance for uncollectible accounts, the allowance account can have a "negative" balance before adjustment. However, it must never have a negative balance after adjustment. A negative balance would indicate that management estimates that it is going to collect more from its customers on account than they actually owe.

expense of $1,250 for the year 2012. The effects upon the accounting equation are:

ASSETS	=	LIABILITIES	+	SE
+ AFUA −1,250				+ Uncollect. Accts. Exp. −1,250

After adjustment, the balance in AFUA becomes $2,250, and accounts receivable (net) will appear in the current asset section of the 12/31/2012 the balance sheet as follows:

Accounts Receivable	$149,000
Less AFUA	2,250
Accounts Receivable (net)	$146,750

Notice that under the balance sheet adaptation of the allowance method, the primary concern is presentation of accounts receivable at net realizable value in the balance sheet, and the determination of uncollectible accounts expense for the period is of secondary consideration.

The income statement adaptation of the allowance method directly calculates an estimate of uncollectible accounts expense for the period based upon a percentage of credit sales for the period, without regard to any existing balance in accounts receivable or the AFUA account. Assume that based upon past experience and current conditions, Behrend estimates that .2% of 2012 credit sales will eventually be uncollectible. The end-of-period adjusting entry directly calculates an estimate of uncollectible accounts expense by multiplying credit sales × estimated % uncollectible (1,000,000 × .2% = $2,000). The effects upon the accounting equation are:

ASSETS	=	LIABILITIES	+	SE
+ AFUA −2,000				+ Uncollect. Accts. Exp. −2,000

After adjustment, the balance in AFUA becomes $3,000, and accounts receivable (net) will appear in the current asset section of the 12/31/2012 balance sheet as follows:

Accounts Receivable	$149,000
Less AFUA	3,000
Accounts Receivable (net)	$146,000

Notice that the primary concern (and calculation) under the income statement adaptation of the allowance method is the amount of uncollectible accounts expense that appears in the income statement, and that the presentation of accounts receivable at net realizable value in the balance sheet is of secondary consideration.

Changes in Estimate

As indicated previously, either adaptation of the allowance method involves recognizing uncollectible accounts expense and adjusting the AFUA account based upon **estimates** of future events—customers' failure to pay. Later in this chapter and future chapters we discuss other instances where estimates of future events are necessary in formulating financial statements. As time passes, information may come to light indicating that previous estimates (and previously issued financial statements) were incorrect. A fundamental accounting issue involves accounting for such "changes in estimate." One alternative is to go back and restate previously issued financial statements.[7] Instead, GAAP requires a different approach—changes in estimate must be accounted for "prospectively." When an accounting change is accounted for prospectively, previously issued financial statements are not changed, only financial statements related to the period of the accounting change and subsequent periods are affected.

Returning to our Behrend example, assume that in 2013 it is determined that actual uncollectible accounts related to 2012 credit sales and year-end 12/31/12 accounts receivable is higher than was previously estimated when making the year-end 2012 adjustments. Had the year-end 2012 estimates been correct, uncollectible accounts expense would have been higher in the 2012 income statement and accounts receivable (net) would have been reported at a lower amount in the 12/31/12 balance sheet. However, once issued, the 2012 financial statements are not revised in accounting for subsequent changes in estimate. Instead a catch-up adjustment is made to the financial statements of the period when the change in estimate occurs (2013).[8] In our example the catch-up adjustment increases 2013 uncollectible accounts

---

[7] Going back and changing previously issued financial statements is referred to as "retrospective" treatment; which will be discussed in a future chapter.

[8] The examples of change in estimate in this chapter are corrected in full by adjusting income for the year of the change in estimate. Future chapters discuss instances where the change in estimate affects income for years beyond the year of change in estimate.

expense beyond the amount that would have been otherwise reported. The understatement of 2012's uncollectible accounts expense is offset by overstating reported uncollectible accounts expense in the 2013 income statement. Although reported income is overstated for 2012 and understated for 2013, after the catch-up adjustment, accounts receivable should be correctly presented at net realizable value in the 12/31/13 balance sheet. If during 2013 it was instead determined that 2012's uncollectible accounts expense had been overstated rather than understated, the opposite would occur. A poor estimate that causes income to be misstated in a particular year is "corrected" by reporting income for the year of the change in estimate to be misstated at an equal amount, but in the opposite direction. In the case of accounting for changes in estimate it seems that standard setters feel that two wrongs **do** make a right!

Sales Returns and Allowances

A return of merchandise by the customer (sales returns) negates the sale. Also, a negotiated reduction in the invoiced amount because of damaged or otherwise unsatisfactory goods (sales allowances) reduces the amount of sales revenue. However, since management is interested in the incidence of sales returns and allowances, a contra revenue account "sales returns and allowances" is generally used rather than reducing sales revenue directly. If sales returns and allowances are material in amount and can be reasonably estimated, the accrual basis of accounting requires that an adjustment must be made at the end of the period to reduce income and present accounts receivable at net realizable value. This estimation and adjustment process is similar to that discussed previously in the case of accounting for uncollectible accounts. Finally, if sales returns and allowances are material in amount but cannot be reasonably estimated, GAAP requires that revenue recognition be delayed until the point that a reasonable estimate can be made or until the customer's right of return period expires.[9]

---

[9] FASB ASC 605-15-25-1; Original pronouncement: Statement of Financial Accounting Standards No. 48, "Revenue Recognition When Right of Return Exists," FASB 1981.

If the amount of sales returns and allowances is deemed to be immaterial, they are typically recognized in the period that the customer returns the goods or the allowance is granted. The following example illustrates the effects upon the accounting equation when the amounts of sales returns and allowances are immaterial: Behrend Corp. sells 200 shirts to a customer at an agreed price of \$10/shirt. Subsequently, the customer returns two shirts for full credit. Also, the customer finds that one shirt is defective but rather than return the shirt, a 40% reduction in price (to \$6) is negotiated with Behrend.

ASSETS		=	LIABILITIES	+	SE	
			Sale of 200 shirts @ \$10 each on account			
+ Accounts Rec.	+ 2,000				+ Sales Revenue	+ 2,000
			Customer returns 2 shirts for full credit			
– Accounts Rec.	– 20				+ Sales Returns	– 20
			Customer and Behrend agree to \$4 allowance			
– Accounts Rec.	– 4				+ Sales Allowances	– 4

Sales (Cash) Discounts

Firms offer cash discounts for a number of reasons (e.g., to encourage prompt payment, industry practice, etc.). Discount terms are abbreviated such as 2/10, n/30 which means 2% of the invoiced amount can be taken as a "discount" if paid within 10 days of the invoice date; otherwise the full gross invoiced amount is due within 30 days. For example a \$100 sale under terms 1/10, n/30 is satisfied by remitting \$99 in 10 days or by paying the full \$100 in 30 days. The customer saves 1% by paying 20 days early. This amounts to a savings rate in excess of 18% on an annualized basis ($1\% \times 365/20$). The effects upon the accounting equation for this example are as follows:

ASSETS		=	LIABILITIES	+	SE	
			Sale of \$100 on account terms 1/10, n/30			
+ Accounts Rec.	+ 100				+ Sales Revenue	+ 100

Payment of $99 received within 10 days

+ Cash	+99	+ Sales Discounts	– 1
– Accounts Rec.	–100		

Payment of $100 received in 30 days

+ Cash	+100
– Accounts Rec.	–100

Note that sales discounts are recognized (in the contra revenue account) only if the customer pays within the discount period.[10]

Accelerating Cash Receipt from Receivables

Should the need for cash arise, firms can use their receivables to accelerate cash inflow. If receivables are considered to be sold (also called factoring), the receivables are removed from the transferor's books and the difference between cash received and the carrying value of the receivables sold is recognized as gain or loss. If receivables are used as collateral in obtaining a loan (referred to as pledging or assigning of receivables), it is considered a secured borrowing. In the case of secured borrowings, the receivables remain on the books of the transferor and the cash proceeds from the loan are recognized in a liability account.[11] Over the term of the loan, interest expense is recognized under the accrual basis of accounting.

Sometimes the exchange contract requires that the transferor guarantee payment in the cases where customers fail to pay. This is referred to as transfer of receivables "with recourse." The fundamental accounting issue involves distinguishing sales of accounts receivable from secured borrowings. Even though the exchange contract may refer to

---

[10] The method illustrated is called the "gross" method, because both sales and accounts receivable are initially recorded at the gross invoiced amount. A theoretically superior but less frequently used method initially recognizes both sales revenue and the receivable at the "net" of the available discount amount. Subsequently customer discounts taken by paying within the discount period are not separately recognized. Instead discounts not taken by customers are recognized as interest revenue. The net method will be illustrated in depth in chapter 3 from the perspective of the customer (purchaser).

[11] Since assets that serve as collateral on loans are not fully available to meet general creditor claims, their amounts must be disclosed in the notes to the financial statements.

the transfer as a "sale," the terms of the agreement may indicate that it actually constitutes a secured borrowing arrangement. This is an example of the concept referred to as "substance versus form." Form is what a particular item is held out to be (e.g., the exchange is termed a "sale" in the contract), whereas its substance is what it actually is (e.g., given the specifics of the exchange contract the arrangement may represent a secured borrowing). Financial reporting strives to present the underlying economic substance of transactions and events regardless of their purported form. In other words, GAAP and IFRS stress "substance over form."

Both FASB and IFRS provide criteria that attempt to identify transfers of receivables with recourse that in substance constitute sales. If the criteria are not met, the transfer is accounted for as a secured borrowing. U.S. GAAP exclusively stresses the issue of control in determining if a transfer of receivables with recourse should be treated as a sale. The FASB identifies three conditions, all of which must be met for a firm to treat the transfer of receivables with recourse as a sale:

1) The transferred asset is legally isolated from the transferor and its creditors, even in the case of bankruptcy,
2) The transferee can pledge or exchange the transferred asset without constraint, and
3) The transferor does not maintain effective control over the transferred assets through an agreement to repurchase or redeem them before maturity.[12]

Contrary to U.S. GAAP's exclusive consideration of the control issue, the IASB stresses the importance of transferring "substantially all risks and rewards of ownership" in determining if the transfer of receivables with recourse qualifies as a sale. Only in situations where the risks and rewards of ownership analysis prove inconclusive, is the secondary issue

[12] FASB ASC 860-10-40-15; Original Pronouncement: Statement of Financial Accounting Standards No. 140, "Accounting for Transfers and Servicing of Financial Assets and Extinguishments of Liabilities," FASB 2000.

of transfer of control considered under IFRS.[13] Due to these differences in GAAP, some transfers of receivables with recourse may be accounted for as sales under the FASB standard but accounted for as secured borrowings under the IASB standard and vice versa.

Economic Consequences of GAAP and Off-Balance-Sheet Financing

Some firms may have debt covenants or other contractual or legal restrictions that may cause them to prefer to account for transfers of receivables with recourse as sales rather than as secured borrowings. For example, consider a firm with \$.4 billion in bonds payable where the bond indenture[14] requires maintaining a maximum debt-to-equity (D/E) ratio of .75 to 1, and violation of the maximum D/E ratio makes the bonds due immediately at the option of the bondholder. Assume that the firm has total assets of \$2 billion, total liabilities of \$.75 billion, and total stockholders' equity of \$1.25 billion. Recall from chapter 1 that the firm's D/E ratio is calculated at .75/1.25 = .6 to 1, and within the limit set in the debt covenant. The firm is in immediate need of \$.25 billion and seeks to get the cash by transferring receivables without recourse. However, the receivables are ultimately transferred with recourse because of the transferee's uncertainty concerning customer uncollectible accounts. If the transfer is accounted for as a sale, the firm can sell as much as \$.5 billion in receivables to generate the required \$.25 billion in cash and in doing so, absorb a loss of up to \$.25 billion and still be within the maximum .75 to 1 D/E ratio (.75/1.00 = .75 to 1). However, if the \$.25 of cash received is accounted for as a secured borrowing, the D/E ratio becomes .8 to 1 (1.00/1.25), and violates the debt covenant, which may cause the firm financial distress.

This is an example of the economic consequences of GAAP—firms may be economically affected by transactions and events differently,

[13] International Accounting Standard No. 39, "Financial Instruments: Recognition and Measurement," IASB.

[14] An indenture is a debt covenant that refers to the contractual arrangement between the debtor and creditor in the case of a bond issue.

depending upon how they are accounted for. In this specific example, the firm will want to structure the transfer of receivables with recourse such that all three GAAP criteria are met so that the transfer will be accounted for as a sale and not as a secured borrowing. If the firm accounts for a transfer as a sale while the underlying economic substance of the transaction is at least in part a secured borrowing, "off-balance-sheet financing" occurs. In the circumstances of our example, the firm has economic incentives to keep debt off its balance sheet. Off-balance-sheet financing has been around for some time. *Forbes* magazine in 1980 said, "The basic needs of humans are simple: to get enough food, to find shelter, and to keep debt off the balance sheet." Standard setters and management are continually involved in conflicting efforts. Standard setters continually attempt to develop rules that make firms present all their liabilities on the balance sheet, while management continually structures transactions that abide by the rules but avoid including debt on the balance sheet.[15] Off-balance-sheet financing will be discussed as it relates to material in future chapters. Accounting for long-term lease commitments as simple rental arrangements is the primary form of "off-balance-sheet financing." Leases are discussed in chapter 6.

Revenue Recognition Later in the Operating Cycle

As stated previously, the general revenue recognition principle identifies the point in the operating cycle when the firm provides goods or services to the customer as the "critical event" in the earnings process

[15] To appreciate the magnitude of off-balance-sheet financing, consider the following incident related to the financial crisis of 2008. Lehman Brothers was able to remove $50 billion of debt from its second quarter 2008 balance sheet by using a "window dressing" practice called "Repo 105." Repo 105 involved "selling" assets for less than their fair value shortly before a balance sheet date, but agreeing to buy them back at fair value shortly thereafter. The cash provided from the "buyer" was used to temporarily pay off debt so that it would not appear in the balance sheet. The sole purpose of Repo 105 transfers was to reduce the amount of debt Lehman reported on its balance sheet. Most would view the underlying substance of Repo 105 transfers as secured borrowing arrangements. However, Lehman successfully used a technicality in the GAAP rules that enabled them to treat Repo 105 transfers as sales. On September 15, 2008 Lehman filed for the largest bankruptcy on record in the history of the United States.

that triggers revenue recognition. Under situations where the firm cannot make reasonable estimates of things like uncollectible accounts, revenue and profit recognition may be delayed to the point of cash collection. In these situations, cash collection is deemed to be the "critical event." Two methods that use the point of cash collection for profit recognition are the "installment sales" method and the "cost recovery first" method. Both of these methods are considered to be relatively "conservative" methods of accounting because they delay or "defer" profit recognition beyond the point of transfer, and in doing so present lower amounts of net assets (stockholders' equity) in the balance sheet.

In discussing these methods, consider the following example: On 9/01/12 Behrend (a calendar year Corp.) sells goods with a cost of $.9 million on account to a customer for a total of $1.2 million with payment to be made in monthly installments of $.1 million at the beginning of each month September 2012 through August 2013.[16] Assume that the customer makes all scheduled payments. The installment sales method recognizes profit with each cash collection proportionate to the gross profit percentage of the sale. The amount of gross profit on the sale is $.3 million ($1.2 million – $.9 million), and the gross profit percentage is 25% ($.3 million/$1.2 million). Each month Behrend will recognize gross profit of $.025 million (monthly cash collected of $.1 million × 25%). Under the installment sales method, $.1 million of gross profit will be recognized in calendar year 2012, and the remaining $.2 million will be recognized in 2013. The cost recovery first method is even more conservative than the installment sales method because no gross profit is recognized until all cost has first been recovered. In our example, the first nine $.1 million customer payments are accounted for as recovery of the inventory's cost ($.9 million) and the last three customer payments

[16] Since this example assumes payments will be made within one year, FASB ASC 835-30-15-3; Original Pronouncement: Accounting Principles Board Opinion No. 21, "Interest on Receivables and Payables," (New York: AICPA 1971), allows interest to be ignored. If payments extend beyond one year, the interest component must be accounted for separately under the accrual basis of accounting.

(June, July, and August 2013) are recognized as gross profit in full. Under the cost recovery first method, Behrend recognizes zero gross profit in 2012, and $.3 million in 2013.

If Behrend can make reasonable estimates of such things as customer uncollectible accounts, they should apply the general revenue recognition principle, and in doing so recognize all $.3 million of gross profit in 2012—when the goods were provided to the customer. The following table illustrates the difference in profit recognition under the three methods:

Profit recognized in	2012	2013	Total
General Revenue Recognition Principle	$.3 mil	$0	$.3 mil
Installment Sales Method	$.1 mil	$.2 mil	$.3 mil
Cost Recovery First Method	$0	$.3 mil	$.3 mil

Notice that in each case the aggregate amount of gross profit recognized is equal in total; it is a matter of when. The most conservative of the three methods is the cost recovery first method and the least conservative (or relatively most aggressive) of the three methods is application of the general revenue recognition principle. Also note that by recognizing profit sooner, stockholders' equity at 12/31/12 will be $.3 million, and $.2 million higher under general revenue recognition than it is under the cost recovery first and installment sales methods, respectively.

Revenue Recognition Earlier in the Operating Cycle

In certain situations, the "critical event" in the earnings process is deemed to occur before goods or services are provided to the customer. Firms recognize profit (or loss) at the "completion of production" even though a sale has not occurred under circumstances where goods are readily salable at determinable prices without substantial effort. This is the case for precious metals and agricultural products. For these industries the critical event is deemed to occur when the metals are mined or when the crops are harvested.

Accounting by Long-Term Contractors[17]

Another area where accelerating profit recognition may be appropriate is the case of long-term contractors such as shipbuilders, bridge construction, etc. Consider the example of Behrend Corp. entering into a contract with the state of Ohio to build a bridge across Lake Erie from Marblehead to Kelley's Island—a distance of about five miles. The fixed contract price is $1 billion, and Behrend estimates it will incur a total cost of about $800 million to construct the bridge over a three-year period. Assume that Behrend's estimates are consistent and ultimately correct—beginning the project in 2012 with completion in 2014 for a total profit of $200 million. Assume also that Behrend's total construction costs of $800 million are incurred as follows: $160 million in 2012, $400 million in 2013, and $240 million in 2014.

One alternative is to account for the project in a manner consistent with the revenue principle, which is called the "completed contract method." Under the completed contract method, no profit is recognized until the contract is complete and transferred to the customer. Under the completed contract method, zero profit would be recognized in 2012 and 2013, and the entire $200 million of profit would be recognized in the year of completion—2014. Remember from chapter 1 that investors and creditors use financial statement information in predicting the amounts, timing, and uncertainty of future cash flows, and that cumulative income and cumulative net cash flows are equal in the long run. It may be difficult for the user to make reasonable predictions of the future profitability (and cash flows) of the firm based upon such erratic earnings reported in the income statement under the completed contract method.

---

[17] Discussion in this section is based upon FASB ASC 605-35, and International Accounting Standard No. 18, "Revenue," IASB. The FASB and IASB have jointly proposed a different model (Proposed Accounting Standard Update, "Revenue Recognition (Topic 605) Revenue from Contracts with Customers," FASB, Revised 1/04/2012. No specific anticipated effective date is provided, but the FASB indicates 2015 at the earliest, with early adoption not permitted. If the proposal becomes GAAP, some changes in accounting by long-term contractors may occur; however, the fundamental procedures presented here will continue under the current language contained in the proposed accounting standard update.

A preferred alternative method of accounting for long-term contracts that is more commonly used in practice is called the "percentage of completion method." The percentage of completion method recognizes a portion of the total contract profit each period during construction based upon the estimated progress toward completion achieved during the period. In determining the estimated progress toward completion, either input or output measures can be used. In our Behrend Corp. example, assume that the length of the bridge is actually equal to 5 miles. Behrend may use this output measure to estimate that each mile of bridge construction constitutes 20% (1/5) progress toward project completion. For each mile of bridge completed during a period, $40 million of profit should be recognized ($200 million × 20%). If Behrend completes 1 mile in 2012, 3 miles in 2013, and 1 mile in 2014, it will recognize profit each year during construction period of $40 million, $120 million, and $40 million, respectively. Output measures are appropriate only if the units of the output measure used are uniform in terms of actual progress toward completion. In our bridge construction example, it is likely that connecting the bridge to land would be relatively more difficult to construct, as would the portion of the bridge built over the deepest part of the lake. In other words, each mile is not equivalent in terms of progress toward completion of the bridge.

For this and other reasons, an input measure called "cost-to-cost" is most commonly used in practice in estimating progress toward completion under the percentage of completion method. Under the cost-to-cost measure, at the end of each reporting period **percentage completed to date** is first calculated:

1) **percentage completed to date** = costs incurred to date/total estimated cost of the project.

The percentage completed to date is next used to calculate **profit to be recognized to date**:

2) **profit to be recognized to date** = percentage completed to date × estimated total profit.

The particular **period's profit** is then calculated:

3) **period's profit recognized** = profit to be recognized to date – profit recognized previously.

The following illustrates the cost-to-cost method for Behrend Corp. assuming that the original cost estimate for the project was correct and never changed from $800 million:

	2012	2013	2014
Contract Price	$1 billion	$1 billion	$1 billion
Cost Incurred to Date	$.16 billion	$.56 billion	$.8 billion
Estimated Cost to Complete	$.64 billion	$.24 billion	$0
Estimated Total Cost	$.8 billion	$.8 billion	$.8 billion
Estimated Total Profit	$.2 billion	$.2 billion	$.2 billion
Percentage Completed to Date—1) above	20%	70%	100%
Profit to be Recognized to Date—2) above	$.04 billion	$.14 billion	$.2 billion
Less Profit Previously Recognized	$0	$.04 billion	$.14 billion
Period's Profit Recognized—3) above	$.04 billion	$.10 billion	$.06 billion

Note that consistent with the completed contract method, total profit recognized is $.2 billion. Assuming that "Cost-to-Cost" is an appropriate measure of progress toward completion, the key to accurately reporting periodic profit under the percentage of completion method is the precision of "Estimated Cost to Complete," which then determines "Estimated Total Cost" and "Estimated Total Profit." In the previous example, estimates are consistently correct, which results in consistently correct profit recognition for each year of construction.

We now consider the effects of erroneous estimates during the construction periods under the two methods of accounting used by long-term contractors. This example will illustrate how changes in estimate of total project cost affect profit recognition each year. We continue to assume that all actual amounts remain unchanged: contract price remains $1 billion, actual project costs incurred each year are still $160 million in 2012, $400 million in 2013, and $240 million in 2014, and the project is completed in 2014 for a total profit of $200 million. However, we now erroneously estimate the total costs to complete the project to be $480 million at 12/31/12, and $140 million at 12/31/13.

Under the completed contract method these errors would not affect reported profit. Since zero profit is recognized until the year of completion, and total profit remains unchanged at $200 million, profit recognition is consistent with the previous example where estimates were consistently correct. Zero profit is recognized in 2012, 2013, and the full $200 million of project profit is recognized in the year of completion, 2014.

The following illustrates how the errors in estimate affect profit recognition under the percentage of completion method using cost-to-cost measures:

	2012	2013	2014
Contract Price	$1 billion	$1 billion	$1 billion
Cost Incurred to Date	$.16 billion	$.56 billion	$.8 billion
Estimated Cost to Complete	$.48 billion	$.14 billion	$0
Estimated Total Cost	$.64 billion	$.70 billion	$.8 billion
Estimated Total Profit	$.36 billion	$.30 billion	$.2 billion
Percentage Completed to Date—1) above	25%	80%	100%
Profit to be Recognized to Date—2) above	$.09 billion	$.24 billion	$.20 billion
Less Profit Previously Recognized	$0	$.09 billion	$.24 billion
Period's Profit Recognized—3) above	$.09 billion	$.15 billion	$–.04 billion

Note that the total amount of profit recognized over the life of the project is once again $200 million. Comparing these reported profit amounts with the previously determined "correct amounts" (observed when the estimates were consistently correct), we can compute each year's understated or overstated profit:

	2012	2013	2014
Profit (Loss) with errors in estimate	$.12 billion	$.15 billion	$–.04 billion
Correct Amounts (no errors in estimate)	$.04 billion	$.10 billion	$.06 billion
Over or Under Reported Profit	$.05 billion	$.05 billion	$–.10 billion

Consistent with our previous discussion, changes in estimate are accounted for prospectively—we do not change previously issued financial statements. The overstatement of profit in 2012 ($50 million) and in 2013 ($50 million), are offset by understating reported profit in 2014 ($–100 million).

It is important to note that there is a direct negative relationship between the degree of error in the year-end "Estimated Cost to Complete" and misstatement of cumulative profit recognized ("Profit to be Recognized to Date"). If year-end "Estimated Cost to Complete" is understated, "Profit (to be) Recognized to Date" is overstated. The underestimation of "Estimated Cost to Complete" at year-end has the dual effect of overstating cumulative reported profit by overestimating both: "Estimated Total Profit" and "Percentage Completed to Date." The opposite effects occur if year-end "Estimated Cost to Complete" is overestimated.

As indicated previously, the percentage of completion method is the preferred method of accounting by long-term contractors. This is consistent under both U.S. GAAP and IFRS. Recall from chapter 1 that information must be both relevant and provide faithful representation to be useful for decision making. The degree to which information is verifiable is considered to be directly related to its representational faithfulness. Information is considered to be verifiable to the extent knowledgeable and independent observers would reach consensus concerning the reported amounts. Since the completed contract method is based upon actual past results, it reports profit amounts that are more verifiable and therefore more faithfully represented measures. However, the percentage of completion method provides more relevant information because profit is reported in a more timely manner—throughout multiyear construction projects. This is an example involving the trade-off between relevance and faithful representation in financial reporting. The percentage of completion method should be used unless the contractor cannot make reasonable estimates of total contract profit and periodic progress toward completion. Under the cost-to-cost method, this is a function of the ability to reasonably estimate "Estimated Cost to Complete." If reasonable estimates cannot be made, it is assumed that the increased relevance of the percentage method is more than offset by its reduced representational faithfulness, making the financial statement information less useful for decision making. Under U.S. GAAP the completed contract method should be used when reasonable estimates of profit and progress cannot be made. Under IFRS, the "cost recovery" method is used when reasonable estimates of profit and progress cannot be made. These methods are very similar with delaying profit recognition until the period of contract completion, and as such are relatively "conservative" when compared with the percentage of completion method.

Additional Issues Concerning Accounting by Long-Term Contractors

Balance Sheet Presentation

Contractors typically make substantial investment in projects and collect cash from customers by billing them during the construction period. Project investments are recognized in an account "construction in progress" (CIP). Customer billings are recognized in an account "progress billings" (PB). These two new accounts do not appear separately in the balance sheet. They are compared on a project by project basis and if CIP > PB, shown net among current assets; whereas if CIP < PB, shown net among current liabilities. Even though projects may extend beyond one year, the balance sheet classification as current is appropriate because of long-term contractors' multiyear operating cycle.

We return to the original Behrend bridge project example (where estimates were consistently correct) to illustrate financial statement impacts using the accounting equation framework. Recall that the contract price was $1 billion and the total contract cost of $800 million was incurred: $.16 billion in 2012, $.4 billion in 2013, and $.24 billion in 2014. It is important to note that we previously determined each year's profit under the completed contract method ($0, $0, $.2 billion, respectively) and under the percentage of completion method ($.04 billion, $.1 billion, $.06 billion, respectively) without regard to customer billing or cash collection. We now assume customer billings for the $1 billion contract price occurred as follows: $.19 billion in 2012, $.41 billion in 2013, and $.4 billion in 2014. In order to simplify the illustration and concentrate on pertinent issues, we assume that the customer (State of Ohio) makes full payment in the year of billing, and all investments in the bridge project are made by paying cash.[18] The following financial statement effects occur in 2012:

ASSETS		=	LIABILITIES		+	SE	
			Incur construction cost in 2012—<u>Both methods</u>				
+ CIP	+.16 bil						
– Cash	–.16 bil						
			Bill customer in 2012—<u>Both methods</u>				
+ Accounts Rec.	+.19 bil		+ PB	+.19 bil			
			Receive 2012 customer payment—<u>Both methods</u>				
+ Cash	+.19 bil						
– Accounts Rec.	–.19 bil						
			Recognize 2012 construction profit—<u>Percentage of completion method only</u>				
+ CIP	+.04 bil					+ Const. Profit[19]	+.04 bil

Note that this last transaction is only recognized under percentage of completion—no profit would be recognized in 2012 under the completed contract method. The other transactions would be recognized under both methods. Since profit recognition increases CIP, its 12/31/2012 balance will be \$.04 higher under the percentage completion method (CIP = \$.2 billion) than under the completed contract method (CIP = \$.16 billion). This results in reporting a net current asset under percentage completion of \$.01 billion (CIP = \$.2 billion; PB = \$.19 billion), whereas a net current liability of \$.03 billion would be reported under the completed contract method (PB = \$.19 billion; CIP = \$.16 billion). As this

[18] Actual bridge construction costs would include various materials inventories (steel beams, concrete, cable, bolts and nuts, etc.), depreciation on machinery and equipment, etc.

[19] Construction profit (or loss) is actually recognized using two income statement accounts: "Construction Revenue" and "Cost of Construction" (an expense similar to cost of goods sold). For example, Construction Revenue would be recognized for \$.2 billion and Cost of Construction would be recognized for \$.16 billion (cost incurred during 2012).

example illustrates, firms that apply the completed contract method report lower liquidity measures (working capital, current ratio, and quick ratio) than firms that use the percentage of completion method. Additionally, since the income statement account "construction profit" would be closed to retained earnings at the end of the year, Stockholders' Equity at 12/31/2012 is \$.04 billion higher under the percentage completion method than under the completed contract method. As this example illustrates, firms using the completed contract method generally report higher debt to equity ratios (total debt/total SE) than firms applying the percentage of completion method.

At the end of 2013 Retained Earnings and CIP will be \$.14 higher under the percentage of completion method. This difference results in reporting a net current asset under percentage completion of \$.1 billion (CIP = \$.7 billion; PB = \$.6 billion), whereas a net current liability of \$.04 billion would be reported under the completed contract method (PB = \$.60 billion; CIP = \$.56 billion).

Although 2014 profit recognized is \$.14 billion higher under the completed contract method, since both methods recognize cumulative profit over the entire construction period of \$.2 billion, the balance sheets are identical once the project is completed. Upon completion of the project, the CIP and PB accounts are closed out—there is no longer any "construction in progress." PB and CIP each have balances equal to the contract price of \$1 billion, PB because the entire contract price has been billed to the customer, and CIP because its two components, construction costs incurred to date (\$.8 billion) plus profit recognized to date (\$.2 billion) sum to the contract price.

Anticipated Project Losses and "Conservatism"

An additional complexity involves anticipated project losses. If an overall project loss is expected ((cost to date + estimated cost to complete) > contract price), the full amount of the loss must be recognized immediately. This is an example of the accounting convention of "conservatism." If a loss is anticipated—recognize it immediately. We will discuss other instances of conservatism as it relates to material in future chapters. This requirement of immediate loss recognition applies regardless of the method used to account for long-term contracts. If the completed contract method is used, the total estimated loss must be recognized during the period in which it is first anticipated. If the percentage completion method is used, a loss equal to the sum of the total anticipated loss plus any profit recognized in previous periods must be recognized during the period in which a loss is first anticipated. The amount of loss recognized is equal to the amount of loss that would be recognized if we assumed the contract was 100% complete at the end of the anticipated loss period.

Going back to our original bridge construction example, let's now assume that at the end of the second year (2013) Behrend estimates the cost to complete the bridge at \$.5 billion (previously we estimated the cost to complete at \$.24 billion). The costs to date (\$.56 billion) + estimated cost to complete (\$.5 billion) now equals \$1.06 billion, which exceeds the contract price of \$1 billion resulting in an estimated overall loss of \$.06 billion. Recall from the original example that no profit (or loss) was recognized in previous periods (2012) under the completed contract method. However, under the percentage completion method \$.04 billion of profit was recognized in 2012 based upon year-end estimates. Under the completed contract method we would recognize a 2013 loss of \$.06 billion. However, under the percentage completion method, a 2013 loss of \$.10 billion would need to be recognized—the sum of the overall anticipated loss (\$.06 billion) + profit previously recognized (2012 profit of \$.04 billion). Recognizing construction loss has the opposite impact upon the accounting equation. Whereas construction profit is recognized with an offsetting increase in CIP, construction loss is recognized by decreasing CIP. When a long-term contractor anticipates an overall project loss during a period, the cumulative effects of accounting entries are the same regardless of whether the completed contract or percentage of completion method is used, and as such should result in identical balance sheets.

Earnings Management

As discussed in chapter 1, the "quality of earnings" concept relates to the usefulness of reported earnings in estimating future earnings (and cash flows). A related topic is called "earnings management." Management choices among available accounting methods (e.g., completed contract versus percentage of completion) and required management estimates of the future (e.g., uncollectible accounts) impact current and future periods' earnings. Managers generally want to report a smooth upward trend in earnings because erratic earnings patterns (even though the data points may result in the same best fitted line under least squares analysis) are perceived to indicate higher risk, which causes higher borrowing rates and lower stock prices. There is also evidence that failure to meet market expectations by reporting earnings at an amount less than anticipated can have a significant negative impact upon the firm's stock price. As such, many believe that it is management's fiduciary duty to make legitimate efforts to manage earnings in order to maximize stockholders' wealth. The issue of earnings management also relates to the concept of "economic consequences." Managers are particularly motivated to report smooth upward earnings performance and meet market expectations if their personal wealth is related to the value of the firm's stock (e.g., as a stockholder, stock option holder, etc.). Some believe that earnings management has gone too far. Former SEC Chairman Arthur Levitt expressed his concern with the earnings management issue by saying, "Earnings reports reflect the desires of management rather than the underlying financial performance of the company."[20]

Legitimate earnings management efforts can provide "high quality" amounts if they are sustainable and therefore indicative of future earnings.[21] Earnings management is a matter of relative degree. The continuum goes from unbiased management choices to legitimate efforts to reasonably manage earnings to fraudulent financial reporting. Consider a firm experiencing between 2 and 3% uncollectible accounts from credit sales in each of the last 10 years, with no discernible pattern or point estimate within the 2–3% range that is more likely to occur. Although the

---

[20] "The Numbers Game," Remarks by Chairman Arthur Levitt, SEC, Delivered at NYU Center for Law and Business, New York, September 28, 1998.

[21] General Electric reported 100 consecutive quarters of increased income from continuing operations through 2000 and had the largest market capitalization at that time ($590 billion). Although GE's management denies it, many believe this was accomplished through effective earnings management.

unbiased estimate would be 2.5%, reasonable estimates of uncollectible accounts expense could be argued to range anywhere from 2% to 3%. Managers wanting to increase reported earnings could use a relatively optimistic 2% estimate, whereas those wanting to decrease reported earnings could use a relatively pessimistic 3% estimate. Unless the creditworthiness of customers making purchases on account has changed during the current period, using a percentage estimate outside the 2–3% range in order to increase or decrease reported income would not be considered reasonable earnings management. There is no "bright line" indicating when reasonable earnings management becomes fraudulent financial reporting along the continuum.

The earnings management issue that relates to material in this chapter concerns management's choice among methods permitted under GAAP, and management estimates that are required when formulating the financial statements.[22] Management incentives to report higher current period earnings can be accommodated by making optimistic estimates of future customers: uncollectible accounts, returns, allowances, and discounts. In the case of long-term contractors, current period earnings can be increased by choosing the percentage of completion method and making optimistic estimates of the cost to complete projects. Current period earnings could instead be managed downward (decreased) by making pessimistic estimates of future events. In doing so, management would create "cookie jar" reserves that could be drawn upon in the future when actual earnings might otherwise be reported at amounts lower than desired by management. Management's ability to manage earnings upward or downward is accommodated by GAAP's requirement to account for changes in estimate prospectively.

In summary, management must make accounting method choices and estimates that affect earnings amounts reported in the current and future periods. Earnings management relates to the degree to which management intentionally influences reported earnings through accounting method choices and estimates. The earnings management continuum

[22] Additional issues involving earnings management (e.g., timing of asset disposals, etc.) will be discussed in future chapters.

goes from unbiased choices to fraudulent financial reporting. Legitimate efforts by management to report a steady increasing pattern of reported earnings may provide "high quality" amounts. However, as earnings management moves toward fraudulent financial reporting, reported earnings become correspondingly less useful to users in estimating future income and cash flows.

CHAPTER 3

Inventory and Cost of Goods Sold

We continue our discussion of current assets and the related income statement effects. In this chapter we concentrate on inventory and its related expense—cost of goods sold. Inventory includes goods held out for sale or held for production in the ordinary course of business. For manufacturing and merchandising firms, inventory is frequently the largest current asset presented on the balance sheet and cost of goods sold the largest expense reported in the income statement. Merchandisers are merchants and simply buy and sell goods in their unaltered finished condition. Manufacturers acquire raw materials and subsequently incur "conversion" costs of labor and overhead in converting the materials into finished goods that are ultimately sold to customers. Manufacturers have three classes of inventory: raw materials, work-in-process, and finished goods. Raw materials have yet to enter the manufacturing process whereas finished goods have completed the manufacturing process and are held for sale. Materials that have entered but not completed the manufacturing process at the balance sheet date are included in work-in-process. Merchandisers have only one class of inventory, which is called merchandise inventory. Although manufacturers' inventory and cost of goods sold accounting is similar to merchandisers', there are differences. Complexities of accounting for inventory by manufacturers are typically addressed in cost accounting books. Our discussion here will be limited to merchandisers.

Given recent information technology advances, most firms utilize a "perpetual inventory" system. This is the system assumed in chapter 1's review where purchases of goods for sale were recorded as increases in inventory, and sales of goods were recorded as reductions in inventory and recognized as cost of goods sold. In such a system the business keeps a continual up-to-date (perpetual) record of how much inventory it should have in stock. You are probably familiar with barcode scanning checkout registers at retailers like Target, Wal-Mart, etc. These "point of sale systems" update the inventory records at the time of sale and are an integral part of a perpetual inventory system for retailers. Actual quantities of inventory on hand will likely differ from the perpetual record amounts because of theft, breakage, etc. Therefore, physical inventory must be taken periodically to determine the quantity of inventory actually held. Taking physical inventory involves counting the items of inventory on hand.[1] Although maintaining a perpetual inventory system does not preclude the need for periodically taking physical inventory, it does enhance internal control. The physical count can be compared with the perpetual record amounts to monitor inventory "shrinkage" due to theft, breakage, etc.

Prior to information technology advances, perpetual inventory systems were more costly to maintain, and frequently considered to be cost ineffective (the perceived benefit from the enhanced information was judged to be less than the cost incurred to provide it). Under such circumstances, firms used a "periodic inventory system," where no perpetual record of inventory is maintained. The amount of inventory appearing in the balance sheet is determined "periodically" by taking physical inventory at each balance sheet date. In a periodic inventory system, a temporary account, "purchases" is used to keep track of inventory acquisitions that occur during the income statement period. The inventory account is not changed until an adjustment is made at the end of the period. Although most firms now use perpetual inventory systems, our discussions sometimes assume a periodic system to better illustrate how inventory related issues impact the financial statements. We will supplement our discussion concerning perpetual versus periodic inventory system implications when appropriate. Exhibit 3.1 illustrates a detailed schedule of Behrend Corp.'s gross profit for 2012. This is an expanded version of Behrend's 2012 income statement previously illustrated in Exhibit 1.2, and adapted to a periodic inventory system.

Exhibit 3.1 shows that "cost of goods available for sale" is the sum of inventory held at the beginning of the period plus purchases of goods that

---

[1] Rather than counting every item of inventory, statistical sampling may be used when a perpetual inventory system is in place.

Exhibit 3.1. Behrend Corp. Partial Income Statement Year Ended 12/31/2012

Net Sales Revenue			$1,900,000
Less Cost of Goods Sold:			
Beginning Inventory		$250,000	
Add Full Cost of Net Purchases:			
Purchases	$1,050,000		
Less Purchases Returns and Allowances	50,000		
Net Purchases	$1,000,000		
Plus Freight-In	100,000	$1,100,000	
Cost of Goods Available for Sale		$1,350,000	
Less Ending Inventory		350,000	
Cost of Goods Sold			$1,000,000
Gross Profit			$900,000

occurred during the period. Beginning inventory is synonymous with inventory at the end of the previous period (see Behrend's 12/31/2011 balance sheet in Exhibit 1.1). Cost of goods available for sale is divided into two parts: ending inventory that appears as a current asset in the 12/31/2012 balance sheet (see Exhibit 1.5), and cost of goods sold, which is recognized as expense in the 2012 income statement. It is important to note that all other things held constant, the larger the asset inventory, the lower the cost of goods sold, and vice versa. We now discuss basic inventory issues, referring to Exhibit 3.1 where appropriate.

What Goods are Included in Inventory

Merchandise inventory includes goods owned by a corporation that are held for sale in the ordinary course of business. Assuming Behrend Corp. is operated as a university bookstore, inventory would include books, supplies, university memorabilia, clothing, etc. Inventory would not include assets that are used in the business but not held for sale (e.g., building, lighting fixtures, display shelves, cash registers, etc). Only goods legally owned by the firm should be included in its inventory. Goods held on consignment are not legally owned by the consignee (firm with physical possession), and should be included on the consignor's balance sheet as inventory. Likewise, goods that are in transit at the balance sheet date may or may not be included in inventory. "Free On Board" (FOB) followed by a location indicates when legal title to goods passes. Terms are either "FOB shipping point" or "FOB destination." While in transit, FOB shipping point goods are owned by and appropriately included in inventory of the buyer, whereas goods shipped FOB destination are owned by and appropriately included in inventory of the seller. Not only does this technicality of title passage affect inventory inclusion, it also affects revenue recognition. Goods that are sold under terms FOB destination should not be recognized as revenue until the exchange takes place—in the period when the goods are transferred to the customer.

Full Cost Principle

Under GAAP all ordinary and necessary costs incurred in getting an asset into its intended usable state are "capitalized," which means included in the cost of the asset. This is commonly referred to as the full cost principle. Under the full cost principle the ordinary and necessary costs of getting inventory to the intended place where it is held for sale are included in the cost of inventory. For example "freight-in" is a capitalized cost of inventory (termed a "product cost") under the full cost principle. Freight-in is the transportation cost incurred by the customer when goods are purchased FOB shipping point. Freight-in is added to purchases in determining cost of goods available for sale under the periodic method illustrated in Exhibit 3.1. Whoever owns the goods while in transit is responsible for the shipping charges. If goods are sold to a customer FOB destination, the seller owns the goods while in transit and is therefore responsible for the delivery charges.

Delivery charges borne by the seller (i.e., sold FOB destination) are considered to be a selling expense that is recognized as a "period cost." Product costs are initially capitalized to inventory and subsequently recognized as cost of goods sold in the income statement. Period costs are recognized as expense in the period incurred, but not as part of cost of goods sold. As an example, assume that Behrend Corp. purchases 100 books at an invoiced price of $110/book from a supplier under terms FOB shipping point. Assume also that since Behrend holds legal title to the books while in transit, they incur $50 for "freight-in" to have the inventory shipped to their location. Under the full cost principle, the cost of each book is $110.50 including the invoiced price of $110/book plus the ordinary and necessary freight charge of $.50/book. If Behrend mistakenly had the books originally shipped to the wrong location, which resulted in an increased freight charge to $90, the cost per book remains at $110.50. Only the ordinary and necessary freight charge of $.50 should be capitalized to inventory; the remaining $40 excess cost incurred should be treated as a period cost and recognized as expense or loss in the period the shipping mistake was made. In a perpetual system, sale of 10 of the books would result in an inventory reduction and cost of goods sold recognition in the amount of $1,105 (10 books @ $110.50/book).

Purchases Returns, Allowances, and Discounts

In the previous chapter we discussed returns, allowances, and discounts from the seller's perspective. These topics are identical here but considered from the opposite (purchaser's) perspective, and for the sake of brevity we do not repeat the discussion of what returns, allowances, and discounts are. Recall from chapter 2 that returns and allowances are presented as contra revenue accounts for the seller. Under the periodic inventory method returns and allowances are treated as contra purchases accounts in arriving at net purchases (see Exhibit 3.1). Inventory on the balance sheet and cost of goods sold on the income statement should be consistent, whether returns and allowances are accounted for using the periodic or perpetual method. Returned goods would be excluded from year-end inventory, and merchandise on hand at the end of the period for which a supplier allowance was granted would be included in inventory at its reduced cost (net of the allowance amount). The recording difference under the perpetual method is that the inventory account would be directly reduced at the time of the return or allowance rather than recording them in separate contra accounts.

When accounting for sales discounts in chapter 2, we assumed the "gross" method was used by the seller. However, our discussion of purchases discounts here will assume the use of the "net" method. We do this not only so that the reader becomes familiar with both methods, but also because comparing the gross and net methods accommodates a discussion of the concept of "management by exception." Under the concept of "management by exception," management directs their attention to areas where things are not going according to plan—"exceptions"—not to areas where things are going as expected.

Consider the following example: Behrend purchases 50 books from a supplier on 7/31/12 at a gross invoice price of $70/book with terms 2/10, n/30. The terms indicate that Behrend can pay the gross invoice amount of $3,500 in 30 days (by 8/30/12), or take advantage of the 2% discount and pay $3,430 by 8/10/12 (20 days earlier). As we discussed in chapter 2, we can annualize the 2% discount rate by multiplying it by 365/20 which results in an annual savings rate > 36%! Given these generous terms, Behrend's management should definitely want to take advantage of discounts by paying within the discount period. The net method records an increase in either purchases or inventory (periodic versus perpetual method, respectively) at the net-of-discount invoice amount ($3,430) with an offsetting increase in the current liability, accounts payable. The net method accommodates monitoring company policy to take advantage of purchase discounts, because when payment is made after the discount period (which should be the "exception") a period expense is recognized—"discounts lost." The effects upon the accounting equation for this example assuming the net method of accounting for purchases discounts and a perpetual inventory system are as follows:

ASSETS		=	LIABILITIES		+	SE
Purchase of $3,500 inventory on account terms 2/10, n/30						
+ Inventory[2]	+3,430		+ Accts. Pay.	+3,430		
Payment of $3,430 made within 10 days						
– Cash	–3,430		– Accts. Pay.	–3,430		
Payment of $3,500 made in 30 days						
– Cash	–3,500		– Accts. Pay.	–3,430		+ Discounts Lost – 70

Recall from chapter 2 that under the gross method the full invoice price is initially recorded. From the purchaser's perspective the current liability, accounts payable is increased by the full gross invoice amount ($3,500) with an offsetting increase in either purchases or inventory. Subsequently under the gross method, if paid within the discount period

[2] Under the periodic method, the purchases account would be increased rather than inventory.

"purchases discounts" is recognized for the $70 discount taken. There is no separate recording of "discounts lost" under the gross method and there is no separate recording of "purchases discounts (taken)" under the net method. Assuming a management policy of taking advantage of purchase discounts, the net method highlights instances of exceptions by recording "discounts lost," whereas the gross method highlights instances when payment is made within the discount period (the expectation) by recording "purchases discounts." The net method accommodates management by exception by alerting management if invoices are not being paid within the discount period, so that they can remedy the situation.

Lower of Cost or Market

Although the primary measurement attribute for inventory is historical cost (as determined under the full cost principle), if cost exceeds "market" value at the balance sheet date, inventory must be written down to market and a loss must be recognized. If the "lower of cost or market" (LCM) write-down loss is considered to be significant, it should be presented as a separate income statement line item or disclosed in the notes to the financial statements. If considered to be immaterial, the write-down can be recognized as an increase in cost of goods sold. Contrary to loss recognition, no gain is recognized if market value exceeds cost, because inventory is not written up to market value under GAAP. This is another example of the "conservatism" convention that was introduced in chapter 2, regarding loss recognition by long-term contractors. Write-down and loss recognition under LCM is required under both U.S. GAAP and IFRS. There is a minor difference between the two in defining "market." IFRS defines market as net realizable value (anticipated selling price minus disposal costs) whereas U.S. GAAP generally defines market as replacement cost.[3]

[3] U.S. GAAP defines market as replacement cost, subject to ceiling and floor limitations. The ceiling is net realizable value (NRV) and the floor is NRV minus normal profit. The ceiling is intended to ensure sufficient loss is recognized from the write-down so that no additional loss is expected in a subsequent period of sale, whereas the floor is intended to ensure the write-down loss isn't excessive such that excessive profit is recognized in the period of sale. All illustrations assume that replacement cost is lower than the ceiling and higher than the floor limitations.

There are three methods used in applying LCM with varying degrees of conservatism regarding their application. The lower the amount of inventory presented on the balance sheet, the larger the associated write-down and loss recognized, and the relatively more conservative the financial statement presentation. Under most circumstances where some inventory items have declined in value (i.e., cost > market), while others have increased in value (i.e., cost < market), the most conservative application of LCM is on an item-by-item basis and the least conservative is application to inventory as a whole. Application to major categories of inventory is the middle ground. To illustrate these three applications of LCM and their impact upon the financial statements, consider the following simplified example: Behrend holds only four items in inventory: an accounting textbook, a dictionary, a sweatshirt, and a notebook.[4] These four inventory items are included in two major categories: textbooks and dictionaries are classified as books, and sweatshirts and notebooks are classified as supplies. Assume physical inventory indicates there are 100 of each inventory item on hand at the balance sheet date with the following unit costs and market values, respectively: textbook—$50, $54, dictionaries—$15, $14, sweatshirts—$15, $12, and notebooks—$5, $6. Using the physical inventory quantities and per unit cost and market values, we develop the information presented in Exhibit 3.2.

The inventory will be presented on the balance sheet at the lowest amount, $8,100 under the item-by-item LCM application basis. Compared with inventory cost of $8,500, a write-down and loss will be recognized in the amount of $400. If we apply LCM to major inventory categories, a loss will be recognized for $200 in order to write the inventory down to market, $8,300. The reason for the reduced write-down is the ability to offset declines in value of inventory items with increases in value of other items, but only within each major category. When LCM is applied on an item-by-item basis, no offsetting is allowed, which results in the most conservative financial statement presentation.

[4] Behrend Corp. would obviously hold more than four items in inventory. The purpose of the simplification here is to illustrate the effects of LCM application with minimal complicating detail.

Exhibit 3.2. Behrend Corp. Lower of Cost or Market (LCM) Methods

	Cost	Market	LCM individual items	LCM major category	LCM total inventory
Accounting Textbook	5,000	5,400	5,000		
Dictionary	1,500	1,400	1,400		
Books Category	6,500	6,800		6,500	
Sweat Shirts	1,500	1,200	1,200		
Notebooks	500	600	500		
Supplies Category	2,000	1,800		1,800	
Total Inventory	8,500	8,600			8,500
LCM			8,100	8,300	8,500

LCM applied to total inventory allows full offsetting without restriction. For Behrend this full offsetting results in no write-down of inventory or loss recognition at all because total market value of $8,600 exceeds total cost of $8,500. No adjusting entry would be made and inventory will be presented in the balance sheet at its cost of $8,500. Notice however that under LCM we do not write up inventory to its market value and recognize a gain. LCM is always considered to be a conservative accounting practice—the three different application methods make it a matter of relative degree.

In addition to the definition of market, there is another difference between U.S. GAAP and IFRS. Under U.S. GAAP, the written-down value of inventory is permanent and becomes "cost" for purposes of applying LCM in subsequent reporting periods. IFRS allows firms whose inventory has increased in value during periods subsequent to its LCM write-down to recover previously recognized loss by recognizing gain, but only to the extent of the previously recognized write-down loss. Recovery of previously recognized write-down loss is not permitted under U.S. GAAP.

Determining Inventory and Cost of Goods Sold Amounts in the Financial Statements

As stated previously, the primary measurement attribute for inventory and cost of goods sold is historical cost (determined under the full cost principle). If inventory units that are available for sale during a period have different costs, the issue of which cost amounts to use for presenting inventory in the balance sheet and cost of goods sold in the income statement needs to be addressed. In discussing this issue, we will use a simplified example of Behrend's purchases and sales of notebooks. We assume that 2011 is their first year of operations, and as such there is no beginning inventory on 1/01/2011. The details of the example appear in Exhibit 3.3. The example indicates 2,500 notebooks available for sale and 1,300 notebooks sold in 2011. As an additional simplification, we assume no notebook inventory shrinkage so that physical inventory at 12/31/2011 indicates 1,200 notebooks are on hand. Regardless of how we assign the total cost of goods (notebooks) available for sale ($8,500) between inventory and cost of goods sold, sales revenue attributed to notebooks will consistently appear in the 2011 income statement at $6,900.

Exhibit 3.3. Behrend Corp. Purchases and Sales—Notebooks Year Ended 12/31/2011

	Units	$/Unit	Total $
Beginning Inventory	0	$0	$0
Purchases			
01/06/2011	1,500	$3	$4,500
08/15/2011	1,000	$4	4,000
Available for Sale	2,500		$8,500
Sales			
02/04/2011	900	$5	$4,500
12/20/2011	400	$6	2,400
Total Sales	1,300		$6,900
Ending Inventory	1,200		

Specific Identification Method

The inventory method that is most intuitively appealing is the "specific identification" (SID) method. Under SID the actual physical flow of goods is used in determining the amounts of inventory and cost of goods sold that appear in the financial statements. Each inventory unit is specifically identified through a serial number, barcode, etc. and has its own individual unit cost amount. In a perpetual system, at the time of sale, inventory is reduced and cost of goods sold is recognized for the cost of the specifically identified unit sold. Physical inventory is taken not only to determine the number of units on hand, but also to specifically identify those units on hand for inventory costing purposes. In a periodic system, the total cost of the specifically identified ending inventory is subtracted from cost of goods available for sale to determine cost of goods sold. Inventory presented in the end of period balance sheet will be the same for periodic and perpetual systems under SID.

The SID method is appropriate for companies whose inventory is composed of unique items, for example, an estate jewelry dealer or an antique/classic car dealership. In these types of businesses it makes an economic difference regarding which item of inventory is being sold, and the specific item's cost should be recognized as cost of goods sold in order to have an appropriate recognition of expense with revenue. However, if a company's goods are interchangeable so that the firm is economically indifferent regarding which unit of inventory is being sold, SID can inappropriately accommodate gross profit manipulation (earnings management).

Assume that the notebooks purchased and sold in Exhibit 3.3 are identical and therefore completely interchangeable. The 2/04/2011 sale is not subject to earnings manipulation and will result in gross profit recognition of $1,800 (sales = $4,500 (900 units @ $5)) and cost of goods sold = $2,700 (900 units @ $3)). The 2/04/2011 sale is not subject to gross profit manipulation because all the notebooks on hand at the time of sale cost $3 each. However, when 400 notebooks are sold on 12/20/2011 there are units on hand with different unit costs. Management can manipulate gross profit on the 12/20/2011 sale by choosing which units to sell—the $3 notebooks, the $4 notebooks, or a combination of the two. Sales revenue will consistently be recognized in the amount of $2,400, but cost of goods sold can be minimized at $1,200 by selling only the $3 notebooks, and can be maximized at $1,600 by selling only the $4 notebooks. At the discretion of management gross profit recognized from the 12/20 sale can be "managed" in a range from a low of $800, to a high of $1,200. This $400 difference would be reflected in the inventory amount appearing on the 12/31/2011 balance sheet. The 1,200 units on hand could be presented at a maximum of $4,600 (200 @ $3 + 1,000 @ $4), and a minimum of $4,200 (600 @ $3 + 600 @ $4). The lower the cost of goods sold, the higher the ending inventory and vice versa.

For reasons of profit manipulation, the SID method should only be used in businesses where inventory is composed of unique items of varying worth. When units of inventory are interchangeable, firms should use an assumed cost flow in determining the financial statement amounts for inventory and cost of goods sold. There is no assumed cost flow under SID because financial statement amounts are determined by the actual physical flow of goods. There are three different assumed cost flow methods allowed under U.S. GAAP. They are "first-in first-out" (FIFO), "average cost," and "last-in first-out" (LIFO). It is important to note that the assumed cost flow doesn't necessarily have anything to do with the actual physical flow of goods. Using the data from Exhibit 3.3 and assuming the periodic method, the gross profit section of the income statement from 2011 notebook sales under each cost flow assumption is developed and illustrated in Exhibit 3.4. The implications

Exhibit 3.4. Behrend Corp. Gross Profit—Notebooks—Periodic Method Year Ended 12/31/2011

	FIFO		Avg. cost		LIFO	
Sales Revenue		$6,900		$6,900		$6,900
Less Cost of Goods Sold:						
Beginning Inv.	$0		$0		$0	
Plus Purchases	8,500		8,500		8,500	
Cost of Goods Available for Sale:	$8,500		$8,500		$8,500	
Less Ending Inv. (1,200 units)	4,600		4,080		3,600	
Cost of Goods Sold		3,900		4,420		4,900
Gross Profit		$3,000		$2,480		$2,000

of using a perpetual system are discussed below as we elaborate on each inventory method. Note that regardless of the assumed cost flow, consistent with specific identification, the financial statement amounts of inventory and cost of goods sold are determined using historical cost amounts.

First-In First-Out (FIFO)

Under the FIFO method it is assumed that the unit costs from the earliest purchases (first-in) should be used in determining the amount of cost that is "first-out" (i.e., out the door)—to cost of goods sold. Another acronym that describes the FIFO cost flow assumption is "Last-In Still-Here" (LISH). Still-Here refers to the costs used in determining the balance sheet amount of ending inventory. LISH indicates that the unit costs from the most recent purchases (last-in) should be used in determining the ending inventory cost. Although FIFO is the more frequently used term, LISH is actually more descriptive of how the financial statement amounts for ending inventory and cost of goods sold are determined. As indicated in Exhibit 3.4, cost of goods available for sale is the sum of beginning inventory cost plus the period's purchases.[5] Physical inventory at 12/31/11 indicates there are 1,200 notebooks on hand. Under LISH we cost these 1,200 units using the most recent acquisition costs. Referring back to Exhibit 3.3 we note the most recent purchase (last-in) occurred on 8/15/11 when Behrend bought 1,000 units @ $4 each. This most recent cost incurred is given primary consideration in determining the total cost of ending inventory. Since only 1,000 units were purchased on 8/15/11, we must next look to the second most recent purchase in costing the remaining 200 units. Referring to Exhibit 3.3, we note that the next most recent purchase occurred on 1/06/11 when we purchased 1,500 units @ $3 each. This is sufficient quantity to determine the cost of the remaining 200 units. Under LISH

[5] Since we assume that 2011 is Behrend's first year of operations, there is no beginning inventory and therefore cost of goods available for sale equals purchases ($8,500) and is consistent across all cost flow assumptions in Exhibit 3.4.

(FIFO) the cost of the 1,200 units in ending inventory is determined to be $4,600 as follows:

Most recent acquisition	8/15/2011	1,000 @ $4/unit =	$4,000
Next most recent acquisition	1/06/2011	200 @ $3/unit =	600
Total units		1,200 Total cost	$4,600

This $4,600 ending inventory cost is then subtracted from cost of goods available for sale of $8,500 to determine cost of goods sold = $3,900. Sales ($6,900) – cost of goods sold ($3,900) = $3,000 gross profit. Gross profit may be expressed as a percentage of sales $3,000/$6,900 = 43.5%. Since cost of goods sold + gross profit = sales, the cost of goods sold percentage can be calculated as 100% – 43.5% = 56.5%, rather than $3,900/$6,900 = 56.5%.

Under FIFO, ending inventory and cost of goods sold will be the same regardless of whether a perpetual or periodic system is used. Using the accounting equation format and data from Exhibit 3.3 we illustrate the financial statement effects from purchases and sales of notebooks under a perpetual FIFO inventory system (we assume all transactions are in cash):

ASSETS		= LIABILITIES +	SE	
Purchase 1,500 notebooks @ $3 each for cash on 1/06/11				
+ Inventory	+ 4,500			
– Cash	– 4,500			
Sell 900 notebooks @ $5 each for cash on 2/04/11				
+ Cash	+ 4,500		+ Sales Revenue	+ 4,500
–Inventory	– 2,700		+ Cost Goods Sold	– 2,700
Purchase 1,000 notebooks @ $4 each for cash on 8/15/11				
+ Inventory	+ 4,000			
– Cash	– 4,000			
Sell 400 notebooks @ $6 each for cash on 12/20/11				
+ Cash	+ 2,400		+ Sales Revenue	+ 2,400
–Inventory	– 1,200		+ Cost Goods Sold	– 1,200

Since there is no inventory shrinkage, the physical inventory and perpetual inventory records agree that 1,200 units are in ending inventory. No adjusting entry is required and balances in ending inventory and cost of goods sold are $4,600 and $3,900, respectively. These amounts are consistent with the FIFO periodic system amounts determined previously. Even if a year-end adjustment to the physical inventory count was needed, the perpetual and periodic system financial statement amounts would be equal since the FIFO ending inventory cost is determined using the most recently incurred costs (LISH).

Average Cost Method

In a periodic average cost system, the average cost of all units available for sale is calculated by dividing goods available for sale (GAFS) in dollars by goods available for sale (GAFS) in units. This average unit cost is used for determining both the cost of units in ending inventory and the cost of units sold. Using the data from Exhibit 3.3 we can calculate this average cost as:

GAFS in $/GAFS in units = $8,500/2,500 units = $3.40/unit.

Under the average cost method, the cost of the 1,200 units in ending inventory is determined to be $4,080 as follows:

1,200 units @ $3.40/unit = $4,080

As indicated in Exhibit 3.4, subtracting ending inventory from cost of goods available for sale determines cost of goods sold to be $4,420. Cost of goods sold can also be calculated by multiplying units sold by the average unit cost (1,300 units @ $3.40/unit = $4,420). Gross profit is $2,480 and the gross profit percentage is 35.9% (cost of goods sold percentage = 64.1%).

Unlike FIFO, the average cost method will provide different results when a perpetual system is used. In a perpetual average cost system (also called the "moving" average cost system), inventory is reduced and cost of goods sold is recognized using the average unit cost of goods available at the time of sale. A new average unit cost needs to be calculated at the time of each purchase based upon goods available for sale in dollars and units immediately following the purchase. Using the data from Exhibit 3.3 we can determine the appropriate unit costs for purposes of reducing inventory and recognizing cost of goods sold at the time of sale in a perpetual average cost system. The 900 units sold on 2/04/11 have an average unit cost of $3 because the only notebooks available for sale at that time were from the 1,500-unit purchase on 1/06/11. Inventory is reduced and cost of goods sold is recognized in the amount of $2,700 (900 units @$3/unit) on 2/04/11. Immediately preceding the 8/15/11 purchase of 1,000 notebooks for $4 each, the perpetual records indicate we should have 600 of the $3/unit notebooks in stock. In determining the new average cost, we divide the GAFS in units = 1,600, into the GAFS in $ (600 units@$3 = $1,800) + (1,000 units@$4 = $4,000) = $5,800. The average cost per unit for purposes of recording the 400-unit sale on 12/20/11 is $3.625 ($5,800/1,600), and inventory is reduced and cost of goods sold is recognized in the amount of $1,450 (400 units @ $3.625/unit).

Using the accounting equation format and data from Exhibit 3.3 we illustrate the financial statement effects of purchases and sales of notebooks under a perpetual average cost inventory system (we assume all transactions are in cash):

ASSETS		=	LIABILITIES	+	SE	
Purchase 1,500 notebooks @ $3 each for cash on 1/06/11						
+ Inventory	+4,500					
- Cash	-4,500					
Sell 900 notebooks @ $5 each for cash on 2/04/11						
+ Cash	+4,500				+ Sales Revenue	+4,500
-Inventory	-2,700				+ Cost Goods Sold	-2,700
Purchase 1,000 notebooks @ $4 each for cash on 8/15/11						
+ Inventory	+4,000					
– Cash	-4,000					
Sell 400 notebooks @ $6 each for cash on 12/20/11						
+ Cash	+2,400				+ Sales Revenue	+2,400
-Inventory	-1,450				+ Cost Goods Sold	-1,450

The perpetual amounts differ from the periodic amounts. In the perpetual system example, ending inventory is higher because it is more heavily weighted by the most recent purchase of 1,000 notebooks at the higher $4 unit cost. The $270 increase in inventory ($4,350 – $4,080) reduces cost of goods sold by an equal amount from $4,420 to $4,150, which in turn increases gross profit. As indicated previously, all other things held constant, the larger the ending inventory, the lower the cost of goods sold, and vice versa.

Last-In First-Out (LIFO)

LIFO is the opposite of FIFO. The most recent acquisition cost is used to determine the amount of cost of goods sold that appears in the income statement, and the earliest acquisition costs are used to determine the amount of inventory that should appear in the year-end balance sheet—"First-In Still-Here" (FISH). Under FISH (LIFO) ending inventory cost is determined by first considering the unit cost of the earliest purchase. Under FISH (LIFO) the cost of the 1,200 units in ending inventory is determined to be $3,600 as follows:

Earliest acquisition	1/06/2011	1,200	@ $3/unit =	$3,600
Total units		1,200	Total cost	$3,600

Based upon the $3,600 ending inventory amount, cost of goods sold is $4,900 and gross profit is $2,000, as presented in Exhibit 3.4. Since there is no inventory shrinkage the cost of goods sold can also be determined by applying the most recently incurred costs to the 1,300 units sold: (1,000 @ $4/unit = $4000) + (300 @ $3/unit = $900) = $4,900. The gross profit percentage is 29% ($2,000/$6,900) and the cost of goods sold percentage is 71%.

Most businesses, particularly sellers of perishable goods like dairy products, try to "rotate" their stock by selling the oldest goods first (a FIFO physical flow). Remember however that an assumed cost flow has nothing necessarily to do with the actual physical flow of goods. Although inventory units physically held at year-end are most likely those most recently purchased, the earliest acquisition costs are applied to determine the year-end inventory amount under the FISH (LIFO) cost flow assumption. Specific to our example, the 1,200 notebooks on hand at 12/31/11 were not actually acquired on 1/06/11. These 1,200 units @ $3/unit constitute a "LIFO layer," that carries forward and is used in determining future year's ending inventory cost because they continue to be "first-in" under FISH (LIFO). In future years this $3/unit LIFO layer will become cost of goods sold only to the extent the inventory quantity falls below 1,200 units.

LIFO originated in 1939 when it first became acceptable for tax purposes. Although the choices of accounting method for financial reporting and tax reporting are usually independent decisions, LIFO is an exception. If a firm wants to use LIFO for tax reporting it must also use LIFO for financial reporting. This is referred to as the "LIFO conformity rule." Firms that experience rising inventory acquisition cost benefit by using LIFO for tax purposes. A rising cost scenario is depicted in the Exhibit 3.3 data, and the effect on gross profit is illustrated in Exhibit 3.4. LIFO cost of goods sold includes the recent higher cost, whereas FIFO cost of goods sold includes the early, lower cost. The average cost method uses an average of the higher and lower costs so that cost of goods sold is between the two—less than LIFO and more than FIFO. Although Exhibit 3.4 indicates a substantial difference between FIFO and average cost, in actuality there is usually little difference in practice. For the sake of simplicity, we assumed only two instances each of sales and purchases of notebooks in 2011. Most firms have frequent purchases and sales of inventory, and use a perpetual inventory system. Under these circumstances, average cost and FIFO provide virtually identical financial statement amounts. This being the case, the following discussion of financial statement differences will concentrate on comparing LIFO with FIFO.

From a tax perspective, cost of goods sold is a deduction that lowers taxable income and the amount of cash paid for taxes. Comparing cost of goods sold for LIFO versus FIFO in Exhibit 3.4, LIFO is $1,000 higher, which results in $1,000 lower gross profit and taxable income. Assuming a tax rate of 40%, Behrend would save $400 in 2011 taxes by using LIFO. The $1,000 lower inventory amount under LIFO will eventually reduce cost of goods sold, which will increase taxable income. However, the delayed tax payment is beneficial from a time value of money perspective.[6] Firms using LIFO usually have experienced rising inventory cost, and do so for the tax benefit. Ironically, LIFO firms generally report lower inventory amounts in the balance sheet, which reduces cumulative net income and retained earnings. However, firm value should be enhanced because the only impact upon cash flows is delayed tax payments. The longer tax payments are delayed, the lesser the present value of the cash outflow for taxes, and the higher the value of the firm. In order to continue delaying tax payment, firms need to "protect" their LIFO layers by maintaining inventory levels.

As the following example will illustrate, it is more difficult for firms to protect their LIFO layers in a perpetual LIFO system. Therefore, firms that use LIFO apply it on a periodic basis. Using the data from Exhibit 3.3, we note that consistent with FIFO and average cost perpetual method illustrations, the 1/06/11 purchase, 2/04/11 sale, and 8/15/11 purchase transactions have the same financial statement impacts under perpetual LIFO. The 1/06/11 purchase increases inventory from zero to $4,500 (1,500 @ $3), the 2/04/11 sale results in inventory reduction and cost of goods sold recognition in the amount of $2,700 (900 @ $3), and the 8/15/11 purchase increases inventory by $4,000 (1,000 @ $4). However, under LIFO the 12/20/11 sale of 400 units reduces inventory and increases cost of goods sold at the most recent acquisition cost. Immediately before the 12/20/11 sale, we had two LIFO layers: the remaining portion of the 1/06/11 purchase (1,500 – 900 = 600 units @ $3/unit) and the entire 12/20/11 purchase = 1,000 units @ $4/unit. Under LIFO, cost of goods sold is determined using the most recent (last-in) cost, which is the 8/15/11 acquisition at $4/unit. Cost of goods sold is recognized (and inventory is reduced) for 400 units @ $4/unit = $1,600.

Using the accounting equation format and data from Exhibit 3.3 we illustrate the financial statement effects of purchases and sales of notebooks

---

[6] Given there is a time value of money, it is beneficial to accelerate tax deductions and delay reporting taxable income when everything else is held constant.

under a perpetual LIFO inventory system (we assume all transactions are in cash):

ASSETS	=	LIABILITIES	+	SE	
Purchase 1,500 notebooks @ $3 each for cash on 1/06/11					
+ Inventory	+4,500				
- Cash	−4,500				
Sell 900 notebooks @ $5 each for cash on 2/04/11					
+ Cash	+4,500			+ Sales Revenue	+4,500
−Inventory	−2,700			+ Cost Goods Sold	−2,700
Purchase 1,000 notebooks @ $4 each for cash on 8/15/11					
+ Inventory	+4,000				
- Cash	−4,000				
Sell 400 notebooks @ $6 each for cash on 12/20/11					
+ Cash	+2,400			+ Sales Revenue	+2,400
−Inventory	−1,600			+ Cost Goods Sold	−1,600

Again, assuming no inventory shrinkage, the perpetual record amounts would appear in the financial statements: cost of goods sold = $4,300 and ending inventory = $4,200. This $4,200 ending inventory has two layers: the remaining portion of the 1/06/11 purchase (1,500 – 900 = 600 units @ $3/unit) and the remaining portion of the 12/20/11 purchase = 600 units @ $4/unit. Recall that 2011 ending inventory under periodic LIFO has only one layer: 1,200 units @ $3/unit = $3,600.

Perpetual LIFO ending inventory is $600 higher (and perpetual LIFO cost of goods sold is $600 lower) than the periodic LIFO amount. This difference relates to the contrasting need to protect LIFO layers in periodic versus perpetual systems. In a periodic system, LIFO layers only need to be protected by year-end when cost of goods sold is determined, whereas under perpetual LIFO the layer(s) require protection throughout the year because cost of goods sold is recognized upon each sale transaction. Under periodic LIFO, Behrend "protected" all but 300 of the 1,500 units purchased on 1/06/11 by purchasing 1,000 units on 8/15/11. Behrend could have protected all 1,500 units @ $3/unit by buying an additional 300 units any time later in the year. For example, assuming no change in sales but that Behrend purchased an additional 300 notebooks during December 2011, the cost of those 300 units would be included in 2011 cost of goods sold, and all 1,500 units on hand at 12/31/11 would be included in ending inventory @ $3/unit. However, under perpetual LIFO, the 1,500 units purchased on 1/06/11 were "unprotected" on 2/04/11 when 900 units were sold. For perpetual LIFO costing purposes, only 600 units @ $3 remain because there is a LIFO layer liquidation of 900 units @ $3/unit on 2/04/11 when cost of goods sold is recognized.

The LIFO conformity rule requires firms using LIFO for tax purposes must also use LIFO for financial reporting. Firms that have experienced rising inventory cost use LIFO for tax purposes because of the benefit derived from delayed tax payments. This tax benefit is maintained only if LIFO layers are protected. Since perpetual LIFO makes it harder to protect LIFO layers, firms do not use it in practice, but instead apply periodic LIFO. As such, perpetual LIFO will not be further discussed. LIFO firms wanting the enhanced benefits that a perpetual inventory system provides assume a different cost flow for perpetual inventory purposes (e.g., FIFO) and then adjust to periodic LIFO amounts at the end of the period for financial reporting and tax return purposes. This adjustment is made using the "LIFO Reserve." The LIFO reserve is generally parenthetically or otherwise disclosed in the financial statements and indicates the inventory amounts that would have been presented using another cost flow assumption (e.g., FIFO).

Summary: Financial Statement Implications of Inventory Method Choice

As discussed previously, the SID method is only appropriate where inventory items are unique and it makes a difference which particular unit is actually sold. Where inventory units are interchangeable (fungible), the SID method is inappropriate. Instead, an assumed cost flow should be used. If there are different unit costs of inventory available for sale, the particular assumed cost flow method chosen will impact the amount of inventory presented in the balance sheet, and the amount of cost of goods sold that appears in the income statement. The assumed cost flow methods commonly applied in practice are FIFO, LIFO, and average cost. FIFO and LIFO will be compared here. Although the average cost method will not be discussed, as indicated previously, financial statement amounts using FIFO are generally identical to those using average cost. Also, a recent survey finds that the predominant inventory methods used are FIFO and LIFO.[7]

FIFO is beneficial from a balance sheet perspective because it applies the most recently incurred cost in determining ending inventory. The most recently incurred cost is usually closest to the fair value of the inventory at the balance sheet date. Most LIFO firms have experienced rising inventory cost and choose its use for tax purposes in order to delay income tax payments. These firms must also use LIFO for financial reporting because of the LIFO conformity rule. LIFO requires that the earliest acquisition costs be used in determining the amount for inventory (FISH), which tends to understate its value on the balance sheet.[8] Inventory undervaluation is a function of LIFO layer quantities and degree to which costs have increased since they were established. Some LIFO firms have inventory layers dating back to the early 1940s, which significantly undervalues their inventory on the balance sheet. Although the LIFO conformity rule requires its use for balance sheet reporting, LIFO firms typically disclosure the inventory amount that would have been reported under another cost flow assumption, for example, FIFO. Knowledge of the inventory cost difference (the "LIFO reserve" discussed above) enables conversion of LIFO inventory amounts to FIFO equivalents for purposes of liquidity analysis.

LIFO generally reports a truer representation of gross profit because it usually applies the most recently incurred costs in reporting cost of goods sold in the income statement. However, as we demonstrate later, this is only the case when inventory quantities are stable. Inventory decreases can cause significant gross profit overstatement under LIFO.

---

[7] Surveyed firms indicate 65% use FIFO, 35% use LIFO, and 29% use average cost. The sum of these percentages exceeds 100% because some firms use different cost flow assumptions for different inventories. American Institute of CPAs, *Accounting Trends and Techniques.* 2010, p. 169.

[8] In instances of decreasing prices LIFO would tend to overstate inventory on the balance sheet if not for LCM's required write-down and loss recognition.

This overstatement results from recognizing much earlier (lower) costs in cost of goods sold while recognizing current selling prices in sales revenue.

Additional Issues Related to LIFO

To consider additional LIFO issues, we will extend our simplified Behrend notebook example beyond 2011 to illustrate how LIFO layers are added and liquidated in subsequent periods, how year-end purchasing decisions directly affect gross profit and accommodate earnings management, and how LIFO financial statement amounts can be converted to FIFO equivalents using the LIFO reserve. We also discuss "Dollar Value LIFO" which is the most commonly used adaptation of LIFO.

Establishing and Liquidating LIFO Layers in Subsequent Periods

Using the 2012 purchases and sales data provided in Exhibit 3.5, we extend our LIFO example beyond 2011. We assume purchases of 2,200 units and sales of 2,000 units (inventory increases by 200 units) during 2012.

Exhibit 3.5. Behrend Corp. Purchases and Sales—Notebooks LIFO Method Year Ended 12/31/2012

	Units	$/Unit	Total $
Beginning Inventory	1,200	$3	$3,600
Purchases			
06/30/12	1,000	$5	$5,000
12/30/12	1,200	$6	7,200
	2,200		$12,200
Sales			
01/10/12	1,100	$7	$7,700
12/14/12	900	$9	8,100
	2,000		$15,800
Ending Inventory			
2011 Layer	1,200	$3	$3,600
2012 Layer	200	$5	1,000
	1,400		$4,600

Exhibit 3.6. Behrend Corp. Gross Profit—Notebooks Periodic LIFO Method Year Ended 12/31/2012

	With 12/30/12 purchase		Without 12/30/12 purchase	
Sales Revenue		$15,800		$15,800
Less Cost of Goods Sold:				
Beginning Inventory	$3,600		$3,600	
Plus Purchases	12,200		5,000	
Cost of Goods Available for Sale:	$15,800		$8,600	
Less Ending Inv. (1,400 versus 200 units)	4,600		600	
Cost of Goods Sold		11,200		8,000
Gross Profit		$4,600		$7,800
GP %		29.1%		49.4%

Since 2012 ending inventory exceeds beginning inventory (1,400 versus 1,200 units), all layers from beginning inventory are included in determining the cost of ending inventory. The cost/unit of the additional 200 units in the new 2012 LIFO layer is determined using the earliest cost incurred during the year (FISH). The first purchase in 2012 occurred on 6/30/12 when 1,000 notebooks were purchased @ $5/unit (Exhibit 3.5). Ending inventory 2012 is calculated as $4,600 and consists of the 1,400 units in two separate LIFO layers:

Earliest acquisition – Beginning Inventory (2011 layer)
1,200 units @ $3/unit = $3600

Next earliest acquisition on 6/30/2012 (2012 layer)
200 units @ $5/unit = $1,000

Total units 1,400 Total cost $4,600

Note that each layer has two characteristics: number of units and cost/unit. The gross profit section of Behrend's 2012 income statement is illustrated in the left-hand columns of Exhibit 3.6.

If ending inventory of 2013 > 1,400 units, the quantity increase and the earliest acquisition cost(s) incurred in 2013 would make up the added

2013 LIFO layer(s). However, if 2013 ending inventory quantity drops below 1,400 units, the reduction (liquidation) is assumed to first come from the 2012 layer. If the 2013 ending inventory quantity falls below 1,200 units, the 2012 layer (200@$5) will be completely liquidated and 2013 ending inventory will be determined using the 2011 layer unit cost. For example, if the 2013 year-end physical inventory indicates 500 units on hand, 2013 ending inventory will appear in the balance sheet at $1,500 and consists of the remaining 2011 layer—500 notebooks @ $3/unit. Once a LIFO layer is liquidated it is not reinstated—if inventory quantity increases in a subsequent year, one or more new LIFO layers are added identifying the quantity increase with the earliest costs incurred during the year in which the quantity increased.

LIFO: Year-End Purchasing Decisions and Earnings Management

The effect of year-end purchase decisions upon LIFO gross profit is illustrated in Exhibit 3.6. Under FIFO, year-end purchases are included in ending inventory (LISH) with no income statement effect. Under LIFO however, being "last-in," year-end purchase costs directly impact cost of goods sold (and gross profit). Using the data from Exhibit 3.5 (with the 12/30/12 purchase of 1,200 units @$6), we generate the gross profit section of Behrend's 2012 income statement (left-hand columns of Exhibit 3.6). The gross profit effects of forgoing the 12/30/12 purchase are illustrated in the right-hand columns of Exhibit 3.6. If the year-end purchase of 1,200 units is not made, purchases is $7,200 less (1,200 units @6/unit), and rather than inventory increasing by 200 units, it declines by 1,000 units (2,000 sold versus 1,000 purchased) to 200 notebooks. For ending inventory costing purposes, these 200 ending inventory units are considered the remainder of the 2011 LIFO layer (200 units @ $3/unit = $600).

More importantly, Exhibit 3.6 illustrates that foregoing the 1,200-unit purchase on 12/30/12 reduces cost of goods sold and increases gross profit by $3,200. This $3,200 difference relates to the different costs applied to the 2,000 units sold. If the 12/30/12 purchase is made, cost of goods sold = $11,200 (1,200@$6 + 800@$5), whereas if the purchase is not made cost of the 2,000 units sold = $8,000 (1,000@$5 + 1,000@$3). If the 12/30/12 purchase is made, those 1,200 units @ $6 = $7,200 are included in cost of goods sold. Without the year-end purchase, cost of goods sold instead includes those 1,200 units at a total cost of $4,000. Specifically it includes the 2012 LIFO layer that is not added (200 units @$5/unit = $1,000), and the 1,000-unit reduction (liquidation) of the 2011 LIFO layer (1,000 units @ $3/unit = $3,000). The difference in cost of goods sold with versus without the 1,200-unit year-end purchase can also be derived on a per unit basis: (200 units @$1 ($6 – $5 per unit) + 1,000 units @ $3 ($6 – $3 per unit)) = $3,200.

With the year-end purchase, the gross profit percentage is 29.1% (almost identical to 2011's LIFO gross profit percentage of 29.0%), but foregoing the year-end purchase increases the gross profit percentage to 49.4%. As indicated previously, a usual benefit of LIFO is recognizing expense (cost of goods sold) using the most recent acquisition costs, resulting in a more accurate measure of gross profit. However, this is the case only if inventory levels are maintained. As Exhibit 3.6 illustrates, LIFO can significantly overstate gross profit in situations of LIFO layer liquidation. The degree of profit overstatement is a function of the quantity decrease and degree to which year-end inventory cost exceeds the costs associated with the liquidated LIFO layers. If a LIFO liquidation has a material effect on income, it must be disclosed in the notes to the financial statements.

There may be adverse tax consequences associated with LIFO layer liquidations. Consider the previous example and assume a 40% tax rate; Behrend will pay $1,280 more in 2012 taxes ($3,200 × 40%) as a result of foregoing the 12/30/12 purchase. If management wants to maintain the tax benefit of LIFO, the layers need to be protected, which may force year-end purchases that would not have otherwise been made. For example, consider a firm experiencing a supply shortage. The supply shortage has driven year-end costs extremely high, but prices are expected to decline early next year. The firm may have sufficient inventory on hand to get through the supply shortage situation. However, in a LIFO liquidation situation, management must weigh the relative costs of paying exorbitant year-end prices versus losing their LIFO tax benefit. This situation might be alleviated if the firms were using "dollar value LIFO" which is discussed later. Absent supply shortages, consider firms that are trying to become "leaner" and more efficient by instituting "Just-In-Time" (JIT) inventory systems. JIT firms make concerted efforts to reduce inventory levels to the bare minimum necessary to conduct business. JIT is particularly important for sellers of "high tech" merchandise that tends to become obsolete in a short period of time (for example, cell phones, computer equipment, etc.). Instituting JIT could require LIFO liquidations, with detrimental tax consequences. Management must weigh the expected benefit of instituting JIT with the negative tax effects of LIFO layer liquidations.

Converting LIFO Financial Statement Amounts to FIFO Equivalents Using the LIFO Reserve

As discussed previously, firms that use LIFO apply it on a periodic inventory basis, and LIFO firms that want the benefits afforded by the perpetual basis usually apply it using another cost flow assumption. For purposes of illustration we will expand the Behrend notebook example assuming that LIFO periodic is used in the financial statements and FIFO perpetual is used for internal reporting. At year-end, the internal perpetual FIFO amounts are converted to LIFO periodic using the "LIFO reserve." The LIFO reserve is the amount by which the FIFO inventory exceeds the LIFO inventory. Recall from our previous discussion that FIFO perpetual and FIFO periodic provide the same financial statement amounts. Beginning inventory 2012 is synonymous with ending inventory 2011. Therefore the LIFO reserve at the beginning of 2012 is $1,000 and is derived from the 2011 ending inventory information in Exhibit 3.4, where FIFO inventory was $4,600 and LIFO inventory was $3,600. Continuing with our example of making or not making the 12/30/12 purchase of 1,200 units @ $6/unit, Exhibit 3.7 shows gross profit under LIFO and FIFO in Panel A (with the 12/30/12 purchase), and Panel B (without the 12/30/12 purchase). All LIFO amounts are taken from Exhibit 3.6.

Notice in both panels that the only difference in amounts presented under the two cost flow assumptions relates to beginning and ending inventory (LIFO reserve amounts). All other elements affecting gross profit (sales and purchases) are (and should be) the same regardless of inventory method used. FIFO in Panel A applies the most recent costs

Exhibit 3.7. Behrend Corp. LIFO Reserve Illustration Year Ended 12/31/12

Panel A—with 12/30/12 purchase					
	LIFO		**LIFO reserve**	**FIFO**	
Sales		$15,800			$ 15,800
Less Cost of Goods Sold:					
Beginning Inventory	$3,600		$1,000	$4,600	
Plus Purchases	12,200			12,200	
Cost of Goods Available for Sale	$15,800			$16,800	
Less Ending Inventory	4,600		$3,600	8,200	
Cost of Goods Sold		11,200			8,600
Gross Profit		$4,600			$7,200
Δ in LIFO Reserve			$2,600		
Panel B—without 12/30/12 purchase					
Sales		$15,800			$15,800
Less Cost of Goods Sold:					
Beginning Inventory	$3,600		$1,000	$4,600	
Plus Purchases	5,000			5,000	
Cost of Goods Available for Sale	$8,600			$9,600	
Less Ending Inventory	600		$400	1,000	
Cost of Goods Sold		8,000			8,600
Gross Profit		$7,800			$7,200
Δ in LIFO Reserve			$ <600>		

(LISH) to the 1,400 units on hand at 12/31/12 to determine the ending inventory amount. The most recent purchase cost of $6 on 12/30/12 is applied to 1,200 units (1,200 @ $6 = $7,200) and the remaining 200 units are included at the 6/30/12 acquisition cost of $5/unit = $1,000. Ending inventory under FIFO = $8,200 and the LIFO reserve at the end of 2012 is $3,600 (FIFO = $8,200 – LIFO = $4,600). In Exhibit 3.7 LIFO amounts (left-hand columns) are converted to FIFO amounts (right-hand columns) by adding the LIFO reserve.

Notice that holding everything else constant, the larger the beginning inventory amount, the larger cost of goods sold amount; whereas the larger the ending inventory amount, the lower the cost of goods sold amount. The LIFO reserves at the beginning and end of the period have opposite impacts upon cost of goods sold. Regardless of its dollar amount, if the LIFO reserve doesn't change during the period, the offsetting effect will cause FIFO cost of goods sold (and gross profit) to be equal to the LIFO amounts. If the LIFO reserve increases, FIFO cost of goods sold will be less than LIFO cost of goods sold, and FIFO gross profit will be higher than LIFO gross profit in an amount equal to the LIFO reserve increase. The exact opposite occurs when the LIFO reserve decreases during the period.

In Exhibit 3.7 Panel A, the LIFO reserve increases by $2,600. Notice that $2,600 is the decrease in cost of goods sold ($11,200 versus $8,600), and increase in gross profit ($4,600 versus $7,200) in going from the LIFO financial statement amounts to their FIFO equivalents. In Panel B, without the 1,200-unit purchase on 12/30/12, ending inventory consists of only 200 units. Under FIFO, these 200 units are costed at $5/unit = $1,000, whereas under LIFO the 200 units are costed at $3/unit = $600 (from Exhibit 3.6). The LIFO reserve at the end of 2012 is $400. The LIFO reserve has now decreased by $600 during the year from $1,000 at the beginning of 2012 to $400 at the end of 2012. Since the LIFO reserve has decreased by $600, FIFO cost of goods sold is $600 higher than LIFO cost of goods sold ($8,600 – $8,000) and FIFO gross profit is $600 lower than LIFO gross profit ($7,200 – $7,800).

As indicated previously, firms that use LIFO generally disclose what inventory would be under another cost flow assumption, for example, FIFO. This information is more useful for purposes of analyzing a firm's liquidity (e.g., calculating the current ratio, working capital, etc.). The change in a firm's LIFO reserve during the period is useful for converting LIFO gross profit to FIFO amounts. A significant decrease in the LIFO reserve indicates LIFO liquidation has occurred and raises the possibility that earnings are being managed upward. The FIFO equivalent income statement amounts may be useful in quantifying the extent of upward earnings management.

Dollar Value LIFO

As discussed previously, firms use LIFO for its tax benefit, and the tax benefit is maintained only if the LIFO layers are protected. In practice, firms usually apply "dollar value LIFO" because doing so makes it easier to protect LIFO layers. If firms apply unit LIFO, goods can be grouped together ("pooled") for purposes of determining quantity changes only if they are considered to be "substantially identical." Firms that apply dollar value LIFO can "pool" together goods that are considered to be "substantially similar." Relative to unit LIFO, dollar value LIFO will result in fewer inventory pools with a greater variety of goods included within each pool. LIFO layers are easier to protect under dollar value LIFO because decreases in some inventory items can be offset by increases in other items within a pool. This is similar to the relative offsetting that is allowed by applying LCM to major categories of inventory instead of applying LCM to individual items of inventory (where no offsetting was allowed).

Under dollar value LIFO, inventory quantity change is not determined by comparing units on hand at the beginning versus the end of the period. Instead, inventory quantity change is determined based upon comparison of constant dollar amounts. At the end of each year, the year-end inventory cost is converted to its price level adjusted (constant dollar) equivalent using a cost index. The cost index can be internally calculated (using a firm's own estimates of inventory cost change) or externally provided (for example, using the applicable "producer price index" or "consumer price index"). Ending inventory in constant dollars is then compared to beginning inventory in constant dollars to determine if quantity has increased or decreased. If it has increased, a new layer is added with two distinguishing characteristics: the constant dollar amount and the cost index for the year. If ending inventory is less than beginning inventory (both expressed in constant dollars), no layer is added; instead, previous layers are liquidated on a LIFO basis. As in unit LIFO, once a layer is liquidated or reduced at year-end, it is not reinstated if inventory increases in a subsequent period; instead, a completely new layer will be added.

To illustrate the mechanics of dollar value LIFO we will consider an entirely new example for Behrend Corp. Assume Behrend began

Exhibit 3.8. Behrend Corp. Dollar Value LIFO Example

Balance sheet date	Inventory at year end cost	Cost index	Inventory at base year cost	Change in inventory base year $	Inventory on year-end balance sheet
12/31/2009	$100,000	100	$100,000	$100,000	$100,000
12/31/2010	$115,500	105	$110,000	$10,000	$110,500
12/31/2011	$116,600	110	$106,000	$<4,000>	$106,300
12/31/2012	$132,250	115	$115,000	$ 9,000	$116,650

operations in 2009 and adopted dollar value LIFO with a single inventory pool for its entire inventory. Year-end inventory and cost index information is provided in Exhibit 3.8. The most important step in applying dollar value LIFO is to express all year-end inventory amounts in constant dollars. In Exhibit 3.8 all year-end inventory costs are converted to base year equivalent dollar amounts by multiplying by a fraction. The numerator of the fraction is the base year index, and the denominator is the particular year's index. Once all year-end inventory amounts are expressed in base year dollars, we compare ending inventory with beginning inventory to determine inventory quantity change. Referring to Exhibit 3.8 we determine the yearly inventory quantity changes (expressed in base year dollar amounts): increased $100,000 in 2009 (its first year of operations), increased $10,000 in 2010, decreased $4,000 in 2011, and increased $9,000 in 2012. This information is fundamental to determining the inventory amounts presented in each year-end balance sheet. We will now illustrate how each year-end balance sheet amount of inventory is determined.

The year-end 2009 inventory has one layer: $100,000 base year dollars @ 100 cost index. Inventory will appear on the 12/31/09 balance sheet at $100,000 base year dollars @ 100/100 = @100,000. On 12/31/10 we note that inventory has increased $10,000 base year dollars, so we add a 2010 LIFO layer. Ending inventory 2010 has two layers: the base layer ($100,000 @ 100), and the 2010 layer ($10,000 @ 105). Ending inventory will be presented in the 2010 balance sheet at $110,500 = ($100,000 × 100/100 + 10,000 × 105/100). In 2011, inventory quantity declines by $4,000 base year dollars. Therefore, we will not add a 2011 layer, but instead need to reduce previously established layers on a LIFO basis. The most recently established layer (2010) has sufficient base dollars ($10,000) associated with it to absorb the $4,000 reduction. Ending inventory 2011 has two layers: the entire base layer ($100,000 @ 100), and the remaining portion of the 2010 layer ($6,000 @ 105). Ending inventory will be presented on the 2011 balance sheet at $106,300 = ($100,000 × 100/100 + $6,000 × 105/100). In 2012 ending inventory increases by $9,000 base year dollars. We add a 2012 inventory layer with the dollar value LIFO characteristics: $9,000 @ 115. Ending inventory 2012 now has three layers. The two LIFO layers from beginning inventory (or 2011 ending inventory) carry over and become part of 2012 ending inventory. Inventory will be presented on the 2012 year-end balance sheet at $116,650 = ($100,000 × 100/100 + $6,000 × 105/100 + $9,000 × 115/100).

IFRS Does Not Allow LIFO

Although IFRS allows firms to use SID, FIFO, and average cost, LIFO is not permitted.[9] This is a major impediment to converging U.S. GAAP and IFRS. U.S. firms that switch their cost flow assumption from LIFO to a method permitted under IFRS for financial reporting purposes will no longer be able to use LIFO for tax purposes because of the LIFO conformity rule. The resulting liquidation of LIFO layers would have significant negative tax consequences for such firms. Unless the IASB changes IFRS to allow LIFO, or the LIFO conformity rule is rescinded, global convergence of GAAP will be difficult to achieve in this area.

[9] International Accounting Standard No. 2, "Inventories," Par. 25, IASB.

CHAPTER 4

Operational Assets

Introduction

Operational assets are long-term assets used by a business in providing goods or services to customers. Operational assets do not include inventory or investments. The function of the asset determines its appropriate balance sheet classification. For example, land upon which a firm's factory is built constitutes an operational asset. However, land held for speculation is considered an investment, and land held for sale by a real estate developer is appropriately classified as inventory. Operational assets fall within three categories: 1) property, plant, and equipment (PP&E), 2) intangibles, and 3) natural resources. PP&E includes land, land improvements (e.g., parking lots, roadways), buildings, machinery, and equipment. Intangibles are long-term assets that lack physical substance and provide the business with certain exclusive rights or other competitive advantages. Intangible assets include patents, copyrights, trademarks, trade names, franchises, goodwill, etc. Natural resources are actually consumed in providing goods or services to customers and include oil and gas wells, coalmines, standing timber, etc.

Operational asset[1] issues will be discussed, including initially capitalized acquisition cost, systematic and rational allocation of cost to expense in the income statement, postacquisition expenditures, impairment losses, and disposals. Each area will be initially discussed in general as it relates to all operational assets and subsequently as it relates to particular operational asset categories.

[1] The term "operational asset" is rarely used in practice. It is used here for convenience when collectively addressing issues concerning "property, plant, and equipment," "intangibles," and "natural resources," the terms actually found in financial statements.

Initially Capitalized Acquisition Cost

The amount initially capitalized as the "historical cost" of an operational asset is generally determined with reference to the fair value of what was given up to acquire it. The full cost principle applies, so that all ordinary and necessary costs incurred in getting an operational asset into its intended usable state are included in the asset's cost. For example, assume a firm acquires a machine for use in its production line with an invoiced price of $50,000, and incurs the following additional costs: freight charges of $1,000, insurance while in transit of $100, and an installation fee of $2,500. The machine's cost is $53,600 under the full cost principle and includes all of these ordinary and necessary costs that were incurred in getting the machine into its intended usable state. If the machine was dropped during unloading and resulted in repair cost of $1,500, that cost should not be capitalized. The $1,500 repair cost should be immediately recognized as a loss because it is not an ordinary and necessary cost of getting the machine installed in the production line. Cash payments made to acquire operational assets are classified as investing activity in the statement of cash flows.

Acquisitions with Delayed Payment

The acquisition cost of assets acquired through cash payments made at or near the time of the exchange is considered to be the amount of cash paid (fair value of what is given up). However, when assets are otherwise acquired, acquisition cost needs to be estimated based upon the cash equivalent purchase price. Consider the case where a firm purchases office furniture by immediately paying $1 million in cash. The historical cost of the furniture is $1 million. However, when cash payment is deferred, time value of money considerations need to be addressed. When the acquiring firm delays payment, the total cash paid exceeds the cash equivalent asset purchase price, with the excess payment attributed to interest. For example, assume that the office furniture supplier agreed to finance the previous transaction by accepting a $1 million 3-year note bearing interest at a 6% annual rate. The amount paid 3 years later would be $1,191,016 ($1 million $\times$ $(1 + .06)^3$). Assuming 6% is a reasonable interest rate, the total amount paid includes two components: the furniture's cash equivalent acquisition cost of $1 million, and $191,016 of interest. In terms of the accounting equation, the transaction should be recognized by increasing both the operational asset "office furniture" and the liability "notes payable" for $1 million. Interest expense of $191,016 is recognized over the 3-year financing period, with an offsetting increase to a liability account. The total liability (including interest) accumulates to $1,191,016 at the end of 3 years, and would be satisfied in full through a cash payment at that time.

Complexity is introduced when assets are acquired by issuing deferred payment promissory notes with unreasonable interest rates. For example, what if the financing note is "noninterest bearing," without specific mention of interest, but simply requires payment of $1,191,016 in 3 years? Since there is no mention of interest, the form of the transaction indicates a purchase of office furniture for a cash payment of $1,191,016. However, recall that GAAP strives to report transactions' underlying economic substance, regardless of their legal form. Although there is no specific mention of an interest element, given there is a time value of money, we know interest is part of the total cash paid and must be appropriately accounted for. Fair value given to acquire the office furniture is the present value of future cash payments discounted using a reasonable interest rate considering the risk of the buyer (borrower). Continuing our example, if a reasonable interest rate is estimated at 6%, the present value of the future payments is $1 million ($\$1{,}191{,}016 / (1 + .06)^3$). At acquisition both the operational asset and the note payable are again recognized at $1 million, and interest expense of $191,016 is recognized over the term of the note. This results in the same financial statement effects discussed previously when the interest component was explicitly stated on the promissory note at a reasonable rate (6%).

In arm's length orderly transactions,[2] it can be assumed that the fair value of what is received is equal to the fair value of what is given; because otherwise, the exchange would not have occurred. This is convenient for accounting purposes because sometimes it is easier to use the fair value of what is received rather than the fair value of what is given in valuing transactions.

[2] Transactions that are at arm's length are those between unrelated parties, and orderly transactions are those where neither party is compelled to enter into the exchange.

Continuing our previous example, we now assume that a fair value for the noninterest bearing note cannot be reasonably estimated. However, the $1 million cash equivalent acquisition value of the office equipment is known with a high degree of certainty. We can use the fair value of what is received (the office furniture) in valuing the transaction. Using time value of money terminology, we now know the future value ($1,191,016), the present value ($1 million), and the term of the note (3 years). This enables calculation of the remaining unknown—the "imputed" interest rate at 6%. Again, financial statement recognition is the same and consistent with the substance of the transaction—the asset and liability are initially recognized at $1 million, and $191,016 of interest expense is recognized over the 3-year term of the note. The assumption of equal fair values given and received in orderly arm's length transactions is particularly useful in determining gain or loss when accounting for assets that are disposed of through exchange for other nonmonetary assets. Disposals are discussed later.

Donated Assets

Although a corporation doesn't directly give anything of value when assets are obtained through donation, an acquisition "cost" must be recognized based upon estimated fair value. Generally, recognizing the increase in assets through donation is required to be offset in the accounting equation through revenue recognition in the period of contribution.[3] Although revenue recognition is permitted in the case of all asset donations, contributions received from governmental units or owners may instead be reported directly in stockholders' equity as paid-in capital.

Basket Purchase

If multiple assets are acquired in a "basket purchase" that is not a business acquisition (discussed later), the total basket cost must be

[3] FASB ASC 958-605-25-2; Original Pronouncement: Statement of Financial Accounting Standards No. 116, "Accounting for Contributions Received and Contributions Made," FASB 1993.

assigned to the particular assets acquired. Assignment of cost to particular assets is important for financial reporting (and tax purposes) because of subsequent accounting issues. In "basket purchase" situations, the total cost is allocated to individual assets acquired based upon their relative fair market values. The fair value of each individual asset acquired needs to be estimated. The sum of these individual fair values is used as the denominator for a series of fractions. The numerator for each fraction is the particular asset's individual fair value. By definition, these fractions sum to one. Each fraction is multiplied by the total cost of the basket purchase to determine each individual acquired asset's historical cost.

For example, assume a firm acquires a parcel of real estate for a total cost of $1,425,000, and the parcel includes land and an office building that the firm intends to use in its operations. The building's cost needs to be distinguished from the cost of the land because in subsequent periods the building will be depreciated but the land will not. Individual fair value estimates are: land = $1,000,000 and building = $500,000. The sum of these individual fair values is $1,500,000. The total historical cost of the basket purchase ($1,425,000) is allocated to the land and building as follows:

1,000,000/1,500,000 × $1,425,000 = $950,000 (cost of land), and
500,000/1,500,000 × $1,425,000 = $475,000 (cost of building).

Note the fractions sum to one (1 million/1.5 million + .5 million/1.5 million = 1) so the total acquisition cost is fully allocated to the individual assets acquired ($.95 million + $.475 million = $1.425 million). Note also that consistent with the conservatism convention, no gain is recognized from this apparent "bargain purchase."

Allocation based upon relative fair value is used frequently in financial accounting regardless of the underlying nature of items being acquired or sold. If in the previous example, the firm made a basket purchase of various inventory items rather than a parcel of real estate, the same allocation procedures would be applied.

Self-Constructed Assets and Other Firm Funded Construction and Development Projects

If a firm constructs an asset for its own use, cost includes the direct costs of material and labor and should also include an appropriate amount of allocated overhead. Consistent with the conservatism convention, if total cost of a self-constructed asset exceeds its fair value, the asset is recorded at fair value, and a loss is recognized.

Some assets require substantial investment over extended periods of time in order to get them ready for use. Consider for example a high-rise office building, or a cruise ship. If a firm buys such an asset, its fair value should include recovery of the full cost incurred by the builder, plus builder profit. One cost the builder would expect to recover is the interest cost incurred on construction related borrowing.[4] When a firm self-constructs or otherwise funds the construction of an asset, interest incurred during the construction period is considered an ordinary and necessary cost of getting the asset into its intended usable state under the full cost principle.[5] Interest cost incurred during the construction period(s) must be included in the historical cost of the asset, rather than being expensed in the period incurred.[6] Interest must be capitalized during periods when three conditions exist: 1) expenditures have been made, 2) the asset is being readied for use, **and** 3) interest cost is being incurred. Given this third condition, only firms with outstanding debt (whether or not related to the asset construction or development) capitalize interest. Interest capitalization is limited to the amount of interest cost incurred during the construction period.

To illustrate interest capitalization, assume that Behrend Corp. wants to construct an office building. They purchase an ideal parcel of land on 1/01/12 for $10 million in cash and simultaneously contract with an

---

[4] Even if no borrowing occurred, the builder would want to be compensated for the opportunity cost of returns foregone as a result of investing otherwise available funds in the construction project.

[5] Capitalization of interest may also apply to assets to be held for sale or lease to others. To qualify for interest capitalization, such assets must be produced as discrete projects—not manufactured on a repetitive basis.

[6] FASB ASC 835-20-05; Original Pronouncement: Statement of Financial Accounting Standards No. 34, "Capitalization of Interest Costs," FASB 1979.

independent builder to immediately begin construction of an office building on the site. Terms of the contract require Behrend to pay the builder a total of $50 million in equal $25 million payments. The first $25 million payment is to be made on 1/01/12 and the second payment is required upon completion of the building. Construction is completed and the second payment is made on 12/31/12. Behrend borrows $30 million at 10% on 1/01/12 to fund the construction project and has other existing debt outstanding in the amount of $20 million @ 10%. Assume that all interest is payable annually on 12/31, and that no debt principal is repaid during the construction period. The total annual interest cost incurred is $5 million ($30 million + $20 million = $50 million × 10% = $5 million) and sets the limit for the amount of interest that can be capitalized during 2012.

All three conditions are met and the interest capitalization period begins on 1/01/12. The interest capitalization period ends on 12/31/12 because the second condition is no longer met (the asset is completed and ready for use). The amount of interest cost to be considered for capitalization is called "avoidable interest," and represents the amount of interest that could have been avoided if debt principal were repaid rather than making construction related expenditures. In our example avoidable interest is calculated as $35 million × 10% = $3.5 million. The $35 million includes the $10 million expenditure for the land and the first $25 million payment to the builder both made on 1/01/12. Since the second builder payment was made on 12/31/12, no interest would have been avoided in 2012 if the expenditure was instead used to repay debt principal. Since avoidable interest ($3.5 million) is less than actual interest of the period ($5 million in 2012) it is included in the cost of the building. The remaining $1.5 million of 2012 interest cost is recognized as expense. Behrend must disclose the total interest cost of $5 million for 2012 and the portion capitalized ($3.5 million) in the notes to the financial statements.

Using the accounting equation format we illustrate the financial statement effects that result from our interest capitalization example (in millions):

ASSETS		=	LIABILITIES	+	SE
Purchase Land for $10 million on 1/01/12					
+ Land	+ 10				
– Cash	– 10				

Pay Builder $25 million on 1/01/12

+ Building + 25
– Cash – 25

Borrow $30 million by Issuing Construction Note Payable on 1/01/12

+ Cash + 30 + Note Payable + 30

Pay Builder $25 million on 12/31/12

+ Building + 25
– Cash – 25

Record Interest Payment of $5 million on 12/31/12

+ Building + 3.5 + Interest Expense – 1.5
– Cash – 5.0

The building's total cost including capitalized interest would be reported in the balance sheet as $53.5 million. Note that although the initial $10 million cost of the real estate parcel is appropriately capitalized to land, it is considered an expenditure that is related to getting the building ready for use. Therefore all interest costs are capitalized to the asset—building. If expenditures were made to prepare land for its intended use (e.g. clearing, grading, etc) those costs would appropriately be capitalized to land, and interest cost incurred during the period that the land was being readied for its intended use would also be capitalized to the asset—land. Once the land is in its intended usable state and the building construction begins, construction and interest costs are capitalized to buildings.

If we change the previous example and assume that Behrend has no debt outstanding other than the $30 million 10% construction loan, the amount of actual interest incurred in 2012 decreases to $3 million ($30 million @ 10%). Although "avoidable interest" remains at $3.5 million, the amount of interest capitalized is limited to the actual $3 million of interest cost incurred in 2012 and the building would be reported at a cost of $53 million. Further, if Behrend had no outstanding debt in 2012, no interest would be capitalized and the building would be reported in the balance sheet at a cost of $50 million. Since interest capitalization occurs only when actual interest cost is being incurred, firms may report identically constructed assets at different amounts in the balance sheet depending upon the degree of debt in their capital structures.

Natural Resources

Accounting for the cost of natural resources is very similar to the accounting used for PP&E. The full cost principle is applied and the capitalized cost of a natural resource includes: 1) the cost of purchased resource rights, 2) exploration costs, 3) development costs, and 4) restoration cost. Firms typically purchase the mineral rights to the natural resource (e.g. coal, oil, natural gas, etc.) then proceed with exploration activities where costs are incurred in trying to locate the resource through drilling, excavating, etc. If exploration is successful, development costs are incurred in making the natural resource accessible for extraction (e.g., building roads, digging tunnels, and mine shafts, etc). After the natural resource is consumed, firms frequently incur substantial restoration costs. These are costs related to restoring the property to an environmentally acceptable condition (e.g., costs of restoring land after a strip mining operation is completed). This liability is referred to as an "asset retirement obligation" and although most commonly associated with natural resources, can also be associated with PP&E (e.g., the cost of closing a nuclear power plant). A firm must recognize the asset retirement obligation when it becomes legally liable. This may occur over the periods of use, but frequently occurs when the asset is placed in service. Recognition of the liability is offset in the accounting equation with an increase in the asset's cost. An asset retirement obligation is initially recognized at the present value of the estimated future cost of restoration activities. Although the asset account is not affected in the future, the liability is increased over time through recognition of interest (accretion) expense, and may be increased or decreased as a result of changes in estimate regarding restoration cost[7] (change in estimate is discussed later).

Intangible Assets—Purchased and Internally Developed

Intangible assets are used in the business and represent certain exclusive rights or otherwise provide competitive advantage to the business.

---

[7] FASB ASC 410-20-35; Original Pronouncement: Statement of Financial Accounting Standards No. 143, "Accounting for Asset Retirement Obligations," FASB 2001.

Identifiable intangibles provide specific benefits and include patents, copyrights, trademarks and trade names, and franchises. Patents provide the exclusive right to produce a product or use a particular process for a period of 20 years. Copyrights are very similar to patents but relate to published works (e.g., paintings, books, songs, etc.) and apply for the life of the creator plus 70 years. Trademarks and trade names refer to symbols and words that uniquely identify a corporation's product or service (e.g., the Nike "swoosh" and Sears "craftsman" tools). Trademarks and trade names are issued for 10-year periods, but can be renewed indefinitely. A franchise is a contractual right to provide particular products or services, usually within a designated geographic area (e.g., a "Subway" or "McDonald's" restaurant).

Consistent with our previous discussion, when identifiable intangible assets are purchased, the full cost principle applies and all ordinary and necessary costs incurred in acquiring the asset (including legal fees) are capitalized. However, if intangibles are internally created, the initial capitalized cost relates only to legal costs and other fees incurred in securing the exclusive rights under the asset (e.g., patent, copyright, etc.). U.S. GAAP generally requires the immediate expensing of underlying "research and development" (R&D) costs incurred during the internal creation of the intangible asset.[8] "Research" is the effort to discover new knowledge that a business can use to develop new products or services. "Development" follows research and involves the planning and designing of new products and services based upon newly discovered or other knowledge.

An exception to the immediate R&D expensing requirement relates to development costs associated with computer software to be sold, leased, or otherwise marketed to others. Once the software development process has reached the point of "technological feasibility" further development costs incurred should be capitalized. Technological feasibility is the point

[8] FASB ASC 730-10-25; Original Pronouncement: Statement of Financial Accounting Standards No. 2, "Accounting for Research and Development Costs," FASB 1974. If R&D expenditures result in assets with "alternative future use" (either in other R&D efforts or outside R&D), the expenditure is initially capitalized, then allocated to R&D expense over the asset's life (cost allocation is discussed later).

at which it is established that "the product can be produced to meet its design specifications..."[9] IFRS differs in its accounting for R&D. Under IFRS, research and development costs must be accounted for separately. Consistent with U.S. GAAP, all research costs must be expensed in the period incurred; however, development costs are capitalized if the firm demonstrates that certain conditions have been met.[10] These conditions are similar but not identical to the technological feasibility requirements that apply exclusively to capitalizing software development costs under U.S. GAAP. Another exception relates to required capitalization of R&D that is purchased in a business acquisition.[11] (Accounting for such purchased R&D is illustrated in our next example).

Firms invest significant funds on R&D, and wouldn't do so unless they anticipate their R&D projects will prove to be cost effective (provide benefits exceeding costs). Successful R&D efforts can result in very valuable patents and other competitive benefits to the firm. The conservative R&D expensing requirements under U.S. GAAP and IFRS can cause intangible assets to be significantly understated in the balance sheets of firms who develop them internally.

Goodwill is termed an "unidentifiable" intangible asset. It represents the worth of an entire business as a going concern that exceeds the fair value of its net identifiable assets. In other words, goodwill is the amount by which "the whole is more than the sum of its parts." Goodwill results from a business' excellent reputation, loyal customer base, highly skilled employees, close supplier relationships, etc. Goodwill is not associated with any particular right or competitive advantage that can be separated and sold or otherwise assigned to another entity without transfer of the business as a whole. Goodwill is developed over time, but due to measurement verifiability issues, all costs incurred in its creation are expensed. Goodwill is recognized as an asset only as a result of a business acquisition. A business acquisition occurs when one corporation acquires the

---

[9] FASB ASC 985-20-25-2; Original Pronouncement: Statement of Financial Accounting Standards No. 86, "Accounting for Cost of Computer Software to be Sold, Leased or Otherwise Marketed," FASB 1985, par. 4.

[10] International Accounting Standard No. 38, "Intangible Assets," Par. 57, IASB.

[11] FASB ASC 805-10-20; Original Pronouncement: Statement of Financial Accounting Standards No. 141 (revised), "Business Combinations," FASB 2007.

Exhibit 4.1. Andover Corp. Balance Sheet at 1/01/2012

Assets:			**Liabilities:**		
Current assets:			Current liabilities:		
Inventory		$80,000	Accounts payable	$100,000	
Long term Assets:			Long-term liabilities:		
Land	$80,000		Long-term debt	200,000	
Buildings (net)	140,000		Total liabilities		$300,000
Equipment (net)	110,000		Stockholders' equity:		
Patent (net)	90,000	420,000	Paid in capital	$50,000	
			Retained earnings	150,000	200,000
Total assets		$500,000	Total liabilities and stockholders' equity		$500,000

assets and assumes liabilities or otherwise achieves control of another business. The amount initially reported as goodwill in the acquirer's balance sheet represents the excess of cost over the fair value of the net identifiable assets acquired.[12]

To illustrate the accounting for a business acquisition, consider the following example: Behrend acquires all of the assets and assumes all of the liabilities of Andover Corp. on 1/01/12 by paying $700,000 in cash. Andover's 1/01/12 balance sheet is illustrated in Exhibit 4.1. Assume that all of Andover's liabilities have fair values approximating book values, but has undervalued (and unrecognized) identifiable assets as follows:

1) Andover's use of LIFO causes inventory to be undervalued by $70,000, inventory is worth $150,000,
2) Patent has an estimated worth of $190,000, and is therefore undervalued by $100,000,
3) Unrecognized internally developed trade names have an estimated fair value of $90,000—when Andover secured the exclusive rights

[12] In rare occurrences where the fair value of the net identifiable assets acquired in a business combination exceeds cost, the "bargain purchase" amount is recognized as a gain, and the identifiable assets acquired and liabilities assumed are recognized at their individual fair values. This contrasts with the method of allocating cost based on relative fair values in the case of "basket purchases" discussed previously.

to its trade names, legal costs incurred were immaterial and were immediately expensed, and

4) Unrecognized In-Process R&D worth $130,000—consistent with GAAP Andover did not capitalize R&D costs but expensed them as incurred.

Using the information above and the information from Exhibit 4.1, the total fair value of all identifiable assets acquired and liabilities assumed is determined to be $.89 million and $.30 million, respectively. Therefore the fair value of the net identifiable assets acquired is $.59 million, and the intangible asset goodwill is recognized for the excess of that amount paid to acquire Andover ($.70 million – $.59 million). The amount of goodwill recognized equals $110,000.

Using the accounting equation format, we illustrate the financial statement effects that result from Behrend's acquisition of Andover Corp. for $.70 million on 1/01/12 (in millions):

ASSETS		=	LIABILITIES		+	SE
– Cash	– .70		+ Accts. Pay.	+ .10		
+ Inventory	+ .15		+ LT Debt	+ .20		
+ Land	+ .08					
+ Buildings	+ .14					
+ Equipment	+ .11					
+ Patents	+ .19					
+ Trade name	+ .09					
+ In-Proc R&D	+ .13					
+ Goodwill	+ .11					

Note that each identifiable asset acquired and liability assumed is recognized at its estimated fair value, but goodwill's fair value is not separately estimated. Goodwill's worth is estimated indirectly as the residual or "plug" amount necessary to maintain the equality of the accounting equation.

Cost Allocation

The periods benefited from asset usage are systematically and rationally allocated portions of capitalized cost as expense under the expense recognition principle. The cost allocation process is referred to as depreciation for plant and equipment, depletion in the case of natural resources, and amortization in association with intangibles. Recognition of expense from cost allocation has no associated cash outflow and therefore does not appear in the statement of cash flows.[13] Allocated costs from operational assets used in manufacturing operations are considered part of "factory overhead," and applied to goods produced as a "product" cost (included in inventory), which eventually appears in the income statement as part of cost of goods sold. Although the methods used for cost allocation are the same, our discussion here will assume nonmanufacturing businesses; therefore, in our presentation, depreciation and amortization appear directly in the income statement as operating expenses. Depletion is considered a product cost and its effects upon the financial statements are presented later. Recognition of depreciation, depletion, or amortization is offset in the accounting equation by reducing the asset's "book value" (BV). The BV of an asset is its capitalized cost less the amount of "accumulated" depreciation, depletion, or amortization. Accumulated depreciation, depletion, or amortization includes all depreciation, depletion, or amortization recognized in all periods preceding the balance sheet date.

It is important to note that depreciation, amortization, and depletion are systems of cost allocation—not valuation. As such:

1) **Depreciation, amortization, or depletion expense reported on the income statement does not represent decline in asset value that occurred during the period, and**
2) **The book value of the asset reported on the balance sheet does not represent its fair value.**[14]

GAAP permits various "systematic and rational" cost allocation methods. All methods require estimates of service life and residual value.

[13] Under the indirect method of presenting operating cash flow, since the period's allocated cost reduces reported net income but has no associated cash outflow, it requires an add-back adjustment in going from income to cash flow from operations. This is illustrated in a future chapter.

[14] Exceptions include the revaluation option allowed under IFRS, and impairments, both are discussed later.

Service life is the firm's estimate of total asset usage, and residual value is the estimated disposal proceeds (at the end of the asset's service life). An asset's economic life may be longer than its service life. For example, a rental car company's policy may require disposal of cars after 2 years (or 30,000 miles) of service, even though the economic life of a car can be much longer (e.g., 10 years or 150,000 miles) depending upon how well the asset is maintained. Another company may place an identical car in service with the intention of using it for six or longer periods. Therefore estimates of service life (and residual value) may justifiably differ across firms. Land is the only tangible asset with "unlimited" life and as such land is generally not depreciated. Intangible assets are usually assumed to have zero residual value.[15] Some intangibles have "indefinite" lives. Such intangibles include trademarks and trade names because they can be renewed indefinitely. Goodwill is another intangible asset with indefinite life. There is no recognition of periodic amortization expense for intangibles with indefinite lives; instead they are periodically tested for impairment (discussed later).

Depreciation

An asset's service life may be expressed in terms of time or activity. Three time-based cost allocation methods are presented here: straight line, declining balance, and sum-of-the-years' digits. Time-based cost allocation methods recognize expense based upon the passage of time; whereas activity-based methods recognize expense as a function of the asset's activity (e.g., units produced, hours of operation, miles driven, etc). Theoretically, under the expense recognition principle, the depreciation method applied should reflect the pattern of relative benefit received from the asset's usage, and firms are permitted to use different methods for various operational assets. Nevertheless, a recent survey indicates that 98% of sampled firms use straight line, and only 11% use another method for financial reporting purposes.[16]

---

[15] Zero residual value for intangibles is required to be assumed unless service life is shorter than economic life and reliable evidence of residual value exists. FASB ASC 350-30-35-8; Original Pronouncement: Statement of Financial Accounting Standard No.142, "Goodwill and Other Intangible Assets," FASB 2001, Par. B55.

[16] "Accounting Trends & Techniques 2010," AICPA, pg. 386. The percentages sum to more than 100% because some firms use multiple depreciation methods.

Exhibit 4.2. Depreciation Example Cost = $45,000 Service Life = 4 Years or 100,000 Miles Residual Value = $5,000

Panel A—Straight line					
Year	**Depreciable cost**		**Straight line rate**	**Depreciation expense**	**BV 12/31**
2011	40,000		1/4	10,000	35,000
2012	40,000		1/4	10,000	25,000
2013	40,000		1/4	10,000	15,000
2014	40,000		1/4	10,000	5,000
				40,000	
Panel B—Sum-of-the-years' digits					
Year	**Depreciable cost**	**Remaining life 1/1**	**SYD fraction**	**Depreciation expense**	**BV 12/31**
2011	40,000	4 Years	4/10	16,000	29,000
2012	40,000	3 Years	3/10	12,000	17,000
2013	40,000	2 Years	2/10	8,000	9,000
2014	40,000	1 Year	1/10	4,000	5,000
				40,000	
Panel C—Double declining balance					
Year	**Depreciable cost**	**BV 1/1**	**DDB rate**	**Depreciation expense**	**BV 12/31**
2011	40,000	45,000	50%	22,500	22,500
2012	40,000	22,500	50%	11,250	11,250
2013	40,000	11,250	50%	5,625	5,625
2014	40,000	5,625	50%	625*	5,000
				40,000	
Panel D—Activity based					
Year	**Depreciable cost**	**Deprecia-tion/mile**	**Miles driven**	**Depreciation expense**	**BV 12/31**
2011	40,000	.40	24,000	9,600	35,400
2012	40,000	.40	21,000	8,400	27,000
2013	40,000	.40	18,000	7,200	19,800
2014	40,000	.40	22,000	8,800	11,000
2015	40,000	.40	19,000	6,000*	5,000
				40,000	

*Depreciation expense is limited to the amount that will reduce book value to residual value.

The financial statement effects of these four depreciation methods are illustrated using the following example: On 1/01/11 Behrend Corp. purchases and places into service a delivery truck. The truck's full acquisition cost is $45,000, and it has an estimated service life of 4 years (or 100,000 miles), with estimated residual value of $5,000. Depreciation schedules for the entire service life of the truck are illustrated in Exhibit 4.2. Before discussing the various cost allocation methods, we note the following consistencies regardless of method:

1) The "depreciable cost" of the asset (cost – residual value = $40,000) is allocated as expense to income statement periods benefited in a "systematic and rational" manner, and
2) The depreciation process reduces the asset's book value (BV) to its residual value.

The Straight Line Method

The formula for determining periodic depreciation under the straight line (SL) method is:

(Cost – Residual Value)/Service Life (expressed in time)
($45,000 – $5,000)/4 years = $10,000 depreciation per year.[17]

As indicated in Exhibit 4.2 Panel A, each period is allocated an equal amount of depreciation expense, which presented graphically over the asset's service life provides a "straight (horizontal) line." From a theoretical perspective, given the predominant use of SL, it would seem most firms anticipate receiving equal benefit during each time period of asset usage. However, more likely firms choose the SL method because of its simplicity. The following illustrates financial statement effects of our SL example in accounting equation form (in 000s):

ASSETS		=	LIABILITIES	+	SE
		Purchase Truck for Cash on 1/01/11			
+ Truck	+ 45				
– Cash	– 45				

[17] Since depreciation is a system of cost allocation—not valuation, depreciation expense presented in the income statement does not indicate decline in asset value.

Record Depreciation Adjustment on 12/31/11

+ Accum. Depr. – 10 + Depr. Expense – 10

Record Depreciation Adjustment on 12/31/12

+ Accum. Depr. – 10 + Depr. Expense – 10

Record Depreciation Adjustment on 12/31/13

+ Accum. Depr. – 10 + Depr. Expense – 10

Record Depreciation Adjustment on 12/31/14

+ Accum. Depr. – 10 + Depr. Expense – 10

The asset "truck" is presented in each year-end balance sheet at its (BV, which is capitalized cost minus the related contra account—accumulated depreciation.[18] In our example, the cost of the truck is consistently $45,000 and accumulated depreciation increases from annual depreciation expense recognition. Under the SL method, each year's income statement includes depreciation expense of $10,000 and year-end accumulated depreciation is $10,000, $20,000, $30,000, and $40,000 on 12/31/11 through 12/31/14, respectively. Year-end BV is $35,000, $25,000, $15,000, and $5,000 on 12/31/11 through 12/31/14, respectively.

Although periodic depreciation expense amounts differ, the financial statement effects of depreciation expense recognition are the same using other depreciation methods discussed below. As such, financial statement effects using the accounting equation format will not be provided.

Sum-of-the-Years' Digits (SYD) Method

SYD applies a decreasing fraction to the asset's depreciable cost to determine each period's depreciation expense. The numerator of the fraction is the number of remaining periods of service life at the beginning of the depreciation period. In our example, on 1/01/2011 there are 4 years of life remaining, there are 3 years remaining on 1/01/12, 2 years remaining on 1/01/13, and 1 year remaining on 1/01/14. The denominator of each

[18] Since depreciation is a system of cost allocation—not valuation, asset BVs presented on the balance sheet do not represent fair value.

fraction is the sum of the numerators. In our example the denominator is: 4 + 3 + 2 + 1 = 10.[19] The full schedule of SYD depreciation for our example is presented in Exhibit 4.2 Panel B. SYD is termed an "accelerated" depreciation method because more depreciation expense is recognized in the early periods of the asset's service life.[20] Regardless of method, the same amount of depreciation expense is recognized over the asset's entire service life (depreciable cost of $40,000). Recognizing higher depreciation amounts in the early periods is offset by recognizing lower amounts of depreciation in the later periods of the asset's service life. This is why accelerated depreciation is also referred to as "decreasing charge." Note that using accelerated depreciation causes firms to present operational assets and stockholders' equity at lesser amounts in the balance sheet. Since debt is not affected, reduced stockholders' equity increases the firm's debt-to-equity ratio.

Declining Balance Method

The declining balance method applies a constant rate (percentage) to a continually declining balance (the asset's BV at the beginning of each depreciation period) to determine each period's depreciation expense. The constant rate applied is a multiple of the straight line depreciation rate. There are different adaptations of the declining balance method (e.g., 125%, 150%, 200%, etc.), which specify the straight line rate multiple. In our example the truck has a 4-year service life, and the straight line rate is 25% (1/4) per year. If we apply 150% declining balance, the constant rate applied to the asset's beginning BV would be 37.5% (150% × 25%). For purposes of illustration, we will assume 200% declining balance (also called double declining balance (DDB)), and the constant rate applied in our example is 50% (200% × 25%). Since BV and cost are equal when the asset is placed in service, 2011 DDB depreciation expense is calculated as:

---

[19] For assets with long service lives, the denominator can be determined as: n (n + 1)/2, where n = service life.

[20] SYD is rarely used in practice. Only 3 of the 500 surveyed firms indicated using SYD (AICPA, Accounting Trends and Techniques, 2010, p. 389). SYD is presented here (and in a future chapter) due to its simplicity in illustrating financial statement effects of applying accelerated depreciation.

$45,000 × 50% = $22,500. The full schedule of depreciation is illustrated in Exhibit 4.2 Panel C. Note that declining balance is the only method that initially ignores residual value in calculating periodic depreciation expense, but eventually takes it into consideration because depreciation is stopped when the asset's BV reaches residual value (see depreciation for 2014 under DDB in Exhibit 4.2). Like sum-of-the-years' digits, declining balance is an accelerated method of depreciation; however, DDB is relatively more accelerated than SYD. This is evidenced by the lower book value amounts presented in the balance sheet on 12/31/11, 12/31/12, and 12/31/13. Note that under all time-based methods of depreciation, book value of an asset at the end of its service life is consistently equal to its residual value. In our example, the BV of the truck on 12/31/14 is $5,000 under straight line, SYD, and DDB.

Depreciation for Tax Reporting Purposes and for Partial Periods

Given time value of money considerations, firms generally prefer using accelerated depreciation for tax reporting purposes. Unlike LIFO inventory, there is no "conformity rule" when choosing depreciation methods (or when making any other accounting method choices). Frequently, firms that use straight line depreciation for financial reporting use an accelerated method for tax purposes. The accelerated depreciation method permitted for tax purposes is the "modified accelerated cost recovery system" (MACRS), which is an adaptation of declining balance. There is no need to estimate service life or residual value under MACRS. Depending on the nature of the asset, specific "cost recovery" periods are prescribed and residual value is assumed to be zero under MACRS. The half-year convention is also generally applied under MACRS. The half-year convention assumes that all operational assets are placed in service and disposed of mid-year regardless of the actual dates. Under MACRS, one half-year's cost recovery deduction (depreciation) is taken in the asset's first year of use and one half-year's depreciation is taken in the year of disposal.

Firms can also apply simplifying assumptions for financial reporting purposes (including the half-year convention) provided they are unbiased. For example, a firm may recognize a full year's depreciation during the asset's first year of use, provided it recognizes zero depreciation in the year of disposal, or vice versa. Alternatively, firms can apply the nearest full month method where a full month's depreciation is taken for assets placed in service during the first half of the month or disposed of in the second half of the month; whereas, for assets placed in service during the second half, or disposed of in the first half of a particular month—no depreciation is recognized for that month. For time-based methods, partial period depreciation can be computed by adjusting full year amounts (e.g., Panels A, B, and C of Exhibit 4.2). For example, assume Behrend uses SYD (Panel B), places the truck in service on 7/05/2011, and computes depreciation to the nearest full month. The truck's 4-year service life begins 7/01/11, and ends 6/30/15. Depreciation expense for 2011 = \$8,000 (\$16,000 × 6/12), for 2012 = \$14,000 (\$16,000 × 6/12 + \$12,000 × 6/12), etc.[21]

Activity Based Depreciation Methods

The formula for determining periodic depreciation under activity-based methods is identical to that used in calculating SL. The difference is how service life is expressed in the denominator. Whereas SL expresses service life in time periods, "activity-based" methods express service life in terms of some activity. In our example, we express the denominator as the total number of miles the truck is estimated to be driven over its service life (100,000 miles). The activity based depreciation formula is:

(Cost – Residual Value)/Service Life (activity based), or
(\$45,000 – \$5,000)/100,000 miles = \$.40 depreciation per mile driven.

Activity-based methods are appropriate when the benefit from an asset is used up from its actual operation rather than the passage of time. A good example would be a rental car company that sells off its automobiles once they are driven 40,000 miles (regardless of age) versus another rental car company that uses automobiles for 5 years (regardless of mileage). The asset's service life can be expressed in input (e.g., hours of operation) or output (e.g., units of production) measures.

[21] In this example, the same depreciation amounts would result applying the half-year convention.

The activity level for the period must be known in order to compute periodic depreciation expense. In our example we assume the truck was driven 24,000, 21,000, 18,000, 22,000, and 19,000 miles in years 2011 through 2015, respectively. The full depreciation schedule is provided in Exhibit 4.2 Panel D.

Unlike the time-based methods, the number of income statement periods charged and the amount of depreciation recognized each period cannot be determined when the asset is placed in service. Note in Exhibit 4.2 Panel D that depreciation is recognized in the fifth year—2015. This is because service life is expressed in miles, and the truck was only driven for 85% of its service life (85,000/100,000 miles) during the first four years of its use. Activity-based depreciation methods are also referred to as "variable charge" methods because periodic depreciation behaves as "variable" cost. Variable costs are those that vary in total proportion to the level of activity, whereas "fixed" costs are those that remain fixed in total regardless of activity level. Note from Exhibit 4.2 Panel D that the activity level for 2012 is 87.5% of 2011's activity level (21,000 miles in 2012 versus 24,000 miles in 2011) and depreciation expense has declined proportionately by 12.5% (from $9,600 in 2011 to $8,400 in 2012). Although periodic depreciation expense may differ from period to period, all time-based methods result in depreciation behaving as a fixed cost that does not change with activity level changes.

Depletion

Depletion is cost allocation associated with the extraction of natural resources and is considered a product cost. Recall from the previous chapter that product costs are capitalized to inventory and subsequently expensed as cost of goods sold (CGS). Depletion is determined using the same formula as activity-based depreciation. However, the activity base for determining depletion is always expressed in terms of quantity. Under activity-based depreciation, this is referred to as the "units of production" method. Service life is expressed in the estimated number of units the asset will produce. Depending upon the natural resource, service life may be expressed as: ounces of gold, tons of coal, barrels of oil, etc. Depletion generally requires geological estimate of extractable quantity. The formula for determining depletion is:

(Cost – Residual Value)/Service Life (estimated extractible quantity of natural resource).

To illustrate depletion assume Behrend Corp. purchases the natural gas rights to a 5 square mile area of Harborcreek Twp. for $10,000 in 2012. Behrend subsequently incurs exploration and development costs totaling $190,000 (also in 2012). Behrend estimates that the well will produce 20 million cubic ft of natural gas, after which restoration costs are expected to be immaterial. Based upon this information, the cost of the natural resource is $200,000. Since Behrend doesn't own the land, residual value is zero. The "depletion base" (cost – residual value) is $200,000. The depletion rate is determined as:

($200,000 – $0)/20 million cubic ft = $.01/cubic ft of natural gas[22]

For purposes of illustration assume that all transactions are in cash, and that in the first year of operation (2012) Behrend extracts 2 million cubic ft and sells 1.5 million cubic ft of natural gas for $25,000. The impacts upon the financial statements under the accounting equation format are (in 000s):

ASSETS		=	LIABILITIES	+	SE	
Record Cost of Gas Well						
+ Gas Well	+ 10					
+ Gas Well	+ 190					
– Cash	– 200					
Record Depletion for 2 million cubic ft. Extracted in 2012						
+ Inventory	+ 20					
+ Accum. Depl.	– 20					
Record Sales (and CGS) of 1.5 million cubic ft. in 2012						
+ Cash	+ 25				+ Sales Rev	+ 25
– Inventory	– 15				+ CGS	– 15

[22] Natural gas is commonly quoted per 1,000 cubic ft, which would result in depletion at $10/thousand cubic ft.

Note that extraction converts a long-term asset—natural resource, to a current asset—inventory.

Amortization

As indicated previously, intangible assets with finite lives are amortized; intangible assets with indefinite lives are not. Generally, firms use the straight line method of amortization unless there is another discernable pattern of relative benefit received. For example, if a purchased franchise agreement limits the number of "name brand" goods that can be sold, a method similar to activity-based cost allocation may be appropriate. Sometimes GAAP mandates a particular method be used. For example, capitalized computer software development cost is periodically expensed as the larger of two amortization method amounts: 1) the straight line method, or 2) the percentage of revenue method (ratio of current period revenue to current and estimated future period revenues).[23] Note that this mandatory accounting for computer software development costs may cause firms to switch from one method to the other from period to period depending upon which results in the larger (and more conservative) amortization charge.

Although obsolescence and similar considerations need to be taken into account when estimating the service lives of tangible operational assets, the issue is particularly important regarding intangibles. Legal or contractual provisions generally set a maximum service life limit (e.g., 20-year legal life of a patent, or a franchise agreement that contractually expires in 50 years). However, technological changes and other factors may cause reasonable estimates of intangible assets' service lives to be much shorter.

Postacquisition Occurrences

The following postacquisition occurrences relating to operational assets are discussed: 1) Changes in estimate, 2) Expenditures, 3) Recognizing changes in fair value, and 4) Disposals.

---

[23] FASB ASC 985-20-35-1; Original Pronouncement: Statement of Financial Accounting Standards No. 86, "Accounting for the Cost of Computer Software to be Sold, Leased or Otherwise Marketed," FASB 1985.

Changes in Estimate

In our discussion of cost allocation we noted the need to make estimates of an operational asset's service life and residual value. With the passage of time, new information and other factors result in revisions of the estimates that were made when assets were initially placed in service. Consistent with our previous discussions (e.g., bad debts), changes in estimate relating to operational assets are also accounted for prospectively. Rather than going back and restating depreciation, depletion, or amortization of previous periods, adjustments are made over the asset's remaining service life. Regardless of when the change in estimate actually occurs during the year, for accounting purposes it is treated as if it occurred on the first day of the year.

To illustrate the accounting for changes in estimate regarding operational assets, we revisit our delivery truck example using straight line depreciation from Exhibit 4.2 Panel A. Recall that the truck cost $45,000 and was placed in service on 1/01/11 with an estimated 4-year service life and $5,000 residual value. Let us now assume that sometime during 2012, new information indicates that the original estimates should be revised, extending the truck's entire service life from four to six years (to 12/31/16) and reducing its estimated residual value from $5,000 to zero. Recall that changes in estimate are accounted for prospectively. We do not go back and revise 2011 depreciation expense of $10,000, nor do we revise the truck's 12/31/11 book value (BV) of $35,000. The revised estimates are used to determine depreciation expense over the asset's remaining service life. Using the revised estimates we determine depreciation for the years 2012–2016 as: (Book Value – Residual)/Remaining Life, or ($35,000 – 0)/5 years = $7,000. Each of the remaining 5 years of life will be allocated $7,000 of depreciation expense, reducing the truck's book value to residual value (zero) at the end of its useful life (12/31/16).

Revising estimates of service life and/or residual value can accommodate earnings management. A current period increase in the estimate of either an operational asset's remaining service life or residual value initially decreases expense (e.g., depreciation or amortization), which initially increases earnings. However, increases in reported income from optimistic changes in estimate will be offset in the future when higher expense amounts decrease reported earnings. The opposite effects occur where pessimistic changes in estimate decrease remaining service life or residual value. As discussed previously, net cash flow and earnings are equal in the long run. Cash paid to acquire an operational asset eventually reduces income (sooner or later).

Postacquisition Expenditures

Postacquisition expenditures are asset related costs that are incurred after the asset is placed in service. The issue for financial reporting purposes is whether or not the expenditure provides future economic benefit **beyond that originally anticipated** from the asset. If the cost merely keeps the asset in its normal operating condition, it is classified as a "revenue expenditure" and expensed in the period incurred. Ordinary repairs and maintenance are examples of revenue expenditures. However, costs incurred that provide future economic benefit should be treated as "capital expenditures." Future economic benefit is evidenced for example when expenditures: 1) increase the quantity of the asset's output, 2) enhance the quality of the asset's output, 3) make the asset operate more efficiently, or 4) extend the asset's service life. Capital expenditures are accounted for by increasing the asset's book value, with subsequent cost allocation to expense over the periods benefited. Revenue expenditures are classified as operating whereas capital expenditures are classified as investing activities in the statement of cash flows.

To discuss revenue versus capital expenditures we refer back to our previous delivery truck example. Revenue expenditures that should be expensed would include changing the truck's oil and repairing a flat tire. Examples of expenditures that would be considered "capital" because they improve the asset include the installation of a navigational system, or a hydraulic lift gate. A major engine overhaul provides an example of capital expenditure that doesn't improve the asset, but extends its estimated service life. Capital expenditures that somehow improve the asset are recorded as increases in the operational asset account, whereas those that merely extend the asset's service life may be recorded by reducing accumulated depreciation. Either way, the asset's book value is increased. It is important to note that all postacquisition expenditures do not fall neatly into the expense versus capitalize category. Firms generally establish policies for treatment of postacquisition expenditures (e.g., expense everything under $1,000), and those policies should be consistently followed.

An issue that may affect the postacquisition expenditure treatment decision is initial cost capitalization. In our previous example we assumed that upon acquisition a single operational asset account was recognized (i.e., delivery truck) and we subsequently recorded depreciation on that single asset. A more precise cost allocation method is applied under "component depreciation." Component depreciation effectively recognizes that when an acquired asset is composed of various elements with different service lives, they should be accounted for separately (as individual components). Consider, for example, the tires on the delivery truck. Although most truck components (engine, transmission, frame, and body, etc.) may be expected to last at least four years or 100,000 miles, the tires likely have a shorter service life. Under component depreciation, a portion of the total truck cost of $45,000 would be initially capitalized as a separate asset—"tires," and depreciation would be based upon a shorter life, assume, for example, two years or 50,000 miles. Assuming straight line depreciation, if the tires are replaced at the beginning of the third year (2013) at a cost of $2,000, the expenditure's treatment would be capitalization under component depreciation. However, if we account for the truck as a single asset, since the new tires do not improve the truck or extend its service life beyond original expectations, the $2,000 tire replacement cost would more likely be expensed. Other examples where component depreciation may be applicable include office buildings (carpeting versus interior/exterior paint versus structure, etc.), or cranes (engine versus cables versus boom, etc). Component depreciation is mandated by IFRS under IAS No. 16. Although allowed, component depreciation is not commonly used by U.S. GAAP firms because it is not required.

Another issue relating to postacquisition expenditures deals with a firm establishing its "turf" when it comes to the "exclusive" rights conveyed under certain identifiable intangibles. Consider, for example, a patent that provides Behrend with the exclusive right to manufacture and sell a new product. If the product is successful, competitors may manufacture and sell a disturbingly similar product. In order to protect its exclusive rights, Behrend will sue the competitor for patent infringement. In doing so, Behrend may incur substantial legal costs. U.S. GAAP acknowledges that infringement attempts are inevitable and therefore legal costs incurred in successful defense are considered ordinary and necessary costs of establishing intangible assets' worth. Legal costs incurred in successfully defending rights under patents, trademarks, etc. are capitalized by U.S. firms. IFRS takes a contrary view by considering successful infringement suit costs as necessary in maintaining (not establishing) intangible assets' worth. Under IFRS, legal costs of successful infringement suits are expensed unless the intangible asset's exclusive rights are expanded or otherwise enhanced. If the infringement suit is unsuccessful, the related legal costs are expensed, and if as a result of the court ruling the intangible is rendered worthless, it should be written off and a loss recognized. This is an example of asset impairment, which is discussed in the next section.

Recognizing Changes in Fair Value of Operational Assets

U.S. GAAP does not allow operational assets to be written up to fair value. However, consistent with the conservatism convention, if operational assets decline in value, they may be written down to fair value with impairment loss recognition. Rules for determining amount and timing of impairment loss recognition differ depending upon operational asset type. Impairment loss will be discussed as it relates to following types of operational assets:

1) Held for sale,
2) Held for use (excluding intangibles with indefinite lives),
3) Held for use intangibles with indefinite lives (excluding goodwill), and
4) Goodwill.

Differences between U.S. GAAP and IFRS for impairment loss recognition will be discussed where appropriate. This section concludes with a discussion of the revaluation method, which is an allowed option under IFRS. Under the revaluation option firms can write-up PP&E for balance sheet presentation at amounts in excess of "amortized cost."

Impairment

"Held for sale" operational assets are separately presented in the balance sheet and are those where management is actively seeking a buyer, and sale in the near future is probable. If the net realizable value (anticipated proceeds from sale less costs to sell) of held for sale assets is less than their book value, they are written down and an impairment loss is recognized. If the sale does not occur before financial statements are issued for a subsequent period, the assets held for sale should be presented in the balance sheet at their revised net realizable value, but gain can only be recognized to the extent of previously recognized impairment loss.

Before discussing impairment loss recognition on assets "held for use," it is important to note that such loss recognition is fairly subjective and frequently at the discretion of management. The timing and amount of impairment loss recognition requires estimates of fair value and may require cash flows estimates into the extended future. These estimates are based upon management's judgment, and can vary widely. Impairment loss recognition reduces earnings in the year of impairment; however, the associated write-down of long-term assets increases future periods' earnings through reduced cost allocation and/or increased gain or decreased loss reported from ultimate disposal. This also results in the shifting of normal recurring operating expense (i.e., depreciation, amortization, or cost of goods sold) to an apparently transitory income statement item—"impairment loss." Given the subjectivity involved in recognizing impairment losses, the user should consider earnings management possibilities and the issue of timing (why now?). Impairment losses should be taken into consideration in assessing the predictive value (quality) of earnings.

PP&E and intangibles with finite lives that are "held for use" are not periodically tested for impairment. Impairment testing for these operational assets is necessary only if conditions indicate that book value may exceed the future economic benefits that will result from their continued use.[24] Under U.S. GAAP there is a two-step process. Step 1

[24] Examples of such conditions are described in FASB ASC 360-10-35-21; Original Pronouncement: Statement of Financial Accounting Standards No. 144, par. 8, "Accounting for Impairment or disposal of Long Lived Assets" and Assets to Be Disposed Of," FASB 2001.

is the "recoverability test" where the asset's book value is compared with the total undiscounted estimated net cash flows that the asset will generate in the future. If the asset passes the recoverability test (future cash flow > book value), no impairment loss is recognized. If the asset fails the recoverability test, an impairment loss is recognized in an amount determined under step 2. The amount of the impairment loss is the excess of asset's book value over its fair value at the balance sheet date. If there is no ready market for the asset, its fair value may be estimated by discounting the future net cash flows (from step 1) to present value (PV). The written-down value of the asset becomes its new cost for purposes of determining future depreciation, amortization, etc. and recovery of the impairment loss is not allowed in future periods regardless of subsequent increases in the asset's value. There are notable differences under IFRS where a single impairment test is applied. If the asset's book value exceeds its "recoverable amount," which is the higher of: 1) net realizable value, or 2) value in use (PV of estimated future cash flows), the excess is recognized as an impairment loss and the asset is written down to the recoverable amount. Also contrary to U.S. GAAP, impairment loss recovery is allowed, but subsequent asset write-up is limited to the book value that would have been presented without the initial write-down to recoverable amount (e.g., net of depreciation effect).

In the case of indefinite life intangible assets except goodwill, impairment testing is required annually under both U.S. GAAP and IFRS. There is no recoverability test under U.S. GAAP and impairment loss is recognized in a one-step process when fair value < book value. Consistent with our previous discussion, the IFRS impairment test is applied by comparing book value with the "recoverable amount," and U.S. GAAP does not allow recovery of previously recognized impairment loss whereas IFRS does.

Recall from our previous discussion that goodwill is only recognized when it is purchased by acquiring another business and paying more than the fair value of the net identifiable assets acquired, with the residual paid determining the goodwill amount recognized. Upon acquisition, goodwill must be assigned to the benefiting unit(s) within the acquiring corp. Assignment of goodwill to the benefiting unit(s) is generally done to accommodate internal monitoring of profitability and cash flow, and is required for impairment testing.

Goodwill must be considered for impairment annually. U.S. GAAP allows firms to first perform a qualitative assessment "to determine whether it is more likely than not" (50% threshold) that the fair value of the benefiting unit is less than its book value. If the qualitative assessment indicates that is not the case, goodwill impairment testing is not required.[25] If the qualitative assessment indicates such is the case, goodwill impairment testing is conducted using a two-step process.[26] The first step compares the fair value of the benefiting unit with its book value. If fair value > book value it is assumed that there is no goodwill impairment; however, if fair value < book value, the second step must be applied. In the second step, the "implied" value of goodwill equals the residual of the fair value of the benefiting unit (determined in step 1) over the fair value of its net identifiable assets. This is the same process we presented earlier in the chapter where goodwill was initially recognized at the time of the business acquisition. If the implied value < book value, goodwill is written down to its implied value and an impairment loss is recognized. In subsequent periods, U.S. GAAP does not allow recovery of goodwill impairment loss.

To illustrate this two-step process, we refer back to our example of Behrend's purchase of Andover Corp. on 1/1/12 for $.70 million. Recall that the fair value of the Andover's net identifiable assets was only $.59 million at that time, so the purchase resulted in goodwill recognition of $.11 million. Assume Behrend continued to operate Andover as a separate autonomous unit, and as such the entire $.11 million of goodwill was assigned to Andover as the benefiting unit. We move forward in time to 12/31/12 and test for goodwill impairment. We now assume that the book value of Andover (including goodwill) has increased from $.70 million to $.75 million, and its estimated fair value is $.78 million. In applying step 1, we note that Andover's fair value ($.78 million) > book value ($.75 million), and therefore it is assumed that goodwill is not impaired. However, if we assume that the fair value of Andover is estimated at only

[25] Accounting Standards Update "Intangibles—Goodwill and Other (Topic 350)" FASB 2011-8, September 2011.

[26] FASB ASC 350-20-35; Original Pronouncement: Statement of Financial Accounting Standards No. 142, "Goodwill and Other Intangible Assets," FASB, 2001.

$.72 million, step 2 must be applied to determine the implied value of goodwill and test for impairment. In order to calculate implied goodwill at 12/31/12 we subtract the fair value of Andover's net identifiable assets from the fair value of Andover as a whole ($.72 million). We assume that the fair value of net identifiable assets (assets (excluding goodwill) – liabilities) is $.65 million. The implied value of goodwill at 12/31/12 is calculated as $.72 million – $.65 million = $.07 million, and goodwill must be written down from its book value ($.11 million) with a $.04 million impairment loss recognized. The following presents the financial statement effects of recognizing goodwill impairment in accounting equation form (in 000s):

ASSETS	=	LIABILITIES	+	SE
Write-Down Goodwill and Recognize Impairment Loss on 12/31/12				
– Goodwill – 40				+ Impairment Loss – 40

Note that with Andover's total fair value estimated at $.72 million, no goodwill impairment loss would have been recognized if the fair value of Andover's net identifiable assets was $.61 million or less because the implied value of goodwill would be at least its book value of $.11 million.

Under IFRS goodwill is tested for impairment annually, and recovery of previously recognized impairment loss is not allowed. Consistent with all other impairment tests, IFRS tests goodwill in a single step. The book value of the (benefiting) unit versus its recoverable amount are compared, and impairment loss is recognized when book value > recoverable amount. This recoverable amount deficiency determines the loss recognized and the necessary goodwill write-down. If the book value of goodwill is insufficient to absorb the entire recoverable amount deficiency, goodwill is written down to zero and the unit's other assets are written down proportionate to their book values.

IFRS's Revaluation Method Option

There can be significant disparity between U.S. and international GAAP in accounting for PP&E. Although PP&E is consistently recognized at full acquisition cost, IFRS allows firms to choose presentation for subsequent reporting under either the "cost" method or the "revaluation" method.[27] The method selected must be applied to all PP&E assets of the same class. A class of PP&E is defined as a group of assets that are "similar in nature and use" in the entity's operations (e.g., machinery, office furniture and fixtures, office equipment, etc.).[28] The cost method is the only method permitted under U.S. GAAP and the most commonly used under IFRS. Under the cost method, assets are presented in the balance sheet as we previously discussed (acquisition cost + capital expenditures – accumulated depreciation – impairment loss). The revaluation model strives to present assets at fair value on the balance sheet. The frequency of revaluation measurement is not specifically dictated, but the amounts should not differ materially from those that would result from revaluation at the balance sheet date. The revaluation model is only permitted if fair value can be reliably measured.

If initial revaluation results in asset write-up, it is offset in the accounting equation by recognition of "other comprehensive income" and presented in the owners' equity as "revaluation surplus." However, if initial revaluation results in asset write-down, it is recognized as a loss in net income and reduces retained earnings. Subsequent reversals of write-downs and write-ups are treated consistent with previous revaluation and recognized either in net income or other comprehensive income. Between revaluations, depreciation is recognized in net income based upon the asset's most recent revaluation amount.

Disposals of Operational Assets

When an operational asset is disposed of, generally the asset's book value is compared with its fair value and the difference is recognized as gain or (loss). This is called "fair value treatment."

Recall from our previous discussion that a transaction can be accounted for based upon the fair value of what is received in the exchange (rather than the fair value of what is given) if it is more clearly determinable. Since depreciation (amortization) is a process of cost

---

[27] International Accounting Standard No. 16, "Property, Plant and Equipment," Par. 29, IASB.

[28] Ibid, Par. 37.

allocation—not valuation—depreciation is recognized in the period of disposal for the portion of the period that the asset was used in operations. This applies whether the asset is disposed of at a gain or a loss. Upon disposal the asset is "derecognized," or taken off the books. This requires removing both the asset itself and any related accumulated depreciation/amortization. If an operational asset is disposed of for cash, the accounting is straightforward—the difference between cash received and the book value of the asset removed is recognized as gain or loss. Consider Behrend's delivery truck depreciated under the straight line method in Exhibit 4.2 Panel A. Recall that depreciation is $10,000/ year and the truck has a book value on 1/01/13 of $25,000 (cost = $45,000 and accumulated depreciation = $20,000). Assume the truck is used in operations up to its sale on 7/01/13 for $17,000. Depreciation is recognized for one half-year in 2013 = $5,000. This increases accumulated depreciation to $25,000 on 7/01/13, reducing book value to $20,000, and results in a loss on sale of $3,000. The following presents the financial statement effects of recognizing depreciation expense for the first six months of 2013 and the sale of the truck on 7/01/13 in accounting equation form (in 000s):

ASSETS		=	LIABILITIES	+	SE	
Record Depreciation expense for the period 1/01/13–6/30/13						
+ Accum. Depr.	– 5				+ Depr. Expense	– 5
Record sale of the truck for $17,000 on 7/01/13						
+ Cash	+ 17					
– Truck	– 45					
– Accum. Depr.	+ 25				+ Loss	– 3

Operational asset exchanges are usually accounted for using fair value treatment. Cash is commonly used to "even up" asset exchanges in cases where the asset values differ. Any cash received or paid in relation to disposal/acquisition of operational assets is classified as an investing activity in the statement of cash flows. To illustrate an exchange, we return to the truck disposal on 7/01/13, but assume the truck is traded in on a new delivery truck with a fair value of $50,000. Continuing to assume the old truck has a fair value of $17,000, Behrend must pay the dealer $33,000 to even up the exchange (fair value given = fair value received). The following presents the financial statement effects of recognizing depreciation expense for the first six months of 2013 and the 7/01/13 exchange in accounting equation form (in 000s):

ASSETS		=	LIABILITIES	+	SE	
Record Depreciation expense for the period 1/01/13–6/30/13						
+ Accum. Depr.	– 5				+ Depr. Expense	– 5
Record trade-in for new truck and payment of $33,000 on 7/01/13						
– Cash	– 33					
+ Truck (new)	+ 50					
– Truck (old)	– 45					
– Accum. Depr.	+ 25				+ Loss	– 3

Exceptions to the usual fair value treatment are made in cases of asset exchange where fair value cannot be determined and those that "lack commercial substance." In these situations, no gain or loss is recognized and the acquired asset's cost is determined based upon the book value of the surrendered asset.[29] This "book value treatment" is consistent under IFRS. A transaction is judged to lack commercial substance if the future expected cash flows from the acquired asset are not anticipated to substantially differ from those that would result from keeping the surrendered asset. To illustrate, assume that on 7/01/13 Behrend exchanged its delivery truck for a similar truck (same year, model, mileage, and condition). Only the color differs. Behrend wants to exchange trucks because the other one is the same color that Behrend uses in its advertising campaigns (like "brown" in the case of UPS). Given the similarity of the trucks, they have equal fair values, so no cash is paid or received in the exchange. This exchange should be given book value treatment because it lacks commercial substance. No gain or loss is recognized, and the "new" truck's cost is recorded at $20,000—the book value of the "old" truck. The following presents the financial statement effects of recognizing depreciation

[29] FASB ASC 845-10-30-6; Original Pronouncement: Statement of Financial Accounting Standards No. 153, "Exchanges of Nonmonetary Assets (an amendment of APB No. 29," FASB 2004.

expense for the first six months of 2013 and the trade-in for the similar truck on 7/01/13 in accounting equation form (in 000s):

ASSETS		=	LIABILITIES	+	SE	
Record Depreciation expense for the period 1/01/13–6/30/13						
+ Accum. Depr.	– 5				+ Depr. Expense	– 5
Record trade for similar truck on 7/01/13						
+ Truck (new)	+ 20					
– Truck (old)	– 45					
– Accum. Depr.	+ 25					

CHAPTER 5

Liabilities: Current, Contingent, and Long-Term Debt

Introduction

In this chapter we initially discuss liabilities and related issues in general. The topic of leases is covered in the next chapter. Debt instruments are discussed from the borrower's perspective here, but the same concepts apply from the lender's perspective, which will be discussed in chapter 7—Investments. Recall from chapter 1 that in financial analysis liabilities are compared with assets in order to assess a firm's liquidity, solvency, and financial flexibility. As we discussed in chapter 1, liabilities are the opposite of assets and represent "probable future economic sacrifices as a result of past transactions and events." Although the "future sacrifice" typically requires cash payment (e.g., accounts payable, taxes payable, salaries and wages payable, etc.), it may require providing goods or services (i.e., unearned revenue). An understanding of the accrual accounting principles (revenue and expense recognition) is necessary to comprehend liability recognition. Under the accrual basis of accounting, revenue is included in the income statement of the period earned (regardless of when the cash is received) and costs associated with revenue of the income statement period are expensed (regardless of when the cash is paid).

Executory contracts (also called unexecuted contracts) are those where parties each agree to provide consideration (something of worth) in the future, but neither party has provided anything yet. Executory contracts are generally not considered to constitute "past transactions or events," and therefore are not typically recognized in the financial statements. For example, if a corporation enters into a contract with its CEO to provide

$12 million in exchange for her services during the next fiscal year, nothing will appear in the current fiscal year-end financial statements because she has not yet provided next year's services, and the corporation hasn't paid her for those services. Partially executed contracts are generally recognized only to the extent of the consideration received or provided. For example, if in the previous example the corporation was to pay the CEO $1 million in advance for the first month of next year's service, the asset "prepaid salaries" would be recognized in the current year-end balance sheet. Recall that financial statements strive to report the underlying substance of transactions and events—regardless of their legal form. Certain leases are unexecuted rental contracts in form; but may be recognized in the financial statements if in substance they are considered to be property transfers with simultaneous financing arrangements. Leases are discussed in the next chapter.

Liabilities Resulting from Normal Operations

Liabilities incurred as a result of normal business operations are discussed first. Since these liabilities are generally satisfied in the near future, they are generally classified as "current" for purposes of balance sheet presentation. We previously discussed accounts payable; a common current liability that arises from the purchase of goods or services on account. Other common liabilities related to normal operations are: employee compensation, income tax, sales tax, warranties, and revenue received in advance. Consistent with balance sheet presentation of receivables in chapter 2, unless there is explicit mention of interest, liabilities resulting from normal operations that are expected to be satisfied within one year appear at undiscounted amounts.[1]

Employee Compensation

With the exception of manufacturing employees, the full cost of employee compensation is recognized as expense in the period the employee provides

---

[1] FASB ASC 835-30-15-3; Original pronouncement: Accounting Principles Board Opinion No. 21 "Interest on Receivables and Payables," AICPA, 1971.

service to the corporation.[2] Generally, there is a time lag between employees providing service and when they are paid. This gives rise to payroll related liabilities. As you are likely aware, an employee's gross pay exceeds their net or "take-home" pay. Employers withhold and subsequently pay portions of the gross payroll to taxing authorities, labor unions, retirement and insurance plans, etc. When financial statements are issued, an adjustment is necessary to recognize compensation expense and the related payroll liabilities for employee services that have been provided but are unpaid at the balance sheet date. For example, assume that Behrend pays all employees monthly on the 15th day of the month following the month of employee service. In preparing its year-end 12/31/12 financial statements Behrend needs to recognize the December 2012 gross payroll (assumed to be $200,000). Employees will only receive $125,000 because of the following various withholdings (W/H): taxes = $54,000 (federal, state, and local income tax = $40,000, social security and Medicare tax = $14,000), medical insurance = $8,000, retirement = $10,000, and union dues = $3,000. The effects upon the accounting equation for this example are as follows (in 000s):

ASSETS		=	LIABILITIES		+	SE	
Make 12/31/2012 adjustment to record December 2012 payroll							
			+ Various W/H Pay.	+ 75		+ Comp. Exp.	– 200
			+ Wage & Sal. Pay.	+ 125			

It is important to note that the entire gross payroll is recognized from the perspective of the employer/corporation—as employee compensation expense. Assuming all amounts are paid on 1/15/2013, the effects upon the accounting equation are as follows(in 000s):

Pay employees and Various Withheld Amounts on 1/15/2013							
– Cash	– 200		– Various W/H Pay.	– 75			
			– Wage & Sal. Pay.	– 125			

[2] Direct and indirect labor costs incurred by manufacturers are treated as product costs which are included in inventory and expensed as "cost of goods sold" in the period of sale. Again in this chapter, our discussion assumes nonmanufacturing businesses and as such employee compensation is treated as a period cost (expensed in the period of employee service).

Because the accounting for satisfaction of current liabilities through cash payment is identical to the previous example, illustration of the accounting equation effects will not be repeated for future examples.

Although amounts withheld from employees pay for social security and Medicare are taxes levied upon the employee, the employer is subjected to a "payroll tax" of an equal amount.[3] In addition to Behrend providing the federal government the $14,000 of social security and Medicare taxes withheld from employees, the employer must pay a matching payroll tax amount. The total social security and Medicare tax paid in association with the December 2012 payroll is therefore $28,000. Employers are also subjected to unemployment taxes levied by both state and federal governments. Additionally, employers typically provide fringe benefits such as paying a portion of medical insurance premiums and contributing to employees' retirement plans. To illustrate, the December 2012 payroll example is expanded by assuming that the employer matches employee contributions to retirement plans, pays half the medical insurance premiums, and is levied unemployment taxes totaling $2,000 (plus $14,000 for social security and Medicare = $16,000 payroll taxes). The effects upon the accounting equation for this example are as follows (in 000s):

ASSETS	=	LIABILITIES		+	SE	
		Make 12/31/12 adjustment to record December 2012 payroll taxes and fringe benefits				
		+ Fringe Ben. Pay.	+ 18		+ Comp. Exp.	– 18
		+ Payroll Tax Pay.	+ 16		+ Payroll Tax Exp.	– 16

Cash bonus plans and stock-based compensation plans are other forms of employee compensation. Stock-based compensation plans will be addressed in chapter 9 (in conjunction with a discussion of stockholders' equity). Cash bonus plan compensation expense is recognized in the period the employee provides services that give rise to the bonus. Managers and other officers are frequently provided with earnings based

[3] During 2011 and 2012, the federal government reduced (by 2%) the employee's social security tax burden. This example ignores this (temporary?) difference in the employee versus employer social security tax burden.

cash bonus plans. For example, Behrend Corp. may provide its president with a cash bonus plan where she is paid 1% of operating income exceeding $100,000 (before deducting the bonus), early in the following year. If Behrend reports 2012 operating income of $195,000, a year-end adjustment is necessary to recognize bonus compensation expense and the current liability—"bonus payable" in the amount of $950 (($195,000 – $100,000) × 1%).

Compensated absence is another form of employee compensation and requires recognition in the period the employee earns the compensated absence by providing service to the corporation; regardless of when the compensated absence is taken.[4] The expense is offset in the accounting equation with a liability that is subsequently reduced when the employee takes the paid time off. For example, assume Behrend Corp. gives each employee one week of paid vacation to be taken in the year following the year of service. During 2012, 10 employees each earned one week's vacation at an average rate of $500/week. The income statement for 2012 needs to include compensated absence expense of $5,000, and the year-end balance sheet must include a liability for compensated absences payable. The effects upon the accounting equation (in 000s) for this compensated absence example are as follows:

ASSETS	=	LIABILITIES		+	SE	
Make 12/31/12 adjustment to record compensated absence earned by employees in 2012						
		+ Vacations Pay.	+ 5		+ Vacation Pay Exp.	– 5

Even though employees take the time off in 2013, it is considered compensation expense of 2012 (when it was earned). As employees take their vacations during 2013, compensation expense is not recognized; instead the liability vacations payable is reduced.

[4] U.S. GAAP requires accrual of a compensated absence liability if: 1) The employee has already rendered the service to earn the time off, 2) The employee's rights to time off vest or accumulate, 3) It is probable that payment of the compensation will be made, and 4) The amount can be reasonably estimated. FASB ASC 710-10-25-1; Original pronouncement: Statement of Financial Accounting Standard No. 43 "Accounting for Compensated Absences," FASB, 1980.

Income Taxes

Corporations are separate legal entities, and as such are subject to federal income tax, and may also be subject to state and foreign income tax. Corporations must pay estimated payments during the year and file a tax return by March 15th of the following year. Taxes expected to be paid on taxable income of the period preceding the balance sheet date are presented among current liabilities. Accounting for income taxes is a fairly complex area that will be discussed in detail in chapter 8.

Sales Taxes

Sales taxes are levied on the purchaser of certain goods and services, but are collected and remitted to governmental authorities by the seller. Sales taxes do not constitute revenue, and since they must be paid in a short period of time, sellers account for sales taxes payable as a current liability. Assume that Behrend sells $100 worth of goods to a customer subject to a 6% sales tax. Assuming a cash sale, Behrend collects $106 from the customer. The effects on the accounting equation are as follows:

ASSETS		=	LIABILITIES		+	SE	
+ Cash	+ 106		+ Sales Tax Pay.	+ 6		+ Sales Revenue	+ 100

Subsequently when the sales tax is paid to the taxing authority, both cash and the liability will be reduced.

Warranties

As a means of enhancing sales, product and service providers frequently promise to repair or replace defective goods or workmanship for a period after sale. The future cost of performing under standard "generic" warranties is required to be estimated and recognized as expense in the period the related revenue is recognized (under the expense recognition principle). Accounting for optional extended warranties differs, and is discussed later. Actual expenditures required under warranty claims may occur in periods following that of revenue recognition. The estimated future cost of performance under generic warranties is presented in the balance sheet as an estimated liability. For example, assume that on 12/31/12 Behrend receives $50,000 from cash sales of goods carrying a 1-year warranty, and estimates the cost of future performance under the warranty at 2% of sales ($1,000). Ignoring cost of goods sold, the effects on the accounting equation (in 000s) are:

ASSETS		=	LIABILITIES		+	SE	
Record cash sale and estimated warranty liability on 12/31/12							
+ Cash	+ 50					+ Sales Revenue	+ 50
			+ Est. War. Liab.	+ 1		+ Est. War. Exp.	– 1

Accounting for estimated warranty liability is similar to the treatment of "allowance for doubtful accounts" that we discussed previously in the case of receivables. In future periods when the repairs and replacements are made, the estimated warranty liability account is reduced, with no income statement effect recognized. Assume that subsequently in 2013, the actual warranty costs incurred equaled the originally estimated $1,000. The effects on the accounting equation (in 000s) would be:

ASSETS		=	LIABILITIES		+	SE
Record performance under warranty during 2013						
– Cash (etc.)	– 1		– Est. War. Liab.	– 1		

The estimated warranty liability account balance needs to be evaluated for reasonableness at each balance sheet date. Any associated change in estimate is accounted for by adjusting warranty expense of the income statement period ending at the balance sheet date. Like accounting for bad debts, this prospective treatment of accounting for change in estimate of warranty costs provides an earnings management opportunity. Also similar to bad debt accounting, mandatory accrual basis treatment of warranty costs under GAAP is not permitted for tax purposes. Tax deductibility of warranty costs must be delayed until the period that actual repair or replacement occurs (recall that bad debts cannot be deducted for tax purposes until they are "written-off"). Using different accounting methods for financial reporting versus tax reporting results in "deferred taxes" (discussed in chapter 8).

Revenue Received in Advance

The revenue principle requires that revenue be included in the income statement period in which it is earned, regardless of when the related cash is received. Revenue is usually considered to be earned in the period that the goods or services are provided to the customer. When providers of goods or services receive cash from customers before the point of revenue recognition, a liability, "unearned revenue" is created. Unlike most liabilities, unearned (deferred) revenue is not usually satisfied through cash payment, but instead by providing goods or services to the customer. From the viewpoint of financial analysis, these are "good" liabilities in the sense that they represent revenue that will appear in future income statements. Examples where revenues are commonly received in advance include "sales" of: newspaper and magazine subscriptions by publishers, "gift cards" by retailers and restaurants, airfares by airlines, etc. To illustrate, assume that Southwest Airlines "sells" two round-trip tickets from Pittsburgh to Orlando on 12/15/12 for a total of $1,000. The flight leaves Pittsburgh on 3/06/13 and returns from Orlando on 3/14/13. The effects on the accounting equation (in 000s) would be:

ASSETS		=	LIABILITIES		+	SE	
			Southwest receives cash from advance "sale" of tickets on 12/15/12				
+ Cash	+ 1		+ Unearned Rev.	+ 1			
			Southwest performs flight service (adjustment at 3/31/13–end of first quarter)				
			– Unearned Rev.	– 1		+ Passenger Rev.	+ 1

Since revenue is commonly earned within a year of the balance sheet date, unearned revenue is usually included among current liabilities.

Extended Warranties

One type of unearned revenue that may provide an exception to current liability classification relates to sales of "extended warranties." Extended warranties are accounted for separately from the provider's generic warranties discussed previously. Returning to our previous warranty example, assume that on 12/31/12 Behrend also sells the customer an optional two-year extended warranty (making the entire term of the warranty three years) for $3,000. Since the extended warranty revenue will not be earned until the second and third years after sale (2014 and 2015—when the extended warranty service is provided), the entire $3,000 is initially reported as a liability—unearned revenue. The financial statement effects of the initial extended warranty sale (in 000s) would be:

ASSETS	=	LIABILITIES	+	SE
Record sales of extended warranties at 12/31/2012				
+ Cash + 3		+ Unearn. War. Rev. + 3		

If expenditures are anticipated to occur fairly evenly over the extended warranty period, revenue is recognized on the straight-line basis.[5] Assuming that is the case, one-half ($1,500) of the extended warranty revenue will be recognized in each year 2014 and 2015 with the following financial statement effects (in 000s):

Adjustment at 12/31/14 to recognize 2014 extended warranty revenue earned		
–Unearn. War. Rev. – 1.5		+ Warranty Rev. + 1.5
Adjustment at 12/31/15 to recognize 2015 extended warranty revenue earned		
–Unearn. War. Rev. – 1.5		+ Warranty Rev. + 1.5

Additionally, expense is recognized when extended warranty related expenditures are incurred (during 2014 and 2015) in accordance with the expense recognition principle. The entire $3,000 of unearned revenue will be classified as a long-term liability in the 12/31/12 balance sheet, whereas $1,500 (one half) will be reclassified as current on 12/31/13, and all of the remaining $1,500 will be classified as current on 12/31/14.

[5] If evidence suggests that the extended warranty related costs will not be incurred evenly, revenue should be recognized proportional to the anticipated pattern of expenditures. This is similar to the cost-to-cost method of applying percentage of completion accounting in the case of long-term construction contracts. FASB ASC 605-20-25-3; Original pronouncement: Technical Bulletin 90-1, "Accounting for Separately Priced Extended Warranty and Product Maintenance Costs," FASB, 1990.

Contingencies

A contingency is a potential increase or decrease in net assets (gain contingency and loss contingency, respectively) that will result ".... when one or more future events occur or fail to occur."[6] A pending civil lawsuit is an example of a loss contingency from the perspective of the defendant and a gain contingency from the perspective of the plaintiff. If the court finds in favor of the plaintiff (i.e., the relevant future "triggering" event occurs), the plaintiff's net assets will increase, and the defendant's net assets will decrease. Contingencies relate to conditions existing at the balance sheet date because of past transactions and events (e.g., a lawsuit is pending or may be brought in the future because an employee was critically injured in a job related accident that occurred before the balance sheet date).

Accounting for gain contingencies differs from the accounting for loss contingencies. Due to the conservatism convention, gain contingencies are only infrequently recognized in the financial statements or disclosed in the financial statement notes.[7] Gain contingencies may be disclosed in the financial statement notes only if there is a high degree of certainty that realization will occur, "... but care shall be exercised to avoid misleading implications as to the likelihood of realization."[8] Loss contingencies are more likely to be recognized in the financial statements and are commonly disclosed in the financial statement notes. Litigation is the most frequently disclosed loss contingency.[9]

---

[6] FASB ASC 450-10-20; Original pronouncement: Statement of Financial Accounting Standards No. 5, "Accounting for Contingencies," FASB, 1975.

[7] An exception relates to tax related gain contingencies (e.g., operating loss carryforwards where benefit will occur only if the firm generates future taxable income), which will be discussed in chapter 8.

[8] FASB ASC 450-30-50; Original pronouncement: Statement of Financial Accounting Standards No. 5, "Accounting for Contingencies," FASB, 1975, par. 17.

[9] To illustrate the relative frequency of contingency disclosures, of 500 recently surveyed companies, 344 had litigation disclosure regarding loss contingencies in 2010, whereas only 13 had litigation disclosure regarding gain contingencies. See *Accounting Trends & Techniques 2011*, AICPA, p. 83.

In contrast, loss contingencies must be recognized if two conditions exist: 1) occurrence of the future "triggering" event is probable, and 2) the amount of the loss can be reasonably estimated. Loss contingencies that are deemed "probable" but cannot be reasonably estimated in amount are required to be disclosed in the financial statement notes. If the likelihood of the triggering event's occurrence is less than probable, but is judged to be "reasonably possible," the loss contingency must be disclosed in the financial statement notes. For loss contingencies where the triggering event's likelihood of occurrence is judged to be "remote," no financial statement recognition or note disclosure is generally required.[10] It is important to note the high degree of judgment involved in accounting for loss contingencies. Assuming the amount of a loss contingency is known with certainty, it can be recognized, disclosed, or ignored depending upon the perceived likelihood that the future triggering event will occur.

Loss contingency recognition can be accompanied by a decrease in assets, or an increase in liabilities. We have discussed two examples where contingent losses require recognition—bad debts and warranties. Accrual accounting requires revenue to be recognized in the period of sale and expenses matched with revenue, without regard to when the related cash flows occur. In the period sales are made on account, there is a loss contingent upon customers' future failure to make payment. Under bad debt accounting, the loss contingency is recognized by increasing bad debt expense and decreasing assets (by increasing the contra asset account—allowance for doubtful accounts). Under accrual accounting for standard generic warranties, contingent warranty loss is recognized in the period of sale by increasing both warranty expense and estimated warranty liability.

---

[10] Some types of loss contingencies must be disclosed even if the likelihood of occurrence is judged to be remote. An example of such mandatory disclosure involves guarantees of other entities' debt. FASB ASC 460-10-50; Original pronouncement: FASB Interpretation No. 45, "Disclosure of Indirect guarantees of Indebtedness of Others," FASB, 1981.

Loss contingencies are termed "provisions" under IFRS. Accounting for loss contingencies (provisions) is similar under U.S. GAAP and IFRS; however, there are two key differences. One difference relates to interpretation of the term "probable" (the threshold for loss recognition). IFRS interprets probable to mean more likely than not—greater than 50%, whereas U.S. GAAP has generally been interpreted to indicate a higher degree of likelihood (80–85%). Another difference involves situations where a recognizable loss contingency amount can only be estimated as a range, where every amount within the range is equally likely. In such situations U.S. GAAP requires loss recognition at an amount equal to the low point of the range, whereas IFRS requires loss recognition at an amount equal to the mid-point of the range.[11] These differences cause IFRS to recognize loss contingencies (provisions) more frequently and at larger amounts than U.S. GAAP.

Subsequent Events

Subsequent events occur during the time lapse between the balance sheet date and the issuance of the financial statements. It usually takes several weeks to accumulate all the necessary information, adjust the accounts and have the financial statements audited. There are two types of subsequent events: 1) those that clarify uncertain conditions existing at the balance sheet date, and 2) those that are unrelated to conditions existing at the balance sheet date. The first category relates to resolution of year-end contingencies. This type of subsequent event should be considered in adjusting the previous year-end financial statements. For example, if a lawsuit is pending on 12/31/12, but is settled before the financial statements are issued on 1/31/2013 with the corporation agreeing to pay $1 million; the 2012 income statement should include the loss, and the 12/31/12 balance sheet should include the liability. Firms do not adjust previous financial statements as a result of subsequent events included in the second category because they do not constitute "past" transactions

[11] IAS No. 37 "Provisions, Contingent Liabilities, and Contingent Assets," International Accounting Standards Board.

or events relative to the balance sheet date. Although these types of subsequent events are not recognized, they may need to be disclosed in order to avoid issuing misleading financial statements. Examples of this type of subsequent event include casualty losses, business combinations, discontinued operations, and stock or debt issuances.

Notes Payable/Receivable

In chapter 2 we discussed sales on "open" account and the related issue of accounts receivable. Such sales involve customers' informal promise to pay (typically in 30–60 days) as evidenced indirectly by purchase orders, shipping, and receiving documents, etc. When a customer has a poor credit history or wants extended payment terms, the seller may want a formal interest bearing note in exchange for providing goods or services. Notes are formal IOUs that document the indebtedness and contractually obligate the debtor to pay cash to the creditor in the future.[12] Such notes involve future receipt of cash and recognition of interest revenue by the seller-creditor, and future cash payment with recognition of interest expense by the buyer-debtor. The accrual basis of accounting is required, with interest recognized in the period earned or incurred, regardless of when it is received or paid. We initially address the topic using an example from the seller (holder of the note) perspective, followed by the same example from the customer (maker of the note) perspective.

Assume that Behrend customarily sells goods to customers on a 30-day open account. However, one customer has requested extended payment terms—6 months. Behrend sells goods costing $5,000 with a normal invoice price of $10,000 to a customer in exchange for a $10,000 6-month note bearing interest at an annual rate of 9%. On 11/01/2012 Behrend provides the goods to the customer in exchange for the note. The note obligates the customer to pay Behrend $10,450 on 4/30/2013. This includes principal of $10,000 and $450 in interest ($10,000 × 9% × 6/12). Note that interest rates are always stated in annual terms

---

[12] A type of long-term note payable is a bond issue, which will be discussed later.

unless specifically indicated otherwise, so that the interest due at maturity is for one half (6/12) of the year. Although the entire $450 of interest is received or paid in 2013, the accrual basis requires interest to be recognized over the term of the note, with 2/6 ($150) recognized in 2012 and 4/6 ($300) recognized in 2013. The effects on the accounting equation (in 000s) from the seller/lender perspective would be:

ASSETS		= LIABILITIES		+ SE	
Record sale on 11/01/2012					
+ Notes Rec.	+10			+ Sales Rev.	+10
– Inventory	–5			+ Cost of Goods Sold	–5
Adjustment at 12/31/2012 to recognize 2012 interest revenue earned					
+ Interest Rec.	+.15			+ Interest Rev.	+.15
Record collection of note's maturity value on 4/30/2013					
+ Cash	+10.45			+ Interest Rev.	+.30
– Notes Rec.	–10.00				
– Interest Rec.	–.15				

The effects on the accounting equation (in 000s) from the customer/borrower perspective would be (closing entries are not presented):

ASSETS		= LIABILITIES		+ SE	
Record purchase on 11/01/2012					
+ Inventory	+10	+ Notes Payable	+10		
Adjustment at 12/31/2012 to recognize 2012 interest expense incurred					
		+ Interest Pay.	+.15	+ Interest Exp.	–.15
Record payment of note's maturity value on 4/30/2013					
– Cash	+10.45	– Notes Pay.	–10.00	+ Interest Exp.	–.30
		– Interest Pay.	–.15		

Corporations also issue notes in exchange for cash in order to meet short-term operating needs. The accounting for such borrowing is the same as illustrated for the customer/borrower above, except the asset—cash—is received (and increased) instead of inventory. Such borrowing is represented by "interest-bearing" notes, because the interest rate is explicitly "stated" on the debt instrument. When the stated (contract) interest rate (9% in our example) is equal to the market rate, the dollar amount written on the note (called "face value") is one and the same as the principal amount, which was the case in our previous example. The market interest rate is discussed in more detail below.

Another way to borrow (and lend) funds is through what are termed "noninterest bearing" notes. The term "noninterest bearing" is a misnomer. In economic substance, all borrowings include an interest element, the only difference between interest and noninterest bearing notes is whether or not the interest element is explicitly stated on the debt instrument itself. An alternative to our previous example is borrowing $10,000 on 11/01/12 by issuing a 6-month noninterest bearing note with a face value of $10,450. The borrower receives $10,000 on 11/01/12 and is required to repay $10,450 on 4/30/13. The difference between total future cash payments to be made and the cash received from note issuance represents interest ($10,450 – $10,000 = $450, in our example). The interest and noninterest bearing notes differ only in form—not substance. Conventional accounting practice records all notes at their face value amounts, which results in slightly different treatment for noninterest bearing notes. To accommodate recording noninterest bearing notes at their face value, accountants use a contra account—"discount on note" payable (in the case of the borrower) or receivable (in the case of the lender). Our discussion here will address the borrower, but similar issues affect the lender.

Noninterest bearing notes include all interest in the face value of the note that is recorded in the contra account "discount on note payable." The carrying value of a note (also called book value) equals its face value minus the discount. At issuance, the carrying value of the note is equal to the original principal amount borrowed, which in our example = $10,000 ($10,450 – $450). Interest expense recognized over the note's term is accompanied by the reduction and eventual elimination of the discount account through a process that is referred to as "amortization." Discount amortization increases the carrying value of the note. For the period 11/01/12–12/31/12, $150 of interest expense is recognized through amortization of discount. This amortization reduces the balance in the contra account to $300 for 12/31/12 balance sheet presentation at its carrying value of $10,150 ($10,450 – $300). From the borrower's perspective, the financial statement effects (in 000s) would be:

ASSETS		= LIABILITIES		+ SE	
Record noninterest bearing note issuance on 11/01/2012					
+ Cash	+ 10	+ Notes Payable	+ 10.45		
		+ Disc. on Note Pay.	– .45		
Adjustment at 12/31/2012 to recognize 2012 interest expense incurred					
		– Disc. on Note Pay.	+ .15	+ Interest Exp.	–.15
Record payment of note's maturity value on 4/30/2013					
– Cash	+10.45	– Notes Pay.	– 10.45	+ Interest Exp.	–.30
		– Disc. on Note Pay.	+ .30		

Although the income statement effects of interest versus noninterest bearing notes are identical, there are slight differences in balance sheet presentation. The interest bearing note provides two separate 12/31/12 balance sheet liabilities: notes payable (at face value) = $10,000, and interest payable = $150, whereas the noninterest bearing note is presented as one liability—its carrying value of $10,150 (face value = $10,450, minus discount on note payable = $300). In both cases, the balance sheet includes a $10,150 in current liabilities related to the note. Balance sheet presentation of noninterest bearing notes is relatively deficient because it doesn't directly communicate the amount of interest that is payable on notes.

A difference in financial statement presentation of interest bearing versus noninterest bearing notes relates to the classification of cash inflow or outflow in the statement of cash flows. Under U.S. GAAP, interest payments or receipts are usually classified as operating activities. However, cash flow from collection or payment of a note's face value is considered to be a financing activity (for the borrower/payer) or an investing activity (for the lender/receiver). Since all interest is included in the face value of noninterest bearing notes, none of the interest paid or received is classified as an operating cash flow. The implications for our example are that in 2013 when the borrower pays $10,450, the entire amount is considered a financing cash outflow in the case of the noninterest bearing note; whereas only $10,000 would be classified as financing and $450 operating cash outflow, in the case of an interest bearing note. Although the amounts are small and likely immaterial in the case of short-term notes, issuing long-term noninterest bearing notes payable (also called "zero coupon" bonds) can significantly enhance reported operating cash flow because all debt related payments made will be classified among financing activities. This disparity may not exist under IFRS because firms are given the option to report interest either paid or received as an operating activity, or as a financing activity when paid and an investing activity when received. Conceptually, interest paid/received is a financing/investing activity, respectively.

Long-Term Debt

Long-term borrowing is generally evidenced by some formal written instrument (note) that indicates the amounts and timing of future cash payments. Common examples of these long-term obligations include bonds, installment notes (mortgage notes and similar debt), and certain leases. Whereas short-term notes generally require both principal and interest to be paid at maturity, long-term notes usually require interest payments to be made periodically over the term of the borrowing.[13] The accounting issues related to various forms of notes involve uniform underlying principles and require an understanding of the time value of money concepts. Although we stress accounting for long-term notes from the borrower/debtor perspective here, the same issues apply to the investor/creditor, which is discussed in chapter 7. Initially bonds are discussed, followed by a discussion of installment notes. Leases are discussed in the next chapter.

---

[13] An exception is previously mentioned "zero coupon" bonds, which will be discussed later.

Bonds

Corporations wanting to borrow large amounts of money commonly do so through bond issues. A bond issue involves the issuance of a number of long-term notes, each usually having a maturity value of $1,000 or $5,000 due in 10–40 years with interest payable semiannually. A corporation wishing to borrow $100 million may do so by issuing 100,000 bonds with a maturity value of $1,000 each, provided that they make periodic payments at the "effective" or "market" rate of interest existing at the date of issuance. The "effective/market" rate of interest is a function of interest rates in general and the perceived riskiness associated with the borrower's likelihood of future payments. There is a positive relationship between risk and return: the higher the risk, the higher the demanded (effective/market) rate of return. The riskiness of a bond issue can be influenced by the debt terms agreed to by the issuer and its creditors in what is called the bond "indenture." Bond indentures may restrict the issuer by: limiting additional borrowing, restricting dividends, specifying a maximum debt to equity ratio, requiring periodic contributions to a trust that is subsequently used to make debt service payments (called a "bond sinking fund"), etc. A trustee may be appointed to assure that indenture terms are adhered to. Some bonds are "secured" where specific assets are pledged as security on the debt. In the case of default, the creditor can force the sale of the pledged assets and use the proceeds to satisfy the amounts due them. Secured debt is generally considered to be less risky than unsecured debt and therefore carries a lower effective/market interest rate. "Debenture" bonds are a form of unsecured notes. Debenture bonds with a high level of risk are termed "junk" bonds.

We will discuss the accounting for bonds using a simplified example. Assume that on 1/01/2011 Behrend Corp issues 3,000, 5-year bonds each with a maturity value of $1,000 and paying interest annually each 12/31 at 6%. This information (that is written on the face of the bonds) determines the amounts and timing of the future cash flows (paid by Behrend and received by the bond investors). Behrend must pay $3,000,000 (3,000 bonds @ $1,000) in 5 years on 12/31/2015, and must pay $180,000 ($3,000,000 × 6% × 12/12) each year for five years 12/31/2011, 12/31/2012, 12/31/2013, 12/31/2014, and 12/31/2015. Time value of money distinguishes two types of future cash flows. The periodic interest payment of $180,000 is considered an annuity, whereas the $3 million maturity value is considered a lump sum. If the market rate of interest for these bonds is equal to their 6% "stated" or "contract" rate, the bonds will be issued at their maturity (face) value. This can be determined using your financial calculator, where N=5, PMT=180,000, FV=3,000,000 and I/Y = 6% (the market or "effective" rate); the PV is calculated at 3,000,000. If the market interest rate exceeds the stated rate of 6%, the bonds will be issued at an amount less than face value, or at a "discount." Using your financial calculator, continue with the same information previously entered, but change the effective rate (I/Y) to 7%; the computed PV now becomes $2,876,994. The bonds are said to be issued at a "discount" of $123,006 ($3,000,000 – $2,876,994). If the opposite relationship exists at issuance (the market interest rate is less than the bonds' stated rate), they will be issued at an amount greater than their face value, which is termed issuance at a "premium." Again, use the same data entered into your financial calculator, except change the effective interest rate to 5%. The bond issue proceeds (PV) is now calculated at $3,129,884, with the bonds issued at a "premium" of $129,884 ($3,129,884 – $3,000,000).

Since future cash flows are contractually set by a bond's face value, term, and stated rate, issuance at a discount or premium is the market's mechanism to adjust for differences between the effective and contract interest rates. Issuance of debt at a particular amount of premium or discount allows the investor to earn and the borrower to incur the effective/market rate of interest regardless of the debt instrument's stated/contract interest rate. Debt issuance at a discount or premium should not be assumed to indicate the credit worthiness of the borrower; it merely represents the relationship between the stated/contract and effective/market interest rates. The 5-year, $3 million, 6% bond issue example discussed above is illustrated in Panels A, B, and C of Exhibit 5.1. The information in each Panel of Exhibit 5.1 is commonly referred to as an "amortization table." Panel A assumes the effective/market rate is equal to the stated/contract rate of 6%. Panel B assumes an effective/market rate of 7%, and Panel C assumes an effective/market rate of 5%. Note that all amounts are rounded to the nearest dollar, and that rounding error affects some amounts presented in the chapter exhibits.

Before discussing the individual scenarios, it is important to note some consistencies in all Panels of Exhibit 5.1. In all cases Behrend pays the same amount of cash (a total of $3,900,000) at the same points in time (interest of $180,000 every year at 12/31 for 5 years = $900,000, and $3,000,000 maturity value paid on 12/31/2015). Remember that the amounts and timing of cash flows paid by Behrend is set by the bond's face value, term, and stated interest rate. Note that the total net cash flow and the cumulative income statement effect are equal within each panel regardless of whether the bonds are issued at face/maturity value, a discount, or a premium. It should also be noted that the bonds are reported in each year-end balance sheet at their carrying/book value which equals maturity/face value minus unamortized discount or plus unamortized premium. The liability will be classified as long term on 12/31/2011, 12/31/2012, and 12/31/2013, but should be classified as current in the year-end 12/31/2014 balance sheet because it is due to be paid within one year.[14] The carrying/book value can also be calculated at any balance sheet date by discounting the maturity value and any remaining interest payments to present value using the "historical" effective/market rate of interest. The historical effective/market rate is the rate in effect at bond issuance (and determined the issue proceeds). Note that the carrying/book value of the bonds will likely differ from their fair market value. Market conditions and other factors will likely cause the effective/market rate to change during the 5-year term of the debt. An increase in the effective/market rate will cause the bonds' fair value to decrease, whereas a decrease in the effective/market rate will cause their fair value to increase. Accounting issues related to changes in fair value of debt will be discussed later in this section.

---

[14] If a sinking fund was established to retire the bonds, both the sinking fund (asset) and the bonds payable (liability) would continue to be classified as long term on the 12/31/2014 balance sheet.

The financial statement effects of issuing bonds at face value, a discount, and a premium will be illustrated using the information from Exhibit 5.1. In Panel A, the bonds are issued at face/maturity value and since the stated/contract rate is assumed to equal the effective/market rate, the amount of interest paid equals the amount of interest expense each interest period. Interest of $180,000 is paid at the end of each interest period at 12/31 of each year for 5 years, which sums to $900,000. The historical effective/market rate in the case of Panel A = 6%, and since that equals the stated/contract rate, the present value of the future cash flows = $3,000,000 (face/maturity value) on each balance sheet date. Each year's income statement will include interest expense of $180,000, and each year-end balance sheet will include the liability "bonds payable" in the amount of $3,000,000.

When the bonds are assumed to be issued at face/maturity value (Panel A), the effects on the accounting equation (in millions) would be:

ASSETS		=	LIABILITIES		+	SE	
Bond issuance on 1/01/2011							
+ Cash	+ 3.00		+ Bonds Payable	+ 3.00			
Record interest expense and interest paid December 31: 2011, 2012, 2013, 2014, and 2015							
– Cash	–.18					+ Interest Exp.	–.18
Record payment of bonds' maturity value Entry on 12/31/2015							
– Cash	– 3.00		– Bonds Payable	– 3.00			

Panel B of Exhibit 5.1 provides the calculated amounts that affect financial statements when 5-year bonds with an annual stated/contract rate of 6% are issued to yield an effective/market rate of return of 7%. As discussed above, the bonds are issued for $2,876,994, which is at a discount of $123,006.[15] Rather than record the principal amount

---

[15] The discount can be calculated directly as the present value of the periodic interest payment deficiency amount of $30,000 (maturity value × interest deficiency = $3,000,000 × (7% – 6%)) discounted at the effective/market rate of 7%. Using your financial calculator the present value of an ordinary annuity (PAY = $30,000, N = 5, and I/Y = 7%) PV is computed = $123,006.

Exhibits 5.1. 5 Year Bonds Maturity Value = $3 Million Annual Interest Payments with Contract Rate = 6%

Panel A					
Market rate = 6%					
Date	**Principal amount (carrying/book value)**	**Year's 6% interest expense**	**12/31 Amount of "interest" paid**	**Change in principal (carrying/book value)**	**Year-end carrying/book value**
1/1/2011	$3,000,000	$180,000	$180,000	$0	$3,000,000
1/1/2012	$3,000,000	$180,000	$180,000	$0	$3,000,000
1/1/2013	$3,000,000	$180,000	$180,000	$0	$3,000,000
1/1/2014	$3,000,000	$180,000	$180,000	$0	$3,000,000
1/1/2015	$3,000,000	$180,000	$180,000	$0	$3,000,000
		$900,000	$900,000		
Pay maturity value on 12/31/2015				($3,000,000)	0
	Total interest paid		$900,000	($3,000,000)	
	Maturity value paid		$3,000,000		
	Total cash paid		$3,900,000		
	Less cash received		$3,000,000		
	Difference		$900,000		

Panel B					
Market rate = 7%					
Date	Principal amount (carrying/book value)	Year's 7% interest expense	12/31 Amount of "interest" paid	Change in principal (carrying/book value)	Year-end carrying/book value
1/1/2011	$2,876,994	$201,390	$180,000	$21,390	$2,898,384
1/1/2012	$2,898,384	$202,887	$180,000	$22,887	$2,921,271
1/1/2013	$2,921,271	$204,489	$180,000	$24,489	$2,945,759
1/1/2014	$2,945,759	$206,203	$180,000	$26,203	$2,971,963
1/1/2015	$2,971,963	$208,037	$180,000	$28,037	$3,000,000
		$1,023,006	$900,000		
pay maturity value on 12/31/2015				($3,000,000)	0
				($2,876,994)	
	Total interest paid		$900,000		
	Maturity value paid		$3,000,000		
	Total cash paid		$3,900,000		
	Less cash received		$2,876,994		
	Difference		$1,023,006		

(*Continued*)

Exhibits 5.1. 5 Year Bonds Maturity Value = $3 Million Annual Interest Payments with Contract Rate = 6%—(Continued)

Panel C					
Market Rate = 5%					
Date	Principal amount (carrying/book value)	Year's 5% interest expense	12/31 Amount of "interest" paid	Change in principal (carrying/book value)	Year-end carrying/book value
1/1/2011	$3,129,884	$156,494	$180,000	$–23,506	$3,106,379
1/1/2012	$3,106,379	$155,319	$180,000	$–24,681	$3,081,697
1/1/2013	$3,081,697	$154,085	$180,000	$–25,915	$3,055,782
1/1/2014	$3,055,782	$152,789	$180,000	$–27,211	$3,028,571
1/1/2015	$3,028,571	$151,429	$180,000	$–28,571	$3,000,000
		$770,116	$900,000		
Pay maturity value on 12/31/2015				$–3,000,000	0
	Total interest paid		$900,000	$–3,129,884	
	Maturity value paid		$3,000,000		
	Total cash paid		$3,900,000		
	Less cash received		$3,129,884		
	Difference		$770,116		

borrowed, accountants record the bonds at their face value and create a contra liability account "discount on bonds payable." The carrying/book value of the bonds at issuance is face value—discount on bonds payable = \$2,876,994 (\$3,000,000 – \$123,006). Total interest expense over the 5-year bond term is equal to the net cash flow of \$1,023,006 (\$3,900,000 – \$2,876,994). Note that the difference in the total interest in Panel B versus Panel A equals \$123,006, the amount of discount. As illustrated in Panel B, the periodic interest expense is determined by multiplying the historical effective/market rate (7%) to the carrying/book value of the debt at the beginning of the interest period. This is called "the effective interest method." The difference between interest expense and cash interest paid determines the amount of "amortization." Amortization eliminates the balance in the discount account so that at maturity it has a zero balance and bonds' carrying/book value equals their maturity value of \$3,000,000. The amortization table in Panel B shows how issuance of 5-year bonds with an annual stated/contract rate of 6% for \$2,876,994 requires the borrower to incur (and allows the investor to earn) interest at the annual effective/market rate of 7%. Note that when bonds are issued at a discount interest expense increases over the bonds' term. Consistent with the concept of compound interest, this is caused by making periodic payments that are less than the interest cost incurred. For example, the amount of interest expense incurred in 2011 is \$201,390 but Behrend only pays \$180,000, which increases the amount of principal for 2012 by this \$21,390 deficiency. The payment deficiency also increases the carrying value of the bonds reported in each year-end balance sheet.

Assuming bond issuance at a discount because the effective/market rate is 7% (Panel B), the financial statement effects (in million's and rounded to the nearest thousand) would be:

ASSETS		=	LIABILITIES		+	SE
			Bond issuance on 1/01/2011			
+ Cash	+ 2.877		+ Bonds Payable	+ 3.000		
			+ Disc. on Bonds Pay.	–.123		

Recognize 2011 interest expense and pay interest on 12/31/2011

– Cash –.180 – Disc. on Bonds Pay. +.021 + Interest Exp. –.201

Recognize 2012 interest expense and pay interest on 12/31/2012

– Cash –.180 – Disc. on Bonds Pay. +.023 + Interest Exp. –.203

Recognize 2013 interest expense and pay interest on 12/31/2013

– Cash –.180 – Disc. on Bonds Pay. +.025 + Interest Exp. –.205[16]

Recognize 2014 interest expense and pay interest on 12/31/2014

– Cash –.180 – Disc. on Bonds Pay. +.026 + Interest Exp. –.206

Recognize 2015 interest expense and pay interest on 12/31/2015

– Cash –.180 – Disc. on Bonds Pay. +.028 + Interest Exp. –.208

Record payment of bonds' maturity value Entry on 12/31/2015

– Cash – 3.000 – Bonds Payable – 3.000

Panel C of Exhibit 5.1 provides the amortization table assuming the 5-year bonds with an annual stated/contract rate of 6% are issued to yield an effective/market rate of return of 5%. As discussed above, the bonds are issued for $3,129,884, which is at a premium of $129,884. Again the bonds are recorded at their face value, but now an "adjunct" liability account "premium on bonds payable" is used to present bonds at their carrying/book value. An adjunct account is the opposite of a contra account in that it is added to, rather than subtracted from the related account. The carrying/book value of the bonds at issuance is face value + premium on bonds payable = $3,129,884 ($3,000,000 + $129,884). Total interest expense over the 5-year bond term is equal to the net cash

[16] Adjusted for rounding.

flow of $770,116 ($3,900,000 – $3,129,884). Note that the difference in the total interest in Panel C versus Panel A equals $129,884, the amount of premium. Like Panel B, periodic interest expense is determined under the effective interest method by multiplying the historical effective/market rate (now assumed to be 5%) to the debt's beginning of period carrying/book value. Again, the difference between interest expense and cash paid determines the amount of "amortization." Amortization eliminates the balance in the "premium on bonds payable" account so that at maturity it has a zero balance and bonds' carrying/book value equals their maturity value of $3,000,000. The amortization table in Panel C shows how issuance of 5-year bonds with an annual stated/contract rate of 6% for $3,129,884 requires the borrower to incur (and allows the investor to earn) interest at the annual effective/market rate of 5%. Note that when bonds are issued at a premium interest expense decreases over the bonds' term. This is the opposite case of when bonds are issued at a discount, and is caused by periodic payments in excess of the interest cost incurred. For example, the amount of interest expense incurred in the first period (2011) is $156,494; however, Behrend makes an end of period payment of $180,000. This $23,506 excess payment represents repayment of principal for purposes of computing interest expense for period 2 (2012). The amount of interest expense decreases by $1,175 in period two ($23,506 × 5%). The excess payments are also reflected in the decreasing amount of bond carrying value (principal) reported in each year-end balance sheet.

The financial statement effects (in millions and rounded to the nearest thousand) when 6% bonds are issued at a premium because the assumed effective/market rate is 5% (Panel C) are:

ASSETS		=	LIABILITIES		+	SE	
			Bond issuance on 1/01/2011				
+ Cash	+ 3.130	+	Bonds Payable	+ 3.000			
		+	Prem. on Bonds Pay.	+.130			
			Recognize 2011 interest expense and pay interest on 12/31/2011				
– Cash	–.180	–	Prem. on Bonds Pay.	–.024	+	Interest Exp.	–.156

Recognize 2012 interest expense
and pay interest on 12/31/2012

– Cash –.180 – Prem. on Bonds Pay. –.025 + Interest Exp. –.155

Recognize 2013 interest expense
and pay interest on 12/31/2013

– Cash –.180 – Prem. on Bonds Pay. –.026 + Interest Exp. –.154

Recognize 2014 interest expense
and pay interest on 12/31/2014

– Cash –.180 – Prem. on Bonds Pay. –.027 + Interest Exp. –.153

Recognize 2015 interest expense
and pay interest on 12/31/2015

– Cash –.180 – Prem. on Bonds Pay. –.028 + Interest Exp. –.152[17]

Record payment of bonds' maturity value
Entry on 12/31/2015

– Cash – 3.000 – Bonds Payable – 3.000

Interest Payments not at Year-end

If bond interest payments are not made at the end of the accounting period, the amortization table amounts are used to determine the appropriate financial statement amounts under the accrual basis. For example, refer to Exhibit 5.1 Panel B, but instead assume issuance on 4/01/2011. The interest periods now begin each 4/01 and end with interest payments on 3/31/2012, 3/31/2013.... with the last interest payment made on the maturity date—3/31/2016. Although no interest is paid in 2011, 9 months of interest expense must be recognized in the 2011 income statement. The effects on the 2011 and 2012 financial statements

[17] Adjusted for rounding.

illustrated in the accounting equation format (in millions and rounded to the nearest thousand) are:

ASSETS	=	LIABILITIES		+	SE
Bond issuance on 4/01/2011					
+ Cash + 2.877		+ Bonds Payable	+ 3.000		
		+ Disc. on Bonds Pay.	–.123		

Note that the bond issuance amounts are exactly the same as originally presented. All that is changed is the assumed issuance date.

Adjustment on 12/31/2011 to recognize 9 months of 2011 interest expense

ASSETS	LIABILITIES		SE
	– Disc. on Bonds Pay.	+.016	+ Interest Exp. –.151
	+ Interest Payable	+.135	

Note that these amounts are equal to 9/12 (April–December 2011) of the Panel B first full period (12 month) amounts (i.e., interest expense = \$201,390 × 9/12 = \$151,049, discount amortized = \$21,390 × 9/12 = \$16,042, and interest payable = \$180,000 × 9/12 = \$135,000). The bonds will appear in the 12/31/2011 balance sheet at their carrying value of \$2,893,036. This is the balance in bonds payable minus unamortized discount (\$3,000,000 – (\$123,006 – \$16,042).

Record first interest payment on 3/31/2012 and to recognize 3 months of 2012 interest expense

ASSETS	LIABILITIES		SE
– Cash –.180	– Disc. on Bonds Pay.	+.005	+ Interest Exp. –.050
	– Interest Payable	–.135	

Note that interest expense recognized and discount amortized are the remaining 3/12 (January–March 2012) of the first full period (12 month) amounts (i.e., interest expense = \$201,390 × 3/12 = \$50,347, discount amortized = \$21,390 × 3/12 = \$5,347) and the current liability interest payable is eliminated with the cash payment.

With reference to Exhibit 5.1 Panel B, similar effects would result from necessary year-end adjustments and subsequent interest payments until the bonds are paid off at maturity on 3/31/2016. These financial statement effects are not illustrated.

Exhibit 5.2. 5 Year Zero Coupon Bonds Maturity Value = $3 Million Effective Annual Rate = 4%

Date	Principal amount (carrying/book value)	Year's 4% interest expense	12/31 Amount of "interest" paid	Change in principal (carrying/book value)	Year-end carrying/book value
1/1/2011	$2,465,781	$98,631	$0	$98,631	$2,564,413
1/1/2012	$2,564,413	$102,577	$0	$102,577	$2,666,989
1/1/2013	$2,666,989	$106,680	$0	$106,680	$2,773,669
1/1/2014	$2,773,669	$110,947	$0	$110,947	$2,884,615
1/1/2015	$2,884,615	$115,385	$0	$115,385	$3,000,000
		$534,219			
pay maturity value on 12/31/2015				($3,000,000)	0
				($2,465,781)	
	"Interest" paid		$0		
	Maturity value paid		$3,000,000		
	Total cash paid		$3,000,000		
	Less cash received		$2,465,781		
	Difference		$534,219		

Zero Coupon Bonds

Zero coupon bonds do not pay periodic interest during their term, so all interest is included in their face value. Therefore zero coupon bonds are issued at a large discount and are also referred to as "deep discount" bonds. Although no interest is paid until their maturity date, GAAP requires the accrual basis of interest expense recognition by applying the effective interest method. To illustrate accounting for a zero coupon bonds, we use our previous example and again (issue 3,000 of $1,000 face value five year bonds on 1/01/2011), but now assume a zero stated/contract rate and an annual effective/market rate of 4%. Using your financial calculators, we determine that the bonds will be issued for $2,465,781 (FV=$3,000,000, N=5, I/Y=4%, PMT=$0), at a discount of $534,219. The amortization table for these zero coupon bonds is illustrated in Exhibit 5.2. Note that total interest expense is again equal to the net cash flow of $534,219, which in the case of zero coupon bonds also equals the original issue discount. Consistent with Exhibit 5.1 Panel B, interest expense increases each period and discount amortization increases the carrying/book value of the bonds to their $3,000,000 maturity/face value at the maturity date. Year-end adjustments would be made to record periodic interest expense and amortize the discount. These financial statement effects are not illustrated.

Bond Issue Costs

Bond issuers can incur substantial amounts of issuance costs. Bonds can be sold through private or public placement. In a private placement, the bonds are sold to a single investor (e.g., a pension fund or insurance company). In the case of a public placement, the corporation usually sells the entire bond issue to an underwriter who then sells them to investors. An underwriter's profit is the spread between its purchase and selling price. Public placement of a bond issue results in substantial SEC registration costs that would be avoided under private placements. Although bond issue costs do not meet the definition of an asset,[18] they are treated as such

[18] Incurring bond issue costs does not provide "future economic benefit."

under U.S. GAAP. Bond issue costs must be capitalized as an asset and amortized to expense over the term of the bonds. Amortization is most commonly done under the straight line method. Expanding again on our original bond example, assume that Behrend incurs $100,000 in issue costs relating to the 5-year 6% bonds sold on 1/01/2011. The effects on the accounting equation (in 000s) are:

ASSETS		=	LIABILITIES	+	SE	
Bond issue costs assumed incurred on 1/01/2011						
– Cash	– 100					
+ Bond Issue Costs	+ 100					
Yearly amortization on 12/31/2011, 12/31/2012, 12/31/2013, 12/31/2014, and 12/31/2015						
– Bond Issue Costs	– 20				+ Bond Issue Exp.	– 20

Annual amortization of $20,000 is derived under the straight line method by $100,000/5 years. The unamortized portion of bond issue costs will be included among the assets on the year-end balance sheets (at $80,000, $60,000, $40,000, and $20,000 on 12/31/2011 through 12/31/2014, respectively). Note that bond issue cost amortization is required regardless of whether bonds are issued at face value, a premium, or a discount.

Callable Bonds

Callable bonds give the issuer the option to purchase bonds at a specified price before their scheduled maturity date. The call price is usually at a premium and is commonly stated as a percentage of face/maturity value. For example, a $1,000 bond callable at 105 can be retired (paid-off) for $1,050 ($1,000 × 105%). Callable bonds enable the issuer to benefit from decreases in the effective/market interest rate. Absent the call feature, if the effective/market interest rate decreases substantially, the fair market value of bonds will correspondingly increase.[19] By limiting the amount

[19] The fair value of debt is the present value of the future cash payments discounted at the effective/market rate that exists at the time of valuation.

the borrower must pay to "retire" the debt, the call feature may enable the issuer to retire bonds at a price less than they would otherwise pay through an open market purchase. The accounting treatment of an "early" debt retirement involves removing all related account balances from the books with the necessary balancing of the accounting equation recognized as gain or loss. To illustrate early retirement, we refer back again to our bond example in Exhibit 5.1 Panel A, but now assume that the bonds are callable at any interest payment date at 104. We also assume that at 12/31/2011 Behrend exercises its call option by retiring the entire bond issue for $3,120,000 ($3,000,000 × 104%). Recall that Panel A illustrates accounting for the 5-year 6% bonds that were issued at face value because the effective/market rate at issuance equaled the stated/contract rate of 6%. The effects on the accounting equation (in millions) would be:

ASSETS		=	LIABILITIES		+	SE	
Bond issuance on 1/01/2011							
+ Cash	+ 3.00		+ Bonds Payable	+ 3.00			
Record interest expense and interest paid 12/31/11							
– Cash	–.18					+ Interest Exp.	–.18
Record exercise of call option and retirement of bonds[20] on 12/31/2011							
– Cash	– 3.12		– Bonds Payable	– 3.00		+ Loss on Early Retire.	–. 12

GAAP requires $120,000 loss recognition in the 2011 income statement because the amount paid exceeds the total book value of the debt retired. It is important to note that the loss typically recognized under GAAP when bonds are retired through exercising a call option is not a reflection of the economic reality. For example, assume that on 12/31/2011 the effective/market rate had decreased to an annual rate of 3%. If there was no call option, the bonds would have a market value of $3,334,539 (FV=$3,000,000, PMT=$180,000, N=4, and I/Y=3%), so

[20] Note that if we instead assumed the bonds were originally issued at a discount (Panel B) or at a premium (Panel C) the unamortized discount or premium on 12/31/2011 would also be written off. Additionally, if we had assumed there were unamortized bond issue costs on 12/31/2011, they would be written off as well.

by retiring the debt for $3,120,000 results in an actual economic gain of $214,539.[21]

Installment Notes

Installment notes are commonly used to purchase specific property items. For example, you may have signed a 4- or 5-year installment note in purchasing a car, or may have signed a 30-year installment note in purchasing a home. These notes typically require monthly payments that include both principal and interest components such that the loan is completely paid off at the end of its term. The note's stated/contract interest rate is usually a fair representation of the effective/market rate so there is no issue concerning premium or discount amortization.[22] Traditionally, installment notes carried a fixed interest rate, but more recently variable rate alternatives are available. Monthly payment amounts will change consistent with changes in interest rates in the case of variable rate loans. Accounting for a variable rate loan is not illustrated. Instead, we will concentrate on fixed rate installment loans by using a simplified example. Assume Behrend Corp. buys a delivery van on 1/01/2013 for $48,000 and finances the entire purchase price by signing a 3-year 10% installment note requiring semiannual payments of $9,457 on 6/30 and 12/31. Recall that interest rates are always stated in annual terms. The semiannual payment can be determined using your financial

---

[21] The economic gain can also be calculated by assuming the retired $3 million bond issue is refunded with $3 million in new 4-year 3% bonds issued on 12/31/2011. Since the stated rate and effective rate on the new bonds are equal at issuance (both at 3%), the bonds will sell at face value, but will only require $90,000 annual interest payments. This annual savings of $90,000/year ($180,000 on the old bonds versus $90,000 on the new bonds) discounted to present value using the effective interest rate of 3% = $334,539. This interest savings gain is reduced by the $120,000 call premium paid providing the economic gain of $214,539.

[22] An exception exists in the case of mortgage lenders that charge the borrower "points." Points reduce the amount loaned/borrowed to an amount less than the face/maturity value of the note. In such cases, the points are treated as original issue discount and the effective/market rate will be greater than the stated/contract rate.

Exhibit 5.3. 3 Year Installment Note with 10% Annual Rate and Semi-Annual Payments

Date	Principal amount (carrying/book value)	6 mo. period's 5% interest expense	End of 6 months period's payment	Change in principal (carrying/book value)	End of 6 months period carrying/ book value
1/1/2013	$48,000	$2,400	$9,457	$–7,057	$40,943
7/1/2013	$40,943	$2,047	$9,457	$–7,410	$33,533
1/1/2014	$33,533	$1,677	$9,457	$–7,780	$25,753
7/1/2014	$25,753	$1,288	$9,457	$–8,169	$17,584
1/1/2015	$17,584	$879	$9,457	$–8,578	$9,007
7/1/2015	$9,007	$450	$9,457	$–9,007	$0
12/31/2015	$0			$–48,000	
	Total	$8,741	$56,741		
	Maturity value paid		$0		
	Total cash paid		$56,741		
	Less cash received		$48,000		
	Difference		$8,741		

calculator: PV = \$48,000, FV = \$0, N = 6, I/Y = 5% (note that the interest rate is half the annual rate—10% × 6/12 = 5%, and N represents the number of interest periods = 6). The amortization table for the example installment note is illustrated in Exhibit 5.3.

The amount of interest expense recognized each period declines because the payments made at the end of each period exceed the period's interest expense which reduces the principal balance in subsequent periods. The accounting is similar to that for bonds issued at a premium, except there is no maturity value due at the end of the note's term. Installment loans satisfy the principal amount borrowed in full through periodic (installment) payments. Interest expenses for years 2013, 2014, and 2015 are \$4,447, \$2,965, and \$1,339, respectively. The aggregate liability represents total principal due at the balance sheet date, with the portion payable in the next year classified as current. The installment loan will appear in the 12/31/2014 balance sheet as a liability of \$17,584—all classified as current; and the 12/31/2013 balance sheet will include a total liability of \$33,533 with \$17,584 classified as long term, and \$15,949 classified as current.

Installment notes are commonly used to finance actual asset purchases. In substance, certain lease arrangements are also considered to be the financing of asset purchases, even though in form, a purchase does not take place. The previously discussed accounting for installment notes used to finance actual asset purchases is identical to that used in accounting for leases that in substance are deemed to constitute the same thing. Leases are discussed in the next chapter.

Fair Value

Bonds and other notes are considered "financial instruments." Most firms report financial instruments that are liabilities in the balance sheet at their carrying/book value (under the effective interest method previously described). However, firms have the option of presenting financial instruments in the balance sheet at fair value, with changes in fair value recognized in net income.[23] This fair value option also applies from the investor perspective to financial instruments that are assets. A detailed discussion of financial instruments and fair value measurement is deferred until we discuss investments in chapter 7. If a firm does not elect the fair value option (and therefore does not recognize fair value changes in income), the financial statements must disclose financial instruments' fair value.[24] In order to provide the financial statement user with information regarding impending cash flow requirements, firms must also disclose maturity values and sinking fund requirements payable in each of the next 5 years.[25]

---

[23] FASB ASC 825-10-35-4; Original pronouncement: Statement of Financial Accounting Standards No. 159, "Fair Value Option for Financial Assets and Financial Liabilities," FASB, 2007.

[24] FASB ASC 825-10-50; Original Pronouncement: Statement of Financial Accounting Standards No. 107, "Disclosures About Fair Values of Financial Instruments," FASB, 1991.

[25] FASB ASC 470-10-50-1; Original pronouncement: Statement of Financial Accounting Standards No. 47, "Disclosure of Long-Term Obligations," FASB, 1981, par. 10.

CHAPTER 6

Leases

Overview

Leases are contractual arrangements where the legal owner of property called the "lessor" (e.g., landlord), allows another party called the "lessee" (e.g., tenant) to use the property in exchange for consideration (usually cash). Leasing is a very controversial accounting area. There are basically two accounting treatments applied to leases. The "operating lease" method treats the arrangement as a rental, whereas the "capital lease" method treats it as a transfer of the property with simultaneous financing. Operating leases result in recognition of rent expense or revenue over the lease term under the accrual basis. Capital lease treatment for the lessee involves recording the leased asset and an equal amount of a liability on their balance sheet. For the lessor, capital lease treatment results in removal of the asset from their books with gain/loss recognition in the income statement if fair value differs from book value.

As we discussed previously, firms may be economically affected by the accounting methods they apply. Bond indenture and other debt obligation restrictions (collectively called debt "covenants") may make it more beneficial for the lessee to apply the operating lease method, and in doing so achieve "off-balance-sheet" financing. On the other hand, dealers and manufacturers may want to apply capital lease treatment in order to record the leased asset's "sale" and recognize gross profit. Leases that are treated as operating by the lessee and capital by the lessor result in the "disappearing asset," because the asset no longer appears on either entity's balance sheet.

Leases are a form of executory contract, and normal GAAP treatment would require financial statement recognition only to the extent that either party has performed under the lease arrangement. This is the required accounting treatment in cases of operating leases. Recall however that

GAAP strives to report the underlying substance of transactions regardless of their legal (contractual) form. GAAP tries to identify those leases that in substance constitute property transfers with simultaneous financing, even though in form, the leased property has not changed hands. Capital leases are accounted for in a manner consistent with the substance of the transaction. The lessee recognizes depreciation expense on the leased asset and interest expense on the lease obligation in its income statement as if they had purchased and financed the asset's acquisition cost.

In order to appreciate the differences in operating versus capital lease accounting treatment consider the following simplified example: Behrend Corp. needs a specialized copying machine that is exclusively distributed by Edinboro Co. The copier has a 4-year life with zero residual value. Edinboro offers to sell the machine to Behrend for $18,000, and finance it at 8% per year or lease the copier to Behrend for four years with lease payments of $5,032 made **in advance**[1] each 1/01 starting on 1/01/2013. Using your financial calculator (remember to set the payments to beginning of each period), note that the calculated PV of the lease payments is equal to the copier's fair value of $18,000 (PMT = $5,032, N = 4, I/Y = 8%, FV = 0). These lease payments are similar to installment note payments we discussed in the previous chapter. The only difference is that this lease example assumes payments are made at the beginning of each period (an annuity due), rather than at the end of each period (ordinary annuity). Given the terms of the lease and the circumstances, in substance this lease constitutes an asset purchase with simultaneous financing and should therefore be accounted for as a capital lease.

Behrend will recognize interest expense related to its lease liability and Edinboro will recognize interest revenue related to its lease asset. Exhibit 6.1 illustrates the installment note amounts that would appear in each year's financial statements by the lessee and lessor under the capital lease method. Since payments are made in advance, the initial 1/01/2013 installment is attributed entirely to principal. Consistent with installment loans, interest declines each period because each payment contains

[1] Lease payments are typically paid at the beginning of each period. You may be familiar with this practice if you rent an apartment on a monthly basis. Rent is due at the beginning of each month.

Exhibit 6.1. Four Year Lease Obligation/Investment Amortization Table Payments at the Beginning of Each Year

Year	Total amount due prior to payment	Beginning of year cash payment	Payment of interest	Payment of principal	Remaining principal due	Year's 8% interest accrual	End of year total principal & interest due
2013	$18,000	$5,032	$0	$5,032	$12,968	$1,037	$14,005
2014	$14,005	$5,032	$1,037	$3,995	$8,973	$718	$9,691
2015	$9,691	$5,032	$718	$4,314	$4,659	$373	$5,032
2016	$5,032	$5,032	$373	$4,659	$0	$0	$0
	TOTAL	$20,128		$18,000		$2,128	

a principal reduction component. No interest expense or revenue is recognized in 2016 because the principal was paid off with the fourth (and last) payment made on 1/01/2016. We will next discuss the lessee (Behrend's) accounting as a capital lease, then as an operating lease; followed by the lessor (Edinboro's) accounting as an operating lease, then as a capital lease.

Lessee Accounting: Capital Lease Example

Assuming the straight-line method, Behrend would recognize $4,500 of depreciation expense in each of the 4 years.[2] Note that total expense recognized by Behrend includes interest of $2,128 (see Exhibit 6.1), and $18,000 of depreciation, which equals total net cash outflow of $20,128 ($5,032 × 4). Applying the capital lease method, the effects on Behrend's financial statements in accounting equation format (rounded to the nearest dollar) would be:

ASSETS		=	LIABILITIES		+	SE	
			Record Acquisition of the Copy Machine on 1/01/2013				
+Leased Copier	+18,000		+Lease Liab.	+18,000			

Although the leased asset and the leased liability are initially recorded at equal amounts at the beginning of the lease term (called the lease "inception"), the subsequent accounting differs. The lease liability is amortized under the effective interest method (Exhibit 6.1), and the leased asset is depreciated over the shorter of the lease term or the asset's service life (our example assumes both are 4 years).

ASSETS		LIABILITIES		SE	
		Record first installment payment on 1/01/2013			
– Cash	– 5,032	– Lease Liab.	–5,032		
		12/31/2013 adjustment to record 2013 interest and depreciation expense			
		+ Int. Pay.	+1,037	+ Int. Exp.	– 1,037
+ Accum. Depr.	– 4,500			+ Depr. Exp.	– 4,500

[2] Recall that straight line depreciation is calculated as (Cost – Residual Value)/Service Life = ($18,000 – $0)/4.

Record second installment payment on 1/01/2014

– Cash	– 5,032	– Int. Pay.	– 1,037		
		– Lease Liab.	– 3,995		

12/31/2014 adjustment to record 2014 interest and depreciation expense

		+ Int. Pay.	+ 718	+ Int. Exp.	– 718
+ Accum. Depr.	– 4,500			+ Depr. Exp.	– 4,500

Record third installment payment on 1/01/2015

– Cash	– 5,032	– Int. Pay.	– 718		
		– Lease Liab.	– 4,314		

12/31/2015 adjustment to record 2015 interest and depreciation expense

		+ Int. Pay.	+ 373	+ Int. Exp.	– 373
+ Accum. Depr.	– 4,500			+ Depr. Exp.	– 4,500

Record fourth (and last) installment payment on 1/01/2016

– Cash	– 5,032	– Int. Pay.	– 373		
		– Lease Liab.	– 4,659		

12/31/2016 adjustment to record 2016 depreciation expense

+ Accum. Depr.	– 4,500			+ Depr. Exp.	– 4,500

Each year includes interest and depreciation expense except for 2016 that exclusively includes depreciation ($4,500). Total expense recognized is $5,537 in 2013, $5,218 in 2014, $4,873 in 2015, and $4,500 in 2016. The 2013, 2014, and 2015 year-end balance sheets will respectively include: the book value of the leased copier (cost – accum. depr.) at $13,500, $9,000, and $4,500 and the total lease related liability (principal + interest) at $14,005, $9,691, and $5,032. The current portion of the total lease related liability at each year-end is $5,032, which represents the installment payment due the first day of the following year.

Lessee Accounting: Operating Lease Example

Accounting under the operating lease method treats the arrangement as a simple rental arrangement, with the lessee recognizing rent expense and the lessor recognizing rent revenue under the accrual basis. In this simple example, since the lease payments occur on the first day of the fiscal year, the cash basis and accrual basis result in the same accounting recognition by both the lessee and the lessor. The lessor continues to carry the asset on its books and recognizes periodic depreciation expense. The lessee does not record an asset acquisition, and more importantly does not record a lease liability. The following shows the financial statement effects under the accounting equation format for Behrend (the lessee) assuming operating lease treatment:

ASSETS		=	LIABILITIES	+	SE	
Record rental payment on 1/01/13 and recognize 2013 rent expense						
– Cash	– 5,032				+ Rent Exp.	– 5,032
Record rental payment on 1/01/14 and recognize 2014 rent expense						
– Cash	– 5,032				+ Rent Exp.	– 5,032
Record rental payment on 1/01/15 and recognize 2015 rent expense						
– Cash	– 5,032				+ Rent Exp.	– 5,032
Record rental payment on 1/01/16 and recognize 2016 rent expense						
– Cash	– 5,032				+ Rent Exp.	– 5,032

As was the case for the capital lease method, the total expense recognized is again equal to net cash outflow of $20,128 with operating lease treatment. Note, however, that under operating lease accounting the amount of each period's expense is equal, whereas the capital lease method "front-loads" expense recognition as a result of the larger interest component in earlier lease periods.[3]

Lessor Accounting: Operating Lease Example

Lessor accounting under the operating lease method mirrors that of the lessee. Edinboro will record each payment received by increasing cash and recognizing rent revenue for $5,032 each year. Edinboro will keep the leased copier on their books and record periodic depreciation. Assuming that Edinboro acquired the copier for cash on 12/21/2012 at a cost of

[3] The front-loading of expense recognition under the capital lease method would be more pronounced if the lessee used accelerated depreciation.

$15,000 and straight line depreciation is used, $3,750 of yearly depreciation will be recognized. The following shows the financial statement effects under the accounting equation format for Edinboro (the lessor) assuming operating lease treatment:

ASSETS		=	LIABILITIES	+	SE	
Record acquisition of the copy machine on 12/21/2012						
+ Inventory	+ 15,000					
– Cash	– 15,000					
Record Reclassification of Inventory to Leased Asset—Copier on lease inception date—1/01/2013						
– Inventory	– 15,000					
+ Leased Copier	+ 15,000					
Record rental receipt on 1/01/2013 and recognize 2013 rent revenue						
+ Cash	+ 5,032				+ Rent Rev.	+ 5,032
12/31/2013 adjustment to record 2013 depreciation expense						
+ Accum. Depr.	– 3,750				+ Depr. Exp.	– 3,750
Record rental receipt on 1/01/2014 and recognize 2014 rent revenue						
+ Cash	+ 5,032				+ Rent Rev.	+ 5,032
12/31/2014 adjustment to record 2014 depreciation expense						
+ Accum. Depr.	– 3,750				+ Depr. Exp.	– 3,750
Record rental receipt on 1/01/2015 and recognize 2015 rent revenue						
+ Cash	+ 5,032				+ Rent Rev.	+ 5,032
12/31/2015 adjustment to record 2015 depreciation expense						
+ Accum. Depr.	– 3,750				+ Depr. Exp.	– 3,750
Record rental receipt on 1/01/2016 and recognize 2016 rent revenue						
+ Cash	+ 5,032				+ Rent Rev.	+ 5,032
12/31/2016 adjustment to record 2016 depreciation expense						
+ Accum. Depr.	– 3,750				+ Depr. Exp.	– 3,750

The lessor recognizes profit equal to net cash flow ($5,128): profit determined as (rent revenue = $20,128 minus depreciation expense = $15,000), and net cash flow as (rent received = $20,128 minus copier cost = $15,000). Profit recognized each year is $1,282, and each year's balance sheet reports the asset at its book value of $15,000 on 12/31/12, $11,250 on 12/31/13, $7,500 on 12/31/14, and $3,750 on 12/31/15. Since the copier is fully depreciated on 12/31/16 it will not appear on the balance sheet.

Lessor Accounting: Capital Lease Example

If the lessor's cost of the asset differs from its fair value (usually the case for manufacturers and dealers) profit is recognized at the inception of the lease under the capital lease method.[4] Such is the case in our example, and Edinboro will recognize profit of $3,000 ($18,000 fair value – $15,000 cost) from the asset's "sale." Interest revenue will be recognized over the lease term under the effective interest method (from Exhibit 6.1 in our example). The following shows the financial statement effects under the accounting equation format for Edinboro (the lessor) assuming capital lease treatment:

ASSETS		=	LIABILITIES	+	SE	
Record acquisition of the copy machine on 12/21/12						
+ Inventory	+ 15,000					
– Cash	– 15,000					
Record sale and cost of goods sold at lease inception 1/01/13[5]						
+ Lease Rec.	+ 18,000				+ Sales Rev.	+ 18,000
– Inventory	– 15,000				+ Cost Goods Sold	– 15,000

Note that gross profit isn't recorded in a specific account. Like normal sales of inventory discussed in chapter 3, gross profit of $3,000 is reported

---

[4] There are two types of capital leases for lessors: "Sales Type" and "Direct Financing." The only difference between the two is whether or not there is profit (or loss) on the asset "sale." Manufacturers and dealers treat capital leases as sales type because there is generally profit on the sale. Banks and other financial institutions may enter into lease agreements where they purchase assets with the sole intention of leasing them to the lessee. Since financial institutions must pay the same price as the end user of the asset, fair value and cost are equal and there is no profit or loss on disposal. Such capital leases are termed "direct financing" type by the lessor.

[5] In the case of a direct financing lease, sales revenue and cost of goods sold would not be recognized. The leased asset would simply be removed from the lessor's books and replaced with lease receivable.

by subtracting cost of goods sold from sales revenue in the income statement.

Record first installment payment on 1/01/13

+ Cash	+ 5,032		
– Lease Rec.	– 5,032		

12/31/2013 adjustment to record 2013 interest revenue

+ Int. Rec.	+ 1,037	+ Int. Rev.	+ 1,037

Record second installment payment on 1/01/14

+ Cash	+ 5,032		
– Int. Rec.	– 1,037		
– Lease Rec.	– 3,995		

12/31/2014 adjustment to record 2014 interest revenue

+ Int. Rec.	+ 718	+ Int. Rev.	+ 718

Record third installment payment on 1/01/15

+ Cash	+ 5,032		
– Int. Rec.	– 718		
– Lease Rec.	– 4,314		

12/31/2015 adjustment to record 2015 interest revenue

+ Int. Rec.	+ 373	+ Int. Rev.	+ 373

Record fourth installment payment on 1/01/16

+ Cash	+ 5,032		
– Int. Rec.	– 373		
– Lease Rec.	– 4,659		

Note that Edinboro's total profit is again equal to its net cash flow of $5,128, but unlike the operating lease method, the lessor front-loads profit recognition by reporting larger amounts in earlier periods. This is not only due to recognition of gross profit in the period of the capital lease inception, but is also caused by larger interest revenue amounts being recognized in earlier periods.[6]

[6] Since there is no gross profit recognized in the case of a direct financing lease, the front-loading of profit recognition is solely due to larger amounts of interest revenue recognized in the earlier lease periods.

Summary

To summarize the financial statement implications of accounting for leases, the lessee generally prefers operating lease treatment in order to keep debt off the balance sheet and to delay expense recognition. Although off-balance-sheet financing is not a motivation for the lessor to apply capital lease treatment, accelerated profit recognition is.

Leases and GAAP

The FASB and IASB are similar in attempting to classify a lease as capital or operating depending upon whether or not substantially all risks and rewards of ownership are transferred under the lease agreement. U.S. GAAP has specified four specific criteria; and if any **one** of the four is met, the lessee must account for the lease as a capital lease. These same criteria apply to the lessor where at least one must be met in order to qualify for capital lease treatment.[7] The four criteria are:

1. Title to the property transfers to the lessee at the end of the lease term.
2. The lessee has the right to exercise a "bargain purchase" option.
3. The lease term is equal to 75% or more of the economic life of the asset.
4. The present value of the minimum lease payments equals 90% or more of the fair value of the leased property.[8]

The following discussion elaborates on each of the four criteria. We discuss these tests assuming that the lessee would prefer to avoid capital lease treatment, whereas the lessor would like to apply capital lease treatment.

If there is a transfer of title to the property, it is straightforward conclusion that the lease constitutes an asset purchase. To avoid meeting the

[7] Two additional tests must be met by the lessor to qualify for capital lease treatment. These will be discussed later in the chapter.

[8] FASB ASC 840-10-25-1; Original pronouncement: Statement of Financial Accounting Standards No. 13, "Accounting for Leases" as amended through 1980, FASB, 1980, par. 7.

first test, the lessee can insist that the lease contract does not stipulate title transfer. The second criterion is a bit more subjective. A "bargain purchase" option exists where the lessee can purchase the asset at a price so much below its anticipated fair value that exercise is reasonably assured. The subjectivity relates to the necessary judgment involved in determining if a bargain purchase exercise is "reasonably assured." Note that if either of the first two tests is met, it is assumed that the lessee will eventually own the asset, and therefore depreciation should be recognized over the asset's service life. However, if the lessee only meets the third or fourth test, lessee ownership of the asset is not assumed, and depreciation should be recognized over the asset's service life or the lease term, whichever is shorter.

In chapter 4 we discussed the subjectivity involved in estimating the service life of an asset. Those same subjectivity issues relate to the 75% of economic life test; however, the third (and fourth) criteria also involve the subjectivity of "lease term" determination. The lease term includes its fixed noncancelable period plus any "bargain renewal option" periods. A bargain renewal option (similar to bargain purchase option) is defined as periods for which the lessee can renew the lease at a rate so much below anticipated fair value that exercise of the option is reasonably assured. The third test's 75% threshold is arbitrary, and there is substantial judgment involved in determining whether this criterion is met. The third test does not apply to assets with 25% or less of economic life remaining at the inception of the lease term.

The fourth criterion defines "minimum lease payments" to include periodic rental payments (excluding "executory costs"), and bargain purchase price or guaranteed residual value. Executory costs are normal ownership costs (e.g., maintenance and repairs, personal property taxes, etc.). If the executory costs are paid by the lessor, their amounts must be estimated and deduced in determining the minimum lease payments. Guaranteed residual value is the amount a party guarantees the lessor will be able to receive from sale of the asset at the end of the lease term. If the lessee is the guarantor, it is considered part of their minimum lease payments. The lessor includes guaranteed residual value in its minimum lease payments whether the guarantor is the lessee or some third party. The present value of minimum lease payments is calculated using the lessee's estimated incremental borrowing rate. The implicit rate being charged by the lessor must be used instead, but only if it is known by the lessee **and** is lower than the estimated incremental borrowing rate. The lessee may be able to avoid capital lease treatment by: assuming a high incremental borrowing rate for discounting the minimum lease payments (reducing present value), and/or not guaranteeing residual value. If the lessor does not want to assume the risk associated with the asset's worth at the end of the lease term and/or wants to meet this fourth test in order to qualify for capital lease treatment, a third party can guarantee the asset's residual value. The extent to which lessees are motivated to avoid capital lease treatment is evidenced by the establishment of a whole industry where the service provided is serving as third party guarantor of leased asset residual value.

IFRS versus U.S. GAAP

IFRS describes situations that are similar to the FASB's four tests but does not identify specific "bright lines" that trigger capital lease treatment (called "finance" leases under IFRS). This is an example of what is called "rules-based" versus "principles-based" GAAP. U.S. GAAP is "prescriptive" because it has many detailed rules that determine what is reported in the financial statements; whereas IFRS describes conceptual objectives in general terms and relies more heavily on judgment in attempting to report the underlying substance of transactions and events in financial statements. For example, IAS 17[9] describes situations that would normally result in a lease being classified as a finance lease, but does not provide rules that automatically mandate finance lease treatment. In describing the situations, IFRS uses more ambiguous terminology such as "the lease term is for the major part of the economic life of the asset..." compared with the FASB's bright line "75% or more." The FASB's bright line: "90% or more" contrasts with IFRS that states "the present value of the minimum lease payments amounts to at least substantially all of the fair value of the leased asset."

[9] International Accounting Standard No. 17, "Leases," par. 10, IASB.

Accounting for Leases: Proposed GAAP Changes

Many financial statement users feel that off-balance-sheet financing will continue unless executory contracts are recognized in the financial statements. The FASB and the IASB are reconsidering accounting for leases in a joint project and agree that the current "all or nothing" model (where the lease is either considered an asset transfer and recorded in full or not recorded at all), be replaced with a "right of use" model. The right of use model would recognize all leases (beyond one year) as assets in that they provide the lessee with the future benefit—the right to use the asset. Along with the asset, a lease related liability would also be recognized. If the proposed right of use model becomes GAAP off-balance-sheet financing through leases will be substantially reduced.

Disclosure Requirements

Current GAAP requires disclosures that provide information that is useful to users in estimating the extent of a firm's off-balance-sheet lease financing through leases. Under U.S. GAAP firms must disclose cash flow amounts in each of the next five fiscal years and in the aggregate. IFRS only requires disclosure of aggregate amounts. Disclosure requirements apply to lessors as well as lessees for both operating and capital/finance type leases.

Lease Accounting Complexities—Lessee

At the inception of a capital lease, the lessee records both the leased asset and the lease liability at the present value of the minimum lease payments. Recall that minimum lease payments may include residual value (only if guaranteed by the lessee[10]) or a bargain purchase price. If the lessee guarantees residual value, both the leased asset and the total lease related liability (lease liability + interest payable) will equal the guaranteed

[10] From the perspective of the lessee, residual value is relevant only to the extent it is guaranteed. Therefore unguaranteed residual value is ignored and has no impact upon the lessee's accounting.

residual value at end of the lease term.[11] The lease related liability may be satisfied in full by transferring the asset to the lessor; however, if the asset's value is less than the guaranteed residual value, a cash payment would also be required and a loss would be recognized. If there is a bargain purchase option, the total lease related liability will equal the bargain price at the end of the lease term, but the leased asset likely will not.[12]

The owner of an asset may want to generate cash through its sale, but may also want to continue using the asset. Such situations may result in a "sale-leaseback" agreement that involves a seller-lessee and a buyer-lessor. If the fair value of the asset doesn't equal its book value at the time of "sale" a gain or loss results. Consistent with the conservatism convention, a loss on sale is recognized immediately. However, under U.S. GAAP any gain is deferred and recognized as reduction of rental expense if the leaseback is an operating lease or reduction of depreciation expense if the leaseback is accounted for as a capital lease. IFRS determines the treatment of gain based upon the classification of the leaseback. IAS 17 requires deferral and recognition over the lease term in the case of leasebacks that are treated as finance leases, but allows immediate recognition in the case of operating lease treatment.

The statement of cash flows effects will differ for the lessee depending upon lease classification. In the case of an operating lease, all cash payments are considered operating activity. If the lessee accounts for a lease as a capital lease, the arrangement is treated as an asset acquisition with related financing. This being the case, U.S. GAAP requires the interest portion of each installment payment be considered an operating activity[13]

---

[11] The leased asset is depreciated to guaranteed residual value over the lease term, and effective interest method reduces the total lease related liability to the guaranteed residual value over the lease term.

[12] If the lease contains a bargain purchase option, the lease term ends when the bargain purchase option is exercisable. The lease related liability is consistently accounted for by applying the effective interest method over the lease term. However, the asset is depreciated over its service life (not the lease term) because it is assumed that the lessee will own the asset through purchase at the bargain purchase price.

[13] As discussed previously, although conceptually interest paid is a financing activity (and interest received an investing activity), U.S. GAAP considers all interest "operating" for statement of cash flows classification. FASB ASC 230-10-45-17; Original pronouncement: Statement of Financial Accounting Standards No. 95 "Statement of Cash Flows," FASB, 1987, par. 22.

and the remainder of each payment (that reduces the "lease liability") is considered a financing activity. Also, in the period of capital lease inception, the lessee reports a capital lease among noncash investing/financing activities for the statement of cash flows (discussed in chapter 10).

Lease Accounting Complexities—Lessor

In qualifying for capital lease treatment, the lessor must meet two additional criteria. These tests relate to revenue recognition criteria discussed in chapter 2. The additional criteria are: 1) Collection of the lease payments is reasonably predictable, and 2) Performance by the lessor is substantially complete with any remaining costs to be incurred by the lessor being reasonably predictable. These two criteria are usually met, and lessors normally apply capital lease treatment when one or more of the four general criteria are met.

Unless one of the first two general criteria is met, residual value is relevant to the lessor whether it is guaranteed or not. When relevant (i.e., only the third and/or fourth criteria are met), its present value is consistently included in the "lease receivable" account recorded at the lease inception date. However, for sales type capital leases, a portion of the asset is considered unsold when residual value is unguaranteed. Therefore, sales and cost of goods sold are both reduced in equal amounts by the present value of any unguaranteed residual value.[14]

The lessor may incur incremental "initial direct costs" that are directly related to specific lease agreements. These costs may include broker's fees, employee commissions, cost of a credit check performed by outside agency, etc. Initial direct costs are treated differently depending upon lease classification. For operating leases they are initially recognized as a separate asset and subsequently expensed over the lease term consistent with rent revenue recognition. For sales type leases, initial direct costs are expensed when sales revenue is recognized. The treatment of initial direct costs is more complex for direct financing leases. They are initially capitalized as part of the "lease receivable" asset, and a new (lower) implicit rate is computed and used to recognize interest revenue over the lease term.

---

[14] Since sales and cost of goods sold are not recognized for direct financing leases, residual value is accounted for the same way, whether guaranteed or not.

In the case of lessor operating leases, all cash receipts are considered operating activities for statement of cash flows presentation. Lessors applying sales type lease accounting also classify all cash receipts as operating because they represent either cash collections from sales to customers, or interest. The lessor's statement of cash flows will differ only when the lease is treated as a direct financing lease. Direct financing lessors report the interest portion of cash receipts as operating, and the remainder (that reduces the "lease receivable" account) is classified as investing. In the period of direct financing lease inception, the lessor reports a capital lease among noncash investing/financing activities for the statement of cash flows (discussed in chapter 10).

CHAPTER 7

Financial Instruments: Investment Securities and Derivatives

Introduction

Financial instruments are defined as: cash, ownership interests in other entities and contractual rights/obligations to receive/deliver financial instruments in the future. We will discuss two forms of financial instruments in this chapter. We first address accounting by investors who hold debt and equity securities of other entities, followed by a discussion of derivatives. Derivatives are financial instruments that "derive" their value from some other item. For example, an option to purchase shares of Ford Motor Co. stock at a set price derives its value from the market value of Ford's stock, while credit default swaps derive their value from the likelihood of borrower default (because they provide contractual rights/obligations in such instances). The required accounting for investment securities and derivatives differs depending upon management intent and/or circumstances. However, firms can elect the "fair value option" in accounting for many financial instruments. The fair value option allows balance sheet presentation at "fair value" while recognizing fair value changes as gain or loss in net income.[1] Although some investment securities and derivatives are already required to be accounted for in that manner under GAAP, others are not. The fair value option is discussed after we present the otherwise required financial statement presentation of investment securities and derivatives under GAAP.

---

[1] FASB ASC 825-10-35-4; Original pronouncement: Statement of Financial Accounting Standard No. 159, "Fair Value Option for Financial Assets and Financial Liabilities," FASB, 2007.

Investment Securities

Firms commonly hold debt and equity securities of other entities as investments. Debt securities include bonds and other notes, commercial paper, etc. Equity securities are stocks and other instruments representing ownership interest in other entities. Debt securities are generally considered "passive" investments in that the investor is only seeking to earn a return on invested funds, not gain the ability to influence the investee firm. Debt security investments are consistently accounted for under the effective interest method with amortization of discount/premium increasing/decreasing the carrying value of the investment to its maturity value at the maturity date. The effective interest method was discussed primarily from the borrower's perspective in chapter 5. Since the investor's application of the effective interest method is the mirror image of that for the borrower, it will not be repeated here. Equity holders may be considered to be passive or "active" investors. Active investors are those with the ability to significantly influence the investee firm. Generally under GAAP, ownership of less than 20% of a firm's voting stock is considered a passive investment, while ownership of 20% or more is considered active. Active investments are accounted for under the equity method or through consolidation, depending upon the degree of investor influence. If the equity security investor can effectively control the investee firm, consolidation is required. The equity method is applied when the investor can significantly influence, but not control the investee firm. Accounting for passive investments will be discussed first.

Passive Investments: Debt and Equity Securities[2]

The accounting for passive investments depends upon management intent. "Trading" (T) securities are those intended to be held for a very short period of time (typically hours or days, but not longer than 3 months). A good example of trading securities is an investment bank

---

[2] The discussion of accounting for passive investments is based upon FASB ASC 320; Original Pronouncement: Statement of Financial Accounting Standard No. 115, "Accounting for Certain Investments in Debt and Equity Securities," FASB, 1993.

that holds debt and equity securities as inventory with the full intention of imminent sale. "Held-to-Maturity" (HTM) securities are those where management has the intent and can demonstrate the ability (financial wherewithal) to hold an investment until its maturity. Since equity securities have no maturity date, HTM securities include only debt instruments. The default, catchall category for passive investment securities is "Available-for-Sale" (AFS). All passive investments that are not classified as T or HTM are accounted for as AFS securities.

Held-to-Maturity (HTM) Securities

HTM securities are presented in the balance sheet at their amortized cost based carrying value (CV) under the effective interest method. Exclusive of default, the market and maturity value of debt securities will be equal at the maturity date. So, if held to maturity, changes in market value are relatively less important. Disposal of HTM securities before maturity should be rare, but if it occurs, gain or loss is recognized in net income as the difference between net proceeds and CV at time of sale.

Trading (T) and Available-for-Sale (AFS) Securities

Contrary to HTM securities, T securities and AFS securities are both presented in the balance sheet at fair value (they are "marked to market"). Publicly traded stocks and bonds that are widely held (called marketable securities) have determinable fair value measures available through quoted market prices.[3] The securities are kept on the books at their cost based CV and are written up or down to fair value (FV) using a "fair value adjustment" (FVA) account. The FVA account relates to the entire portfolio of T or AFS securities, serving as a negative/contra asset account if portfolio's FV < CV or a positive/adjunct asset account if the portfolio's FV > CV. On the balance sheet date, the FVA account is adjusted to its

[3] Nonmarketable equity securities are outside the scope of ASC Topic 320, and are generally not marked to market, but instead presented in the balance sheet at cost. Under ASC Topic 320, nonmarketable debt instruments are considered to have determinable fair values computed by discounting the future cash flows using estimated effective interest rates at the date of the financial statements.

appropriate amount and offset in the accounting equation through "unrealized" holding gain or loss recognition.

The key distinction between T and AFS securities is how unrealized gain or loss is recognized in the financial statements. Recall from previous discussion that there are two components of comprehensive income (CI): net income (NI) and other comprehensive income (OCI). Recall also that most U.S. GAAP firms choose to present OCI in the statement of owners' equity—not in combination with the income statement.[4] For T securities unrealized holding gain/loss is recognized in NI (and subsequently closed to retained earnings), whereas unrealized holding gain/loss on AFS securities is recognized in OCI (and subsequently closed to accumulated other comprehensive income (AOCI).

Gain or loss is not considered "realized" until the security is sold or otherwise disposed of. Realized gain or loss from the sale of T and AFS securities is recognized in NI in full, and computed as the difference between sale proceeds and the individual security's cost-based CV. To avoid double counting, previously recognized unrealized holding gain or loss must be reversed in the period of sale. The income reversal is consistent with the original treatment of unrealized gain/loss recognition when the securities were marked to market (i.e., T securities in NI and AFS securities in OCI). Although the reversal entry can be made at the time of sale, it is typically done when the entire portfolio is marked to market through an adjusting entry made at the end of the period.

Interest and dividends from both T and AFS securities are recognized as investment revenue and included in NI. The effective interest method is applied to determine investment revenue from debt securities[5] whereas dividends from equity securities are recognized in investment revenue upon declaration by the investee firm.

---

[4] As indicated in chapter 1, for fiscal years beginning after December 15, 2011, U.S. GAAP will no longer allow presentation of OCI in the statement of stockholders' equity (Accounting Standards Update No. 2011-05, June 2011 "Comprehensive income (Topic 220) Presentation of Comprehensive Income)."

[5] Since trading securities are held for a very short period of time, and unrealized holding gain or loss is recognized in NI, many firms do not amortize discount or premium on trading debt securities under the materiality constraint.

Example

The following example is used to illustrate the accounting differences due to HTM, T, and AFS classification. On 1/01/12 Behrend Corp. purchased debt and equity securities of Gannon Corp. Behrend paid $100,000 in exchange for 100 of Gannon's $1,000 bonds that pay 10% interest annually on 12/31, and mature on 12/31/13.[6] Behrend also buys 1,000 shares of Gannon Corp stock for $100/share. Behrend held no other investments on 1/01/12, therefore its total portfolio CV at 1/01/12 = $200,000 ($100,000 in debt securities and $100,000 in equity securities). Assume that on 12/31/12 Gannon's bonds are trading at 94[7] and their stock is trading at $120/share (total portfolio FV = $214,000). In addition to paying interest due on 12/31/12 Gannon also declares and distributes a dividend of $5/share (interest and dividends earned and received = $15,000). On 12/31/13 Gannon pays both maturity value ($100,000) and interest on its bonds, and also declares and pays a $6/share dividend on its stock (interest and dividends earned and received = $16,000). The Gannon stock is trading at $99/share on 12/31/13 (portfolio FV = $99,000 versus CV = $100,000). Behrend sells its entire investment in Gannon Corp. stock on 7/22/14 for $102/share ($102,000).

Held-to-maturity (HTM) accounting—Debt securities only

This example will initially assume that Behrend's debt security investment is classified as HTM. Since HTM securities include only debt instruments, the illustration exclusively depicts Behrend's accounting for its investment in Gannon bonds. With HTM classification, we assume Behrend's management has the intent and can demonstrate the ability to hold the Gannon Corp. bonds until their maturity on 12/31/13. We

---

[6] Note that since Behrend buys the bonds at their face value, the effective rate is equal to the stated rate of 10% so that no discount or premium amortization issues exist.

[7] Bond prices are frequently quoted as a percentage of par so that a $1,000 bond trading at 94 has a market value of $940 ($1,000 × 94%), and a $1,000 bond trading at 105 has a market value of $1,050 ($1,000 × 105%).

illustrate the financial statement implications of HTM classification using the accounting equation format (in 000s):

ASSETS	=	LIABILITIES	+	SE

2012

HTM Debt Security (Bond) purchase on 1/01/2012

+ HTM Sec.	+ 100		
– Cash	– 100		

The statement of cash flows will include an investing cash outflow of $100,000.

HTM Security—Record 2012 interest received 12/31/2012

+ Cash	+ 10	+ Invest. Rev. (NI)	+ 10[8]

Note that HTM securities are **not marked to market.** HTM securities appear on the balance sheet at carrying value with no recognition of unrealized gain or loss. Since the maturity date is one year from 12/31/12, the HTM investment would be included among current assets. To illustrate how stockholders' equity is affected in the balance sheet, temporary account closing is also presented:

HTM Security—Close related temporary accounts on 12/31/2012

		– Invest. Rev. (NI)	– 10
		+ Retained Earnings	+ 10

2013

HTM Security—Record 2013 interest received 12/31/2013

+ Cash	+ 10	+ Invest. Rev. (NI)	+ 10

HTM Security—Record Bond maturity on 12/31/2013

– HTM Sec.	– 100		
+ Cash	+ 100		

Consistent with the accounting by the borrower in chapter 5, no gain or loss is recognized by the investor when a debt security's

[8] Note that if the bond investment was purchased at a discount or premium, interest revenue would have been increased or decreased for amortization and the HTM security investment account balance increased or decreased, respectively to the maturity value at the maturity date.

maturity value is collected at the maturity date. Recording the receipt of debt's maturity value simply involves recording an increase in cash and removing the security from the books. Note that cumulative net income recognized equals the $20,000 total net cash flow from the bond investment.

HTM Security—Close related temporary accounts on 12/31/2013

		– Invest. Rev. (NI)	– 10
		+ Retained Earnings	+ 10

Trading (T) and Available-for-Sale (AFS) Accounting—Debt or Equity Securities

We now use the same example information to compare and contrast the accounting assuming T or AFS security classification. Financial statement effects are first presented assuming T security classification and then presented assuming AFS classification. Since T securities are bought and sold within a very short period of time, assuming a 2-year holding period is unreasonable from a technical perspective, and is only provided for illustrative purposes. The financial statement implications of applying T versus AFS classification are presented using the accounting equation format (in 000s):

ASSETS		=	LIABILITIES	+	SE
2012					
T Securities purchased on 1/01/2012					
+ T Debt Sec.	+ 100				
+ T Equity Sec.	+ 100				
– Cash	– 200				
AFS Securities purchased on 1/01/2012					
+ AFS Debt Sec.	+ 100				
+ AFS Equity Sec.	+ 100				
– Cash	– 200				

Note that financial statement effects are identical except for security portfolio classification as T or AFS.

T Securities—Record 2012 interest of $10,000 and dividends of $5,000 received on 12/31/12

+ Cash	+ 15	+ Invest. Rev. (NI)	+ 15

AFS Securities—Record 2012 interest of $10,000 and dividends of $5,000 received on 12/31/12

+ Cash	+ 15	+ Invest. Rev. (NI)	+ 15

Financial statement effects are identical. Dividends from both T and AFS equity securities are recognized as investment revenue when declared. Investment revenue is consistently recognized under the effective interest method whether debt securities are classified as T, AFS, or HTM.

T Securities—Mark to market on 12/31/2012 and recognize unrealized holding gain/loss in NI

+ FVA (T) Sec.	+ 14	+ Unreal. Gain (NI)	+ 14

AFS Securities—Mark to market on 12/31/2012 and recognize unrealized holding gain/loss in OCI

+ FVA (AFS) Sec.	+ 14	+ Unreal. Gain (OCI)	+ 14

The fair value adjustment (FVA) account is increased from 0 to $14,000 and represents the difference between the portfolio's CV ($100,000 + $100,000 = $200,000) and its FV ($94,000 (bonds) + $120,000 (stock) = $214,000). Since FV > CV, the FVA account will serve as a positive/adjunct asset account and be added to the portfolio's CV of $200,000 for balance sheet presentation at $214,000 (FV). Although T and AFS securities are both presented on the balance sheet at FV, the offsetting recognition of unrealized holding gain or loss is different. NI for 2012 will be $14,000 less under AFS classification because the net unrealized gain is only recognized in OCI—not in NI.

T Security—Close related temporary accounts on 12/31/2012

		– Invest. Rev. (NI)	– 15
		+ Retained Earnings	+ 15
		– Unreal. Gain (NI)	– 14
		+ Retained Earnings	+ 14

AFS Security—Close related temporary accounts on 12/31/2012

		– Invest. Rev. (NI)	– 15
		+ Retained Earnings	+ 15
		– Unreal. Gain (OCI)	– 14
		+ AOCI:AFS Sec.	+ 14

Since retained earnings and AOCI are both stockholders' equity accounts, total stockholders' equity is consistently increased by $29,000 in 2012 regardless of T or AFS classification. The difference relates to the entire amount being included in retained earnings under T security classification, whereas retained earnings and AOCI are increased by $15,000 and $14,000 respectively under AFS security classification.

2013

T Securities—Record 2013 interest of $10,000 and dividends of $6,000 received on 12/31/13

+ Cash	+16	+ Invest. Rev. (NI)	+ 16

AFS Securities—Record 2013 interest of $10,000 and dividends of $6,000 received on 12/31/13

+ Cash	+ 16	+ Invest. Rev. (NI)	+ 16

The financial statement effects are identical and similar to those from recognizing 2012 investment revenue except dividends increased from $5/share = $5,000 to $6/share = $6,000 in 2013.

T Securities—Record cash receipt from bond maturity on 12/31/2013

– T Debt Sec.	– 100
+ Cash	+ 100

AFS Security—Record cash receipt from bond maturity on 12/31/2013

– AFS Debt Sec.	– 100
+ Cash	+ 100

Consistently applying the effective interest method (regardless of T, AFS, or HTM classification) causes the debt security's CV to equal its maturity value at the maturity date, and no gain or loss is recognized.

T Securities—Mark to market on 12/31/2013 and recognize unrealized holding gain/loss in NI

– FVA (T) Sec.	– 15	+ Unreal. Loss (NI)	– 15

AFS Securities—Mark to market on 12/31/2013 and recognize unrealized holding gain/loss in OCI

– FVA (AFS) Sec.	– 15	+ Unreal. Loss (OCI)	– 15

The FVA account only relates to the remaining security—the Gannon Corp. stock. The FVA account has a positive/adjunct balance before adjustment of $14,000 (see the 12/31/12 mark to market adjustment). Since the FV of the Gannon stock is $99,000 at 12/31/13 ($99/share) and has a cost-based CV of $100,000, the FVA account should have a negative/contra balance of $1,000 after adjustment. We must reduce it by $15,000.

T Security—Close related temporary accounts on 12/31/2013

		– Invest. Rev. (NI)	– 16
		+ Retained Earnings	+ 16
		– Unreal. Loss (NI)	+ 15
		– Retained Earnings	– 15

AFS Security—Close related temporary accounts on 12/31/2013

		– Invest. Rev. (NI)	– 16
		+ Retained Earnings	+ 16
		– Unreal. Loss (OCI)	+ 15
		– AOCI: AFS Sec.	– 15

Total stockholders' equity is consistently increased in 2013 by $1,000 regardless of T or AFS classification. The entire increase is included in retained earnings under T classification, whereas under AFS classification, retained earnings is increased by $16,000 and AOCI is decreased by $15,000. Note that after closing, the AOCI:AFS securities account has a negative $1,000 balance (consistent with the negative balance in the FVA account) and will appear in the 12/31/2013 balance sheet as a contra stockholders' equity account.

When securities are sold, realized gain or loss is determined based upon sale proceeds versus the cost based CV of the investment without regard to any existing balance in the FVA account. This is the case across all investment classifications.

2014

T Equity Securities sold on 7/22/2014

– T Equity Sec.	– 100	+ Real. Gain (NI)	+ 2
+ Cash	+ 102		

AFS Equity Securities sold on 7/22/2014

– AFS Equity Sec.	– 100	+ Real. Gain (NI)	+ 2
+ Cash	+ 102		

Assuming no further passive investment activity during 2014, Behrend has no investment securities at 12/31/2014 (CV = FV = $0). The FVA account needs to be brought to a zero balance, and since all gain or loss is now realized (and recognized), unrealized gain or loss is reversed to avoid double counting. The cumulative unrealized loss of $1,000 ($14,000 gain recognized in 2012 and $15,000 loss recognized in 2013) is reversed consistent with initial recognition (NI for T securities versus OCI for AFS securities). A year-end adjustment is necessary to remove the FVA account balance and reverse cumulative unrealized loss as follows:

T Securities—Adjustment at 12/31/14

+ FVA (T) Sec.	+ 1	+ Unreal. Gain (NI)	+ 1

AFS Securities—Adjustment at 12/31/2014

+ FVA (AFS) Sec.	+ 1	+ Unreal. Gain (OCI)	+ 1

Closing the related temporary accounts has the following effects on stockholders' equity:

T Securities—Close related temporary accounts on 12/31/2014

– Real Gain (NI)	– 2
– Unreal. Gain (NI)	– 1
+ Retained Earnings	+ 3

AFS Securities—Close related temporary accounts on 12/31/2014

– Real Gain (NI)	– 2
+ Retained Earnings	+ 2
– Unreal. Gain (OCI)	– 1
+ AOCI:AFS Sec.	+ 1

Before closing, the AOCI:AFS securities had a negative balance of $1,000. After the closing, there is no balance in the AOCI related to the

AFS securities. Note also that upon entire investment portfolio liquidation, cumulative net income of $33,000 is reflected in retained earnings regardless of T or AFS classification.

Net cash flow of $33,000 (2012 = <$185,000>, 2013 = $116,000, 2014 = $102,000) is equal to cumulative net income over the entire investment period. Net income amounts differ between T and AFS classification each period but in total equal the $33,000 net cash flow (T: 2012 = $29,000, 2013 = $1,000 and 2014 = $3,000 versus AFS: 2012 = $15,000, 2013 = $16,000 and 2014 = $2,000).

Additional Issues Regarding Passive Investments

We next discuss how changes in passive investment securities classification are accounted for with related discussion of earnings management opportunity. We then describe financial statement presentation issues related to passive investment securities.

As indicated previously, classification of passive investment securities is based upon financial circumstances and management intent. Classifications need to be reassessed when financial statements are issued, which may result in reclassification of investment securities. For example, financial conditions may indicate that debt securities previously classified as HTM must be reclassified as AFS or T because the firm can no longer demonstrate the ability to hold them to maturity. When reclassification occurs, the security is marked to market when transferred to the new category. Depending upon the type of transfer, the accounting differs with regard to the treatment of related unrealized gain or loss. All transfers into or out of the T category require recognition in NI.[9] All transfers between HTM and AFS require recognition in OCI.[10]

[9] Transfers to the T security classification will result in NI recognition of the full amount of unrealized gain or loss since acquisition. Transfers from the T classification will affect NI only to the extent that value has changed since previously being marked to market (since previous changes in FV will have already been recognized in NI).

[10] A complicating issue relates to transfers of debt securities from AFS to HTM. The fair value at time of transfer becomes the CV of the debt and a new effective rate is determined. Over the remaining term of the debt interest revenue is recognized using the new effective rate but is adjusted for amortization of any unrealized gain or loss recognized in OCI at the time of transfer.

Firms with AFS securities have the capability of increasing or decreasing NI[11] by selling particular securities from their AFS and HTM portfolios or reclassifying them as T. Holding gain or loss on AFS and HTM securities impacts NI in the period realized through their sale or reclassification as T securities. Since the period of sale or reclassification can be a matter of management discretion, accounting for AFS and HTM securities provides an earnings management opportunity. In our previous example, management can increase 2012 income by as much as $20,000 (by selling or reclassifying as T its entire investment in Gannon stock) or decrease income by as much as $6,000 (by selling or reclassifying as T its entire investment in Gannon bonds). Choosing to sell or reclassify particular AFS and HTM securities in order to manage earnings is sometimes referred to as "cherry picking." This opportunity doesn't exist for securities initially classified as T because market valuation—not management discretion, determines the holding gain or loss included in NI.

Passive investments in T securities appear among current assets on the balance sheet. HTM securities are presented as long-term assets unless maturity is within one year of the balance sheet date. AFS securities should be presented as current assets if management holds them as a ready source of cash should the need arise. If management intends to hold AFS securities for more than one year they should be included among long-term assets. For purposes of the statement of cash flows, all dividends and interest received are considered operating under U.S. GAAP, but are classified as either operating or investing under IFRS. Cash flows from purchase and sale of passive investments should be included in investing cash flows. The only exception may relate to T securities. If purchase and sale of T securities is considered part of normal operations (e.g., an investment banking firm), all related cash flows should be considered operating.

Active Investments

Investment in equity securities may enable the investor to influence the operating and financing decisions of the investee firm. Depending upon the degree of influence, the investor may be required to either apply the

[11] Recall that only items included in NI affect reported earnings-per-share amounts.

equity method or issue consolidated financial statements. Consolidated financial statements are required when the investor controls the investee firm. The equity method is applied when the investor has the ability to significantly influence (but not control) the investee firm. We initially discuss the equity method of accounting and subsequently address issuance of consolidated financial statements.

Equity Method of Accounting

Since dividends are included in NI under AFS accounting, its use is inappropriate in cases where the investor holds a sufficient voting interest to influence the dividend making decisions of the investee firm. Dividends are declared at the discretion of a firm's board of directors. If the investor can influence the dividend making decisions of the investee firm, they can indirectly control the timing and amount of investment revenue reported in its own income statement under AFS accounting. Unlike AFS accounting, the equity method does not treat dividends as investment revenue, but instead treats dividends as reductions of CV (dividends are treated as a return **of** capital, not return **on** capital). Equity method investment income or loss is recognized as a proportionate share of the investee's reported income or loss for the period, and is offset in the accounting equation with an increase or decrease in the investment's CV. Equity method investments are not marked to market so there is no recognition of unrealized gain or loss, and realized gain or loss recognition is the difference between sale proceeds and CV of the investment sold.

The equity method is deemed appropriate in instances where the investor has the ability to exercise "significant influence" over the investee firm. Unless there is evidence to the contrary, GAAP assumes that owning a voting interest between 20 and 50% indicates that significant influence exists and the equity method is appropriate. The equity method can be applied in situations where voting interest is less than 20% and not applied in situations where voting interest is 20–50%; however, the burden of proof is on the investor firm to show that significant influence does or does not exist, respectively. Consider these situations: 1) if an investor holds 18% of a firm's voting stock, but the remaining 82% is widely held with the next largest holder owning only .01%, the equity method may be appropriate; and 2) if an investor holds 30% of a firm's voting stock, but the remaining 70% is owned by another entity that acts without regard to the 30% investor's interests, the equity method may not be appropriate.

To illustrate the equity method, consider the case of Behrend Corp. purchasing 25% of the stock of FWC Corp. on 1/01/12 for $50,000. The balance sheet of FWC Corp. on 1/01/12 is illustrated in Exhibit 7.1. Note that FWC's total book value (or net assets = assets – liabilities) at 1/01/12 is $200,000 ($1,000,000 – $800,000), and Behrend pays an amount equal to the book value acquired ($200,000 × 25% = $50,000). Also, we initially assume that all assets and liabilities of FWC have fair values equal to their book values. During 2012 FWC reports income of $100,000 and pays dividends of $40,000 as reported in the combined statement of income and retained earnings illustrated in Exhibit 7.2. The fair value of Behrend's investment in FWC Corp. stock on 12/31/12 is $70,000.

Exhibit 7.1. FWC Corp. Condensed Balance Sheet 1/01/2012 (All Amounts in 000s)

Assets:		
Cash	$100	
Accounts Rec. (net)	100	
Inventory	300	$500
Operational assets (net)		500
Total Assets		$1,000
Liabilities:		
Accounts Payable	$300	
Long-Term Debt	500	$800
Stockholders' Equity:		
Paid in Capital	$100	
Retained Earnings	100	200
Total Liabilities and Stockholders' Equity		$1,000

Exhibit 7.2. FWC Corp. Combined Statement of Income and Retained Earnings Year Ended 12/31/2012 (All Amounts in 000s)

Revenue	$700
Cost of Goods Sold	–400
Gross Profit	$300
Operating Expenses (Including Depreciation)	–150
Income from Continuing Operations Before Tax	$150
Income Tax	–50
Net Income	$100
Retained Earnings 1/01/2012	100
Less Dividends 2012	– 40
Retained Earnings 12/31/2012	$160

The financial statement implications of applying the equity method are presented using the accounting equation format (in 000s):

ASSETS	=	LIABILITIES	+	SE

Behrend records its equity method investment in FWC Corp. purchased on 1/01/2012

+ Invest. in FWC	+ 50
– Cash	– 50

Note that FWC makes no entry related to sales/purchases of its stock in the secondary market.[12]

FWC dividends declared and received by Behrend during 2012

+ Cash	+ 10
– Invest. in FWC	– 10

Although dividends received under the equity method are not recognized in NI, consistent with T and AFS securities, dividends are considered operating for purposes of presentation in the statement of cash flows.[13]

[12] Trading of stocks and bonds between investors is referred to as the "secondary market." Initial issuance of stocks and bonds by a corporation is referred to as the "primary market." With the exception of the fair value option for a firm's debt, trading by investors in the secondary market is not reflected in the issuing firm's financial statements.

[13] FASB ASC 230-15-55-10; Original pronouncement: Statement of Financial Accounting Standard No. 95, "Statement of Cash Flows," FASB, 1987, par. 131.

FWC reports income of $100,000 for 2012

+ Invest. in FWC + 25 + Invest. Rev. (NI) + 25

Under the equity method, investment revenue is recognized in the amount of the proportionate reported income of the investee firm (25%). Since investments are not marked to market under the equity method, FWC's market value of $70,000 at 12/31/12 is ignored. Note that the book value of FWC increased by $60,000 during 2011 (Income of $100,000 – dividends of $40,000), and the investment in FWC account increased proportionately ($60,000 × 25% = $15,000) under the equity method ($25,000 – $10,000).

Investee firms usually have a fair value greater than their book value, requiring the investor to pay an amount in excess of the proportionate share of net assets reported in the investee firm's balance sheet at the time of acquisition. The excess payment should be explained to the extent possible by identifying differences in book value and fair value of the investee's assets and liabilities at the time of acquisition, with any remaining excess attributed to goodwill. Subsequently, investment revenue recognized under the equity method will require adjustment for related income statement effects (e.g., a difference in book and fair value associated with inventory would impact cost of goods sold in the period of sale, any difference associated with operational assets would impact depreciation or amortization expense over its remaining service life, any difference associated with long-term debt would impact interest expense over the remaining term of the debt, etc.).

We continue the FWC equity method example with a simple introduced complication. Although FWC presents the same balance sheet on 1/01/12 (Exhibit 7.1), we now assume that Behrend pays $80,000 for its 25% voting stock interest, and that FWC has equipment included in operational assets that is undervalued by $40,000 (fair value = $140,000 and book value = $100,000) with remaining service life of 5 years. We continue to assume all other FWC assets and liabilities have fair values equal to their book values. The payment in excess of book value is first identified with specific assets and liabilities that are under/overvalued, and any remaining unidentified excess payment attributed to goodwill. Recall from chapter 4 that goodwill is determined as the residual amount paid over the fair value of a business's net identifiable assets acquired.

In chapter 4 we assumed the entire business (100%) was acquired. Here we adapt that procedure since only 25% of FWC is purchased.

Amount paid:	\$80,000
Book value acquired	50,000 (\$200,000 × 25%)
Excess payment	\$30,000
Undervalued equipment	−10,000 (\$40,000 × 25%)
Goodwill	\$20,000

Since FWC uses its assets' book values to determine income statement expense amounts, an adjustment for FWC's understated depreciation is needed. The equipment's annual depreciation expense (included in operating expenses) recognized by FWC = \$20,000 (\$100,000/5 years), whereas from Behrend's perspective (since it paid fair value—not book value) depreciation should be \$28,000 (\$140,000/5 years). Behrend will reduce investment revenue by \$2,000/year for 5 years with offsetting reduction of the investment account's carrying value. The underlying logic for the adjustment is that from the investor's perspective, FWC's income each year 2012–2016 is overstated by \$8,000 and Behrend's share is 25% (8,000 × 25% = \$2,000). Recall from chapter 4 that the intangible asset goodwill is not amortized because it has "indefinite life." Therefore no goodwill related adjustment to investment revenue is made under the equity method.[14] The following adjustment to investment revenue and the investment account for each year 2012–2016 (in 000s) is as follows:

ASSETS	=	LIABILITIES	+	SE
Behrend adjusts 2012, 2013, 2014, 2015 and 2016 investment revenue for understatement of FWC's depreciation expense				
– Invest. in FWC −2				– Invest. Rev. (NI) −2

The amount of investment revenue recognized in 2012 is \$23,000, and is equal to FWC's adjusted income of \$92,000 (\$100,000 – \$8,000) × 25%. Note that after five years, the balance in the investment account

[14] Unlike goodwill that appears as an intangible asset in the balance sheet, the implied goodwill amount included in the investment account under the equity method is not annually tested for impairment.

will be equal to 25% of FWC's book value plus the $20,000 originally attributed to goodwill. With the possible exceptions of recognizing "impairment loss" or electing the "fair value option" (discussed later), postacquisition changes in fair values are ignored under the equity method.

The equity method of accounting is referred to as a "one line consolidation." The reason for this terminology will become apparent after we next address consolidated financial statements.

Consolidated Financial Statements

In chapter 4 we discussed how one firm gains control of another through direct purchase of its assets and assumption of its liabilities. In such instances, the form and the substance of the business acquisition are one and the same. The acquired firm ceases to exist as a going concern, and the acquiring firm records the acquired firm's assets and liabilities directly on its books. Consolidated financial statements are required when one firm controls another firm indirectly, usually through a majority ownership interest in another firm's voting stock. Holding a majority interest in a firm's voting stock enables the investor to select the investee firm's board of directors who hires and fires the managers who make the day-to-day operating decisions of the investee firm. In form, two separate legal entities continue to exist (and maintain their own self balancing set of books); however, in substance there is one economic entity. In majority voting interest situations, the investor firm is referred to as the "parent" (P) and the investee firm is called a "subsidiary" (S). The objective of consolidation is to issue one complete set of financial statements for the P and its one or more S(s) as if there was just one set of books maintained by the one economic entity (as was the case in chapter 4 with direct purchase of assets and assumption of liabilities).

There are many reasons why a corporation may want to indirectly control another firm rather than hold a direct ownership interest. One reason may involve minimizing legal liability. For example, assume that "FWC" stands for FireWorks Complete and FWC is a manufacturer and distributor of fireworks. By holding stock of FWC rather than owning it outright, if FWC is sued, Behrend may be able to protect its own assets and limit potential loss to the amount of its investment.

Also, a firm can gain control of 100% of a firm's operations by acquiring less than 100% of its stock, and in doing so leverage its investment dollar.

Although the P does not record the assets and liabilities of the S directly in its own accounts, it must somehow keep track of its investment in the S for record keeping purposes. GAAP dictates financial reporting requirements but recordkeeping is at the discretion of the firm.[15] For purposes of illustration we will assume that the P applies the equity method of accounting for internal record keeping purposes and subsequently applies procedures that result in consolidated financial statements.[16]

We continue using FWC Corp. as our example based upon its 1/01/2012 balance sheet presented in Exhibit 7.1. We initially assume that Behrend acquires 100% of FWC's stock for its book value of $200,000, and all FWC assets and liabilities have fair values equal to their book values. Behrend records the investment in FWC as follows (amounts in 000s):

ASSETS		=	LIABILITIES	+	SE
Behrend records its equity method investment in FWC Corp. purchased on 1/01/2012					
+ Invest. in FWC	+ 200				
– Cash	– 200				

Exhibit 7.3 illustrates a consolidation worksheet immediately after acquisition. The consolidation worksheet is a tool used in transforming the individual account balances on the books of the P and its S(s) to the appropriate consolidated amounts as if there were just one set of books maintained by the one economic entity. We assume the books are closed on 12/31/2011 and the FWC stock acquisition is Behrend's first transaction in 2012. As such, only balance sheet information is included.

[15] Recall from chapter 1 discussion that there are no "Generally Accepted Recording Principles" (GARP).

[16] Consolidation accounting is covered extensively in the advanced financial accounting course. Most advanced accounting texts primarily assume the P's use of the equity method for internal recordkeeping purposes.

Exhibit 7.3. Consolidation Worksheet At 1/01/2012 Purchase 100% of FWC Stock at BV (In 000s)

	P Behrend Corp.	S FWC Corp.	Consolidation adjustments	Consolidated amounts
Assets:				
Cash	1,800	100		1,900
Accounts Receivable (net)	500	100		600
Inventory	500	300		800
Investment in FWC	200	–	<200>	–
Operational assets (net)	2,000	500		2,500
Total Assets	5,000	1,000	<200>	5,800
Liabilities:				
Accounts Payable	500	300		800
Long-Term Debt	500	500		1,000
Stockholders' Equity:				
Paid In Capital	1,000	100	<100>	1,000
Retained Earnings	3,000	100	<100>	3,000
Total Liabilities and SE	5,000	1,000	<200>	5,800

Behrend's amounts are assumed except for the "investment in FWC" account balance of $200,000 resulting from the FWC stock acquisition illustrated above. Note again that FWC makes no entry related to the acquisition of its stock by Behrend, so its amounts are consistent with those presented in Exhibit 7.1. A consolidated balance sheet should include the combined assets and liabilities of the P and its S(s) (Behrend and FWC in our example). The worksheet sums across from left to right, where the far right column is usually a summation of the P and S amounts (e.g., consolidated cash of $1,900,000 includes the P's cash of $1,800,000 and the S's cash of $100,000), which appears in the consolidated balance sheet. If the summation is not the appropriate consolidated amount, a worksheet "adjustment" is made. Since the S's assets and liabilities are included in the consolidated balance sheet amounts, also including the P's investment in S (FWC) account would be double counting; so a worksheet "adjustment" eliminates "Investment in FWC" so that it does not appear in the consolidated balance sheet. Also, since the P's stockholders are the owners of the economic entity, the equity accounts of the S are eliminated so that consolidated owners' equity is that of the P.

Before proceeding to the other consolidated statements, we reintroduce the complication of Behrend paying more than the book value acquired because FWC has equipment on its books that is undervalued by $40,000. Any remaining excess payment is again attributed to goodwill. In our equity method example, we assumed that Behrend paid $80,000 for a 25% interest. We now assume that on 1/01/2012 Behrend pays $320,000 for 100% of FWC's stock.[17] We again assume FWC has equipment with undervalued book value of $40,000 that has a remaining service life of 5 years. Similar to our equity method example, we determine the amount of goodwill at acquisition as the unidentifiable excess amount paid:

Amount paid	$320,000	
Book value acquired	200,000	($200,000 × 100%)
Excess payment	$120,000	
Undervalued equipment	–40,000	($40,000 × 100%)
Goodwill	$80,000	

Behrend records the investment in FWC as follows (amounts in 000s):

ASSETS	=	LIABILITIES	+	SE

Behrend records its equity method investment in FWC Corp. purchased on 1/01/2012

+ Invest. in FWC	+ 320
– Cash	– 320

Exhibit 7.4 illustrates a consolidation worksheet immediately after acquisition with the excess payment of $40,000 specifically assigned to undervalued equipment and $80,000 attributed to goodwill. Note that the consolidated balance sheet includes the S's identifiable assets

[17] Investors may need to pay a higher amount (a premium) to gain control of another firm. Such "control premium" generally results in higher amounts of goodwill reported in the consolidated balance sheet. For purposes of simplification, control premium is ignored in this example.

Exhibit 7.4. Consolidation Worksheet on 1/01/2012 Purchase 100% of FWC Stock at $120,000 More Than BV (In 000s)

	P Behrend Corp.	S FWC Corp.	Consolidation adjustments	Consolidated amounts
Assets:				
Cash	1,680	100		1,780
Accounts Receivable (net)	500	100		600
Inventory	500	300		800
Investment in FWC	320		–320	–
Operational assets (net)	2,000	500	+40	2,540
Goodwill	–	–	+80	80
Total Assets	5,000	1,000	–200	5,800
Liabilities:				
Accounts Payable	500	300		800
Long Term Debt	500	500		1,000
Stockholders' Equity:				
Paid In Capital	1,000	100	–100	1,000
Retained Earnings	3,000	100	–100	3,000
Total Liabilities and SE	5,000	1,000	–200	5,800

and liabilities at FV (operational assets are increased by $40,000 for the undervalued equipment) and goodwill of $80,000 is also included. Note also that consistent with Exhibit 7.3, consolidated stockholders' equity is that of the P and the investment in FWC account is eliminated.

Assuming the equity method is used for recordkeeping purposes Behrend's accounts would be affected as follows in 2012 (in 000s):

Dividends declared and received from FWC during 2012

+ Cash + 40
– Invest. in FWC – 40

FWC reports income of $100,000 for 2012

+ Invest. in FWC +100 + Invest. Rev. (NI) + 100

Again under the equity method, since FWC uses its assets' book values to determine NI, we recognize an annual adjustment associated with the understatement of depreciation expense on the undervalued equipment. As discussed previously, the equipment's annual depreciation expense (included in operating expenses) recognized by FWC = $20,000 ($100,000/5 years); whereas from Behrend's perspective (since it paid fair value—not book value) depreciation should be $28,000 ($140,000/5 years). Since Behrend owns 100% of FWC it reduces investment revenue by the full $8,000 per year for 5 years with offsetting reduction of the investment account's carrying value. Again, the intangible asset goodwill is not amortized because it has "indefinite life," so no goodwill related adjustment to investment revenue would be made under the equity method. Assuming the equity method is used for recordkeeping purposes Behrend's accounts would be affected each year 2012–2016 as follows (in 000s):

ASSETS	=	LIABILITIES	+	SE
Behrend adjusts 2012 (2013, 2014, 2015 and 2016) investment revenue for understatement of FWC's depreciation expense				
– Invest. in FWC – 8				– Invest. Rev. (NI) – 8

Note that the investment in FWC account balance is now $372,000 (320,000 + 100,000 – 40,000 – 8,000) and investment revenue is $92,000 (100,000 – 8,000).

The consolidation worksheet in Exhibit 7.5 includes the income statement accounts of P and S for the year 2012 and the individual balance sheet accounts of the P and S on 12/31/2012. FWC's income statement and retained earnings related accounts were taken from Exhibit 7.2. All remaining FWC account balances are assumed. All of Behrend's account balances are assumed with the exception of investment in FWC = $372,000 and investment revenue = $92,000.

Concentrating on the income statement, note that the revenues and expenses of FWC are included in the consolidated income statement with one adjustment that increases operating expenses by $8,000. This is the adjustment necessary to report the appropriate amount of depreciation expense on the undervalued equipment. This same adjustment will be made for the consolidated income statements of 2013, 2014, 2015, and 2016. The equipment will be fully depreciated by the end of 2016 and no longer require adjustment (FWC's book value based depreciation will

Exhibit 7.5. Consolidation Worksheet Year Ending 12/31/2012 Purchase 100% of FWC Stock at $120,000 More Than BV (In 000s)

Statement of income and retained earnings—2012	P Behrend Corp.	S FWC Corp.	Consolidation adjustments	Consolidated amounts
Revenue	2,908	700		3,608
Cost of Goods Sold	1,000	400		1,400
Gross Profit	1,908	300		2,208
Operating Exp. (Incl. Depr.)	800	150	+8	958
Operating Income	1,108	150		1,250
Investment Revenue–FWC	92	–	–92	–
Income Before Tax	1,200	150		1,250
Income Tax	400	50		450
Net Income	800	100		800
Retained Earnings 1/1/2012	3,000	100	–100	3,000
Less Dividends 2012	500	40	–40	500
Retained Earnings 12/31/2012	3,300	160	–160	3,300
Balance Sheet at 12/31/2012				
Assets:				
Cash	2,000	150		2,150
Accounts Receivable (net)	450	350		800
Inventory	550	100		650
Investment in FWC	372	–	–372	–
Operational assets (net)	1,900	450	+32	2,382
Goodwill	–	–	+80	80
Total Assets	5,272	1,050	–260	6,062
Liabilities:				
Accounts Payable	472	290		762
Long-Term Debt	500	500		1,000
Stockholders' Equity:				
Paid In Capital	1,000	100	–100	1,000
Retained Earnings	3,300	160	–160	3,300
Total Liabilities and SE	5,272	1,050	–260	6,062

thereafter equal depreciation expense from the perspective of the economic entity). Notice also that the investment revenue account ($92,000) does not appear in the consolidated income statement. This prevents double counting of the S's 2012 income in consolidated net income. The following FWC income items will appear in the consolidated income statement:

Revenue	$ 700,000
Cost of Goods Sold	– 400,000
Operating Expense (including depreciation)	– 158,000 (150,000 + 8,000 depreciation adjustment)
Income Tax	– 50,000
S's Consolidated Net Income Effect	$92,000

This is why the equity method is referred to as a "one line consolidation" in reporting investment revenue. Under the equity method, $92,000 of investment revenue is included in the investor's income statement; whereas the S's detailed income statement elements are included in a consolidated income statement.

Regarding the statement of retained earnings, note that consolidated amounts relate exclusively to the P. In cases of 100% ownership interest, the P's stockholders are the owners of the economic entity.[18] S dividends paid to the parent are nonevents from the viewpoint of the economic entity and they do not appear in the statement of cash flows because no cash has left the consolidated entity. Consolidated stockholders' equity is that of Behrend (the P), the S's stockholders' equity accounts are eliminated through consolidation adjustment.

The consolidated balance sheet excludes the investment in FWC account. Instead, the individual assets and liabilities of the S are included. As we discussed in chapter 4, goodwill needs to be tested for impairment annually. We assume no goodwill impairment exists at 12/31/2012 and therefore it continues to be included in the consolidated balance sheet at $80,000. Consolidation adjustment increased operational assets by $40,000 on 1/01/2012, but only by $32,000 at 12/31/2012. The original $40,000 undervaluation of equipment has been recognized to the extent of 2012's consolidation adjustment that increased depreciation

[18] Less than 100% ownership complications will be discussed later.

by $8,000. As discussed above, the remaining $32,000 undervaluation will be recognized by increasing depreciation expense over the next 4 years at $8,000/year. The adjustment to increase operational assets will be $24,000, $16,000, and $8,000 at 12/31/2013, 12/31/2014, and 12/31/2015, respectively. No consolidation adjustment to operational assets will occur at 12/31/2016 and beyond because the original $40,000 undervaluation will have been fully recognized. The 12/31/2012 consolidated balance sheet includes the following assets and liabilities related to FWC:

Cash	$150,000	
Accts. Rec. (net)	350,000	
Inventory	100,000	
Operational Assets (net)	482,000	(450,000 + 32,000 consolidation adj. for undervalued equipment)
Goodwill	80,000	(entirely through consolidation adj.)
Accounts Payable	– 290,000	
Long-Term Debt	– 500,000	
Net Assets Included	$372,000	

Note that $372,000 is the balance in the investment in FWC account that would be presented in the investor's balance sheet under the equity method of accounting. This is the rationale for terming the equity method a "one line consolidation" as it relates to the balance sheet.

Additional Issues Related to Consolidation

In this section we first discuss the required accounting when the P Corp. owns less than 100% of the S's stock. We then discuss the consolidation issues related to transactions between separate legal entities of the consolidated economic entity. Specifically we discuss "intercompany" sales and "intercompany" payables/receivables.

Consolidated financial statements are usually required when a P owns more than 50% of another firm's voting stock. When a P controls the S with less than 100% ownership, the consolidated income statement still includes all revenues and expenses of the S, and the consolidated balance sheet still includes all of the S's assets and liabilities.[19] Therefore the portion of the S not owned by the parent, termed "noncontrolling interest" needs to be presented in the consolidated balance sheet and the "noncontrolling interest's share of S income" must be deducted to arrive at the consolidated net income to the "controlling interests." We again use Behrend's acquisition of FWC on 1/01/2012 to illustrate. Previously, we assumed that Behrend purchased 100% of FWC's stock for \$320,000. Let's now assume that Behrend purchased 75% of FWC's stock for \$240,000 (\$320,000 × 75% = \$240,000). The consolidated balance sheet on 12/31/2012 will include the same asset and liability amounts as presented in Exhibit 7.5. However, consolidated stockholders' equity will include "noncontrolling interest" in the amount of \$93,000. This equals the noncontrolling interest's share in S net assets that are included in the consolidated balance sheet (\$372,000 × 25%). The consolidated income statement will include the S's revenues and expenses as depicted in Exhibit 7.5. Recall that the S's contribution to consolidated net income was \$92,000. Noncontrolling interest's share of S income in the amount of \$23,000 (\$92,000 × 25%) will appear as a deduction (similar to an expense) in determining consolidated net income to the "controlling interest." Also, even though consolidated dividends are those of the parent (as depicted in Exhibit 7.5), the dividends paid by the S to the noncontrolling interest are included in the statement of cash flows as a financing cash outflow. The P's stockholders constitute the "controlling interest," and consolidated financial statements are intended to meet their decision making needs. The separate financial statements of the S are better suited to meet the decision making needs of noncontrolling shareholders.

Frequently the P and S engage in "intercompany sales." Intercompany sales are those between the separate legal entities that make up the one economic entity. From the viewpoint of the economic entity, the

[19] Including only the P's portion (e.g., 75%) is referred to as "proportionate consolidation." Proportionate consolidation is not permitted under U.S. GAAP. Previously, proportionate consolidation was an allowed alternative to the equity method for firms under IFRS. However, consistent with U.S. GAAP firms with significant influence must now apply the equity method under IFRS.

consolidated income statement should not include any sales revenue or cost of goods sold (gross profit or loss) from intercompany "sales" until it is legitimately realized through sale to an unrelated third party, and inventory should be included in the consolidated balance sheet at its true cost to the economic entity. If the P and S record intercompany transfers in their separately maintained books, adjustments will be required in the consolidation worksheet to assure that the consolidated financial statements report the correct (realized) amounts. For example, assume that Behrend records an intercompany cash "sale" of inventory with a cost of $100,000 to FWC for $140,000 on 11/30/2012. The intercompany sale would affect the accounts of Behrend and FWC as follows (in 000s):

ASSETS		=	LIABILITIES	+	SE	
Behrend records intercompany sale of inventory costing $100,000 to FWC for $140,000 on 11/30/2012						
+ Cash	+ 140				+ Sales Revenue	+ 140
– Inventory	– 100				+ Cost Goods Sold	– 100
FWC records the intercompany purchase of inventory from Behrend for $140,000						
+ Inventory	+ 140					
– Cash	– 140					

If FWC continues to hold the inventory on 12/31/2012, a legitimate sale has not occurred because the inventory continues to be held within the economic entity. A worksheet adjustment must be made reducing sales revenue by $140,000 and cost of goods sold by $100,000. Without adjustment consolidated gross profit would be overstated by $40,000. Also, since FWC carries the inventory on its books at its cost of $140,000, a worksheet adjustment must be made to reduce inventory by $40,000. After adjustment, the inventory would be included in the consolidated balance sheet at its true cost to the economic entity of $100,000. Note that cash would not require a worksheet adjustment because it is retained within the economic entity.

The worksheet adjustment would be different if the inventory is sold by year-end to an unrelated firm. Let's now assume that FWC sells the inventory for cash to ABC Corp. on 12/30/2012 for $160,000. The following additional effects on the books of FWC to record the sale are (in 000s):

ASSETS		=	LIABILITIES	+	SE	
FWC records sale of inventory to unrelated third party for $160,000 on 12/30/2012						
+ Cash	+ 160				+ Sales Revenue	+ 160
– Inventory	– 140				+ Cost Goods Sold	– 140

The revenue is realized through sale to an outsider, but to avoid overstatement of both sales and cost of goods sold an adjustment is required. Without adjustment sales would be $300,000 ($140,000 recorded by Behrend, and $160,000 recorded by FWC) and cost of goods sold would be $240,000 ($100,000 recorded by Behrend, and $140,000 recorded by FWC). The legitimate related amounts of consolidated sales revenue and cost of goods sold are $160,000 and $100,000, respectively; therefore, adjustments reducing both sales and cost of goods sold by $140,000 would be made on the consolidation worksheet. Note that no consolidation worksheet adjustment of inventory would be necessary because neither Behrend nor FWC carries it on their books at year-end.

Sales by the P to the S are termed "downstream," and "sales" by the S to the P are termed "upstream." In cases where the P controls multiple Ss, sales by one S to another S are termed "horizontal." Regardless of intercompany sale direction, the consolidation worksheet adjusts related income statement and balance sheet accounts to present the appropriate amounts in the consolidated financial statements. However, unrealized profit or loss adjustments on intercompany sales are **"attributed to"** the shareholders of the transferor firm (i.e., the P in the case of downstream transfers and the S in cases of upstream and horizontal transfers). Therefore noncontrolling interest's share of S income that appears in the consolidated income statement and non-controlling interest that appears in the consolidated balance sheet must be adjusted to reflect the S's realized profit (or loss) from upstream and horizontal transfers.

Another intercompany issue relates to amounts owed to/from entities within the consolidated entity. The related payable/receivable should not appear in the consolidated balance sheet because from the viewpoint of the economic entity, a firm cannot owe itself money. For example, if instead of paying cash, assume that FWC purchased the inventory on account from Behrend on 11/30/2012 and the amount remained unpaid at year-end. FWC would have $140,000 in accounts payable on its books and Behrend would have $140,000 in accounts receivable on its books on 12/31/2012. The consolidation worksheet would include an adjustment decreasing both accounts payable and receivable in the amount of $140,000. In cases where intercompany amounts owed to/from involve interest bearing instruments (e.g., a note payable/receivable) the worksheet adjustments would also eliminate related interest expense and interest revenue.

Variable Interest Entities

Firms sometime want to avoid consolidation of firms they effectively control in order to achieve off-balance sheet financing and accommodate earnings management. Consider Behrend's acquisition of FWC on 1/01/2012 illustrated in the consolidation worksheet in Exhibit 7.3. Note that Behrend's D/E ratio without consolidation of FWC (far left column) is .25 to 1 ($1,000,000 of debt/$4,000,000 of SE). Since FWC is highly leveraged, with consolidation (far right column) the D/E ratio increases to .45 to 1 ($1,800,000 of debt/$4,000,000 SE). If Behrend were to apply any of the other methods of accounting for its investment (T, AFS, or equity) it would report its FWC investment in one asset account and in doing so, keep the investee's debt off its balance sheet. Also, if they applied AFS (or T) classification accounting, they could report profit from "sales" of goods or services to the "passive" investee firm.

Traditionally, consolidated financial statements have been required when there is a parent–subsidiary relationship. Under ARB 51 consolidated statements are required given the financial control the P has over the S through an ownership of the majority (greater than 50%) of its voting stock.[20] In most situations, this is appropriate because the degree of relative stock ownership is indicative of the relative degree of control held by the equity holder. The relative amount of equity held also generally

[20] FASB ASC 810-10-25; Original pronouncement: ARB No. 51, "Consolidated Financial Statements," AICPA, 1959, par. 5.

indicates the extent of risk and reward of ownership. If the investee corporation does well, the equity holder benefits through an increase in the worth of its investment, whereas if the investee does poorly, the equity holder's investment correspondingly decreases in value.

Firms like Enron were establishing entities in which they had effective control and the accompanying risks and rewards of ownership, but they structured the entities such that they had little, if any equity ownership. Under strict compliance with ARB 51, since they did not have a majority equity ownership in the created entity, they did not consolidate the financial statements of the created entity with their own. This provided the investor firm (that had effective control in **substance**) with the opportunity for off-balance-sheet financing (by having the created entity purchase and finance assets on the controlling company's behalf), and the opportunity to report fictitious earnings (by making sales to the controlled entity at a profit). Recall from our previous discussions of consolidated financial statements that this would not be possible with consolidation because debt of all affiliates would appear in the consolidated balance sheet, and "intercompany profit" would be eliminated for purposes of the consolidated income statement.

In response to these types of financial reporting abuses, the FASB issued Interpretation No. 46 (FIN 46) in January 2003 and revised it December 2003 (FIN 46R)[21] and again in 2009[22]. The objective of these ARB 51 interpretations is to identify instances where majority equity interest is not indicative of the true underlying control and the risks and rewards of ownership. This is determined to be so in the case of "Variable Interest Entities" (VIEs). For VIEs, equity ownership is deemed to **not** be indicative of relative control, and therefore majority stock ownership is not used to determine if consolidation is appropriate. Once an entity has been identified as a VIE, other factors are used to determine if there is a "primary beneficiary" of the VIE. If so, the primary beneficiary consolidates the VIE and issues consolidated financial statements.

---

[21] Interpretation No. 46 (Revised), "Consolidation of Variable Interest Entities," FASB, 2003.

[22] Statement of Financial Accounting Standards No. 167, "Amendments to FASB Interpretation 46(R)," FASB, 2009.

Two fundamental issues are addressed. The first involves identification of an entity as a VIE. If an entity exists under certain conditions, it is determined to be a VIE. A VIE is one "in which equity investors do not have the characteristics of a controlling financial interest or do not have sufficient equity at risk for the entity to finance its activities without additional subordinated financial support or, as a group, the holders of the equity investment at risk lack any one of the following three characteristics: (a) The power, through voting rights or similar rights, to direct the activities of an entity that most significantly impact the entity's economic performance (b) The obligation to absorb the expected losses of the entity (c) The right to receive the expected residual returns of the entity."[23] If an entity has been identified as a VIE, the second issue addressed is determining if there a "primary beneficiary" of the VIE. All those with a "variable interest" in the VIE are considered as a potential "primary beneficiary" of the VIE. An enterprise must consolidate a VIE if it has both of the following characteristics: "1) The power to direct the activities of a variable interest entity that most significantly impact the entity's economic performance, and 2) The obligation to absorb losses of the entity that could potentially be significant to the variable interest entity or the right to receive benefits from the entity that could potentially be significant to the variable interest entity."[24]

In the case of VIEs, intercompany profit and loss is consistently "attributed to" the primary beneficiary—not to the noncontrolling interests, so unrealized profit or loss on intercompany transactions affects consolidated net income in full. The primary beneficiary is precluded from manipulating reported income by entering into transactions with the VIE. Also, inclusion of all VIE debt on the consolidated balance sheet precludes the primary beneficiary from achieving off balance sheet financing by having the VIE incur debt on its behalf.

---

[23] FASB ASC 810-10-05-8; Original pronouncement: Statement of financial Accounting Standard No. 167, par. 3a.

[24] FASB ASC 810-10-25-38; Original pronouncement: Statement of financial Accounting Standard No. 167, par. 3b.

Accounting for Investment Securities Under IFRS

U.S. GAAP and IFRS have been very similar in their required accounting for investment securities.[25] However, the IASB recently issued IFRS No. 9, which must be applied for fiscal years beginning on or after January 1, 2015.[26] Accounting for active type investments will continue to require using the equity method in instances where the investor has "significant influence" and also continue to require consolidated financial statements when the investor has "control" over the investee firm. However, the accounting for passive type investments will significantly change under IFRS No. 9. Rather than "available for sale" constituting the default category, the default category will instead be "trading" with changes in market value recognized in net income (termed "fair value through profit or loss" (FVTPL) under IFRS).

In the case of debt security investments, available for sale accounting treatment is not permitted at all under IFRS No. 9. Under IFRS No. 9, debt investments must be accounted for as trading securities (FVTPL) unless specific criteria are met, which will allow "held for collection" accounting treatment.[27] Held for collection debt securities are accounted for the same way as "held to maturity" securities discussed previously. Held for collection debt securities are not marked to market but are accounted for under the effective interest method, with balance sheet presentation at amortized cost. Investment revenue continues to be recognized in net income each period using the effective interest method for all debt investment securities under IFRS No. 9.

Dividends received from all passive equity investments continue to be recognized in net income under IFRS No. 9. However, FVTPL treatment

---

[25] FASB ASC 320; Original Pronouncement: Statement of Financial Accounting Standard No. 115, "Accounting for Certain Investments in Debt and Equity Securities," FASB, 1993; and International Accounting Standard No. 39, "Financial Instruments: Recognition and Measurement," IASB.

[26] Early adoption of IFRS No. 9 is permitted. International Financial Reporting Standard No. 9 "Financial Instruments," IASB.

[27] There are two criteria that require that: 1) the instrument will provide exclusively interest and principal payments in the future, and 2) the firm's business model indicates the objective is to hold the debt security in order to collect contractual cash flows.

is required for all passive equity security investments under IFRS No. 9 unless management makes an irrevocable election at the time of acquisition to account for them as "fair value through other comprehensive income" (FVTOCI). If the election is made, the securities are accounted for similar to "available for sale" securities discussed previously—they are marked to market with unrealized gain and loss recognized in other comprehensive income. However, a significant difference involves the accounting for sales of FVTOCI securities. No gain or loss is recognized in net income as a result of sales of FVTOCI securities under IFRS No. 9. In the period of sale, cumulative unrealized gain or loss related to security being sold is transferred directly from accumulated other comprehensive income to retained earnings, without recognition in net income. Recall that earnings-per-share is computed based exclusively upon amounts reported in net income—not amounts reported in "other comprehensive income." This required treatment that disallows income statement recognition of realized gain or loss from sales of FVTOCI securities under IFRS No. 9 will effectively eliminate the earnings management opportunity previously accessible through sales of "cherry picked" available for sale securities.

Derivative Securities[28]

As described at the beginning of this chapter, derivatives are financial instruments that derive their value from some other measure of worth (called the "underlying"). The value of a derivative is a function of the underlying and the contracted amounts (called the "notional amounts"). Derivatives are consistently presented on the balance sheet at fair value, and those with positive value are presented as assets and those with negative value are presented as liabilities. If a firm presents a derivative on its balance sheet as an asset, the other party involved in the derivative contract (called the "counterparty") should be presenting an equal amount

---

[28] The discussion of derivative accounting is based upon FASB ASC 815; Original pronouncement: Statement of Financial Accounting Standards No. 133, "Accounting for Derivative Instruments and Hedging Activity," FASB, 1998; and International Accounting Standard No. 39, Financial Instruments: Recognition and Measurement," IASB.

on its balance sheet as a liability. Common types of derivatives include options, swaps, and forward/futures contracts.

Forward and futures contracts **require** the holder to buy or sell some "notional amounts" of an underlying (e.g., commodities such as crude oil or wheat, or units of a foreign currency like Japanese yen or Euros) in the future at a predetermined price.[29] The most common type of derivative is an interest rate swap. Issuers of fixed rate debt may want to "swap" their fixed interest payments for interest payment amounts that would otherwise have been required had they carried variable rate debt, and vice versa. In the case of interest rate swaps, the "underlying" is interest rate changes and the "notional amounts" include the debt principal and time until maturity. If the variable interest rate increases (decreases), the party swapping from a variable to a fixed rate experiences an increase (decrease) in worth, whereas the "counterparty" that swapped from a fixed to a variable rate experiences a decrease (increase) in worth. Depending upon whether interest rates have increased or decreased since inception, the swap instrument will have a positive or negative value. The swap instrument's worth is a function of interest rate change, the principal amount involved and the time until maturity.

Options allow, **but do not require** the holder to sell (called a "put" option) or to buy (called a "call" option) something in the future at a predetermined "strike" price. Options will only be exercised if they are "in the money"; that is, if the strike price exceeds the market price of a put option, or if the market price exceeds the strike price of a call option. Options that are "out of the money" will expire unexercised because the holder is not required to buy for more or sell for less than market value of the underlying. Therefore, although the maximum value of an option to its holder is unlimited, it cannot have a negative value and will never appear in the holder's balance sheet as a liability. The option holder's loss is limited to the option's cost. Contrary to the option holder, the option writer is exposed to the risk of unlimited

---

[29] Two key distinctions between futures and forward contracts are: 1) forwards specify a certain date for the future sale or purchase whereas futures are exercisable over a span of time, and 2) futures are traded on organized market exchanges whereas forwards are privately negotiated contracts.

negative value, whereas their gain is limited to the proceeds from the option's issuance.

Derivatives differ from other investment securities in that they generally have little if any initial investment cost but can subsequently have substantial market value (positive or negative) depending upon changes in the underlying and the notional amounts involved. Also, derivatives are typically settled at net amounts rather than directly exercising/fulfilling the rights/obligations otherwise provided per the derivative security. For example, assume that Behrend Corp. holds a forward contract to purchase 100 ounces of gold on 12/31/2012 at $1,000 an ounce and the market price of gold is $1,100 on 12/31/2012. Rather than buying the 100 ounces of gold for $100,000 and then immediately selling it at the market price of $110,000, Behrend receives a net settlement where the counterparty simply pays them $10,000. The net settlement feature significantly reduces transaction costs.

Although the balance sheet presentation of derivatives at market value is consistent, the offsetting effects in double entry accounting differ depending upon the circumstances. Changes in fair value of derivatives that are held for speculation are recognized as gain or loss in net income (NI) (similar to the accounting for trading securities discussed previously). Frequently, firms enter into derivative arrangements in an attempt to reduce risk. For example a firm with variable rate debt may want to eliminate or reduce the risk associated with increases in interest rates by entering into a swap arrangement whereby it converts to fixed rate interest payments. The process of trying to eliminate or reduce risk by taking an offsetting position is called "hedging." In accounting for derivatives under GAAP there are two types of hedges: "cash flow" hedges, and "fair value" hedges. Interest rate swaps provide a good example to distinguish cash flow from fair value hedges. The example just discussed where a firm with variable rate debt swaps for fixed rate debt payments is termed a cash flow hedge if it is intended to eliminate the risk of fluctuating cash flows (interest payments) due to changes in interest rates. The counterparty to the swap arrangement that exchanges their fixed rate debt to get variable rate debt may be doing so as a fair value hedge. The fair value of a debt instrument is the present value of future payments discounted using the market interest rate. Whereas the fair value of fixed rate debt changes with changes interest rates,[30] the fair value of variable rate debt does not fluctuate as widely. Therefore swapping fixed rate debt for variable rate debt in order to reduce the risk associated with changes in the debt's fair value is referred to as a fair value hedge.

Fair value hedge accounting is available in hedging risk associated with recognized assets and liabilities, and "firm commitments." Cash flow hedge accounting is available in hedging risk associated with recognized assets and liabilities, and "forecasted transactions." Fair value hedges are accounted for similar to the accounting for trading securities, with change in a derivative's fair value recognized in net income (NI). The hedged item in a fair value hedge must also be marked to market and presented as an asset or liability on the balance sheet, with change in fair value recognized in NI regardless of how the hedged item would otherwise be accounted for under GAAP. For example, in the case of interest rate swaps, although debt is normally presented on the balance sheet at amortized cost, if a swap is designated as a fair value hedge, both the derivative (swap) and the fixed rate debt (the hedged item) will be presented on the balance sheet at fair value with changes in each recognized in NI. The intention of this special treatment is that gains on the derivative instrument should offset losses in the hedged item, and in the case of perfect hedges the effect on NI should be zero. Cash flow hedges are accounted for similar to the accounting for available-for-sale securities, with change in a derivative's fair value recognized in other comprehensive income (OCI). Unlike fair value hedges, cash flow hedges account for the hedged item consistent with general GAAP, and defer recognition in NI to the period(s) income is otherwise effected by the hedged item. In order to qualify for special hedge accounting treatment, management must identify (and document) their cash flow or fair value hedge intention when the derivative arrangement is entered into, and the derivative must be judged "highly effective" in reducing risk consistent with management's intent. The hedge instrument is considered highly effective if the correlation between the change

[30] There is a negative relationship between changes in interest rates and the fair value of debt instruments. If interest rates increase, the fair value of debt instruments decreases, and vice versa.

in value of the hedged item and the change in value of the derivative instrument is at or near −1.

Example

To illustrate hedge accounting we provide as an example a firm entering into a forward contract to hedge the risk due to changes in commodity prices of a "firm commitment" (fair value hedge), and of a "forecasted transaction" (cash flow hedge). Assume that Behrend mines and sells gold. On 12/15/12 Behrend's salesman indicates that a customer (a jewelry manufacturer) intends to purchase 1,000 ounces of gold on 1/01/13 at its market price on that date. The market price of gold on 12/15/12 is $1,000 per ounce and because Behrend believes that the market price of gold will decline before 1/01/13 it enters into a forward contract requiring the sale of 1,000 ounces of gold on 1/01/13 for $1,000 per ounce. If a formal contract documenting the exchange is signed, it is considered a "firm commitment" and accounted for as a fair value hedge, whereas if there is no such contract, it is considered a "forecasted transaction" and accounted for as cash flow hedge. Since the forward contract price agreed to equals the market price of gold on 12/15/12, we assume its market value (and cost) is zero. We assume further that the price of gold actually increases to $1,050 per ounce on 12/31/12, and remains at that value on 1/01/13, so that Behrend receives $1,050,000 from the customer for the cash sale of the gold. Also on 1/01/13, Behrend pays the counterparty $50,000 (1,000 ounces at $50 per ounce ($1,050–$1,000)) in net settlement of the forward contract.

Fair Value Hedge Accounting

We initially provide the accounting as a fair value hedge where both the derivative instrument (forward contract) and the hedged item (firm commitment) are marked to market with change in value recognized in NI. The financial statement implications of fair value hedge treatment are presented using the accounting equation format (in 000s):

ASSETS	=	LIABILITIES	+	SE

Fair value hedge—Behrend enters into forward contract on 12/15/12

Since there is no cost or fair value of the forward contract, Behrend's accounts are unaffected.

Fair value hedge—Behrend marks both the forward contract and the firm commitment to market on 12/31/12, and recognizes change in value of each in net income (NI)

	+ Fwd. con. + 50	+ Loss on fwd. con. (NI)	– 50
+ Firm com. + 50		+ Gain on firm com. (NI)	+ 50

Recall that all derivative instruments (e.g., the forward contract) are consistently presented on the balance sheet at fair value, and in the case of fair value hedge accounting: 1) the hedged item (the firm commitment) must also appear on the balance sheet at fair value regardless of how it would otherwise be accounted for under GAAP, and 2) changes in fair value of both the derivative instrument and the hedged item are recognized in net income. Although firm commitments are "executory contracts" and not normally recognized in the financial statements, fair value hedge accounting requires recognition of the hedged item at fair value regardless of how it is otherwise accounted for under GAAP. Since the price of gold has increased, the firm commitment has positive value and is included on the year-end balance sheet as an asset. Because the forward contract requires Behrend to sell gold at less than its market price, it has negative value and is presented in the year-end balance sheet as a liability. Note that this is an example of a "perfect" hedge and in such cases the overall effect on net income is zero because any gain (loss) that otherwise would have occurred due to the increase (decrease) in value of the firm commitment is precisely offset by the loss (gain) on the derivative instrument. Note that if the hedge was not perfect, the "ineffective" portion would affect reported net income.[31]

Fair value hedge—Close related temporary accounts on 12/31/2012

– Loss on fwd. con. (NI)	+ 50
– Gain on firm com. (NI)	– 50
Retained Earnings	0

[31] If the forward contract required Behrend to sell 1,500 ounces of gold, the commitment to sell the additional 500 ounces of gold for $1,000 per ounce would be considered "ineffective" and treated as a derivative held for speculation resulting in recognition of a net loss of $25,000 in net income.

Note that since our example involves a perfect hedge, there is no impact upon year-end stockholders' equity when accounted for as a fair value hedge.

Fair value hedge—Behrend records the sale, net settlement of the forward contract on 1/01/13

+ Cash	+ 1,050			+ Sales (NI)	+ 1,050
– Cash	– 50	– Fwd. con.	– 50		
– Firm com.	– 50			– Sales (NI)	– 50

Initially the 1/01/13 sale of 1,000 ounces of gold at its market price of $1,050 per ounce is recorded. The second item records net settlement of the forward contract liability by paying the counterparty $50,000. The third item removes the firm commitment asset from the books and reduces sales revenue.[32] The amount of sales reported in the income statement is $1 million, which is equal to the amount Behrend locked in when they entered into the forward contract requiring them to sell 1,000 ounces of gold for $1,000 per ounce.

Fair value hedge—Close related temporary accounts on 12/31/2013

				– Sales (NI)	– 1,000
				+ RE	+ 1,000

After closing the overall effect on the financial statements is an increase in both cash and retained earnings (RE) in the amount of $1 million.

Cash Flow Hedge Accounting

We next illustrate the accounting for a cash flow hedge by assuming there was no formal agreement entered into by Behrend, and the anticipated sale was merely a forecasted transaction.[33] Under cash flow hedge accounting, only the derivative instrument (forward contract) is marked to market, and change in its value is recognized in OCI. The financial

[32] Rather than reducing sales, Behrend could include the $50,000 loss elsewhere in the operating section of the 2013 income statement.

[33] To qualify for cash flow hedge accounting treatment a forecasted transaction must be deemed "likely to occur."

statement implications of cash flow hedge treatment are presented using the accounting equation format (in 000s):

ASSETS	=	LIABILITIES	+	SE	

Cash flow hedge—Behrend enters into forward contract on 12/15/12

Since there is no cost or fair value of the forward contract, Behrend's accounts are unaffected.

Cash flow hedge—Behrend marks the forward contract to market on 12/31/12 and recognizes change in value in other comprehensive income (OCI)

ASSETS		=	LIABILITIES	+	SE	
+ Fwd. con.	+ 50				+ Loss on fwd. con. (OCI)	– 50

Again, the derivative instrument (e.g., the forward contract) is presented on the balance sheet at fair value, but under cash flow hedge accounting, changes in its fair value are recognized in OCI. Also under cash flow hedge accounting, the hedged item appears in the financial statements consistent with how it is accounted for under GAAP. Forecasted transactions are not recognized in the financial statements under GAAP. Note again that this example involves a "perfect" hedge and in such cases the full change in the derivative's value is recognized in OCI. If the hedge was not perfect, the change in fair value of the derivative not effectively hedging the forecasted transaction would be considered held for speculation and recognized in NI, not OCI.[34]

Cash flow hedge—Close related temporary accounts on 12/31/2012

ASSETS	=	LIABILITIES	+	SE	
				– Loss on fwd. con. (OCI)	+ 50
				– AOCI: Cash flow hedge	– 50

Recall that OCI is closed to accumulated comprehensive income (AOCI), not retained earnings (RE). As such, AOCI: Cash flow hedge

---

[34] Assuming again that the forward contract required Behrend to sell 1,500 ounces of gold at $1,000 per ounce, the effective portion of the hedge would reflect the requirement to sell 1,000 ounces of gold, and the ineffective portion would be the requirement to sell 500 ounces of gold. If that was the case, a $50,000 loss would still be recognized in OCI, but an additional loss of $25,000 loss would be recognized in NI.

will appear as a contra stockholders' equity account in the year-end balance sheet.

Cash flow hedge—Behrend records the sale and net settlement of the forward contract on 1/01/13

+ Cash	+ 1,050			+ Sales (NI)	+ 1,050
– Cash	– 50	– Fwd. con.	– 50		
				+ Gain on fwd. con. (OCI)	+ 50
				– Sales (NI)	– 50

The first two financial statement effects are the same as those for the fair value hedge accounting. The first recognizes the sale of 1,000 ounces of gold at its market price of $1,050 per ounce, and the second records the forward contract liability's net settlement by paying the counterparty $50,000. The third recording does two things: 1) It reverses the loss recognized in 2012's OCI by recognizing a gain in 2013's OCI, and 2) it reclassifies the loss previously recognized in 2012's OCI to NI by reducing 2013's sales revenue.[35] Note that consistent with fair value hedge accounting, sales revenue of $1 million appears in the 2013 income statement that reflects the amount locked in when Behrend entered into the forward contract on 12/15/12.

Cash flow hedge—Close related temporary accounts on 12/31/2013

				– Sales (NI)	– 1,000
				+ RE	+ 1,000
				– Gain on fwd. con. (OCI)	– 50
				+ AOCI: Cash flow hedge	+ 50

After the 2013 related temporary accounts are closed, again the overall effect on the financial statements is an increase in both cash and retained earnings in the amount of $1 million. Note that the balance sheet account "AOCI: cash flow hedge" is brought to a zero balance.

---

[35] Again, rather than adjusting sales, Behrend could include the $50,000 loss elsewhere in the operating section of the 2013 income statement.

The Fair Value Option[36]

GAAP allows firms the option to report certain investment securities and derivative instruments on the balance sheet at fair market value with changes in fair value recognized in net income. As discussed previously in this chapter, that accounting treatment is already required in the case of 1) trading securities, 2) derivatives held for speculation, and 3) derivatives held as fair value hedges. The fair value option is not available for investments that are accounted for as consolidations. Therefore, if elected, the fair value option affects financial statement presentation of: 1) held to maturity securities, 2) available for sale securities, 3) equity method securities, and 4) derivatives held as cash flow hedges. The fair value option must be elected (and specifically documented) at the time of acquisition. The option is available for election on a security-by-security basis, but once made, it is binding and irrevocable.

In the case of held to maturity and available for sale securities, if the fair value option is elected the investor accounts for the investment as trading securities and also classifies them as trading securities in the balance sheet. If the fair value option is elected for what otherwise would be accounted for as equity method securities, the investor accounts for the securities as if they were trading, but includes them on the balance sheet among equity method (long-term) investments. If the fair value option is elected for derivatives that would otherwise be accounted for as cash flow hedges, the investor accounts for the derivative as a speculative investment.

In the previous chapter we discussed bonds and other forms of notes payable. The fair value option is also available in the case of these forms of financial instruments. If the fair value option is elected for liabilities, increases in their value results in loss recognition in the net income, whereas decreases in their value results in gain recognition in net income.

---

[36] The discussion of the fair value option is based upon FASB ASC 825-10-35-4; Original pronouncement: Statement of Financial Accounting Standards No. 159, "Fair Value Option for Financial Assets and Financial Liabilities," FASB, 2007; and International Accounting Standard No. 39, Financial Instruments: Recognition and Measurement," IASB.

CHAPTER 8

Accounting for Postretirement Benefits and Income Taxes

Introduction

The accrual basis of accounting is consistently applied in accounting for postretirement benefits and income taxes. In the case of postretirement benefits, expense is recognized in the period of employee service to the corporation—not when the benefits are paid. In the case of accounting for income taxes, any tax effects of income statement items are recognized in the period they are included in the GAAP-based income statement, which may or may not be the period in which they are reported in the tax return. These topics are discussed together here due to some common characteristics:

1) Each may result in balance sheet presentation among either assets or liabilities,
2) The time lapse between expense recognition and cash outflow may be very long relative to accrual accounting topics discussed in previous chapters, and
3) Each involves complex applications of accrual basis accounting affected by a number of changing underlying factors.

Postretirement benefits are discussed first.

Postretirement Benefits[1]

Employees provide service to the firm in exchange for compensation. Employee compensation includes salaries, wages, commissions, etc. and is generally paid when the work is performed or shortly thereafter.[2] In some cases, employees accept lower amounts of salaries, wages, etc. in exchange for pension and other compensation benefits that are received in retirement.[3] The expense recognition principle requires that compensation expense be recognized in the period(s) of employee service regardless of when payment is made to the employee or on their behalf. We initially discuss two main categories of postretirement benefits: 1) pension plans, and 2) other postretirement benefits from a U.S. GAAP perspective. We conclude the discussion by comparing U.S. GAAP with IFRS.

Pension Plans

Federal regulations require that pension plans be "funded." The employer "funds" the plan by making contributions to an independently maintained trust.[4] Trust fund contributions are invested with expectation of providing returns so that pension benefit payments to retirees exceed the amounts initially contributed to the plan. There are two basic types of pension plans: defined "benefit" plans, and defined "contribution" plans. Regardless of the type of plan, over its entire life the aggregate amount

---

[1] The U.S. GAAP discussion in this section is based upon FASB ASC 715 (Compensation – retirement Benefits), and ASC 712 (Compensation – Nonretirement Postemployment Benefits); Original pronouncements: Statement of Financial Accounting Standards No. 87, "Employers' Accounting for Pensions," FASB 1985, and Statement of Financial Accounting Standards No. 158, "Employers' Accounting for Defined Benefit Pension and Other Postretirement Benefits," FASB 2006, and Statement of Financial Accounting Standards No. 106, "Employers' Accounting for Postretirement Benefits Other Than Pensions," FASB 1990. The IFRS discussion is based upon International Accounting Standard No. 19, "Employee Benefits," IASB.

[2] Employers' accounting for payroll is discussed in chapter 5.

[3] In chapter 9 we discuss additional forms of compensation such as stock options.

[4] The employer always makes contributions to the pension plan. The terms "contributory" versus "noncontributory" relate to the employees' funding. If the plan is exclusively funded by the employer it is called a "noncontributory" pension plan, whereas if employees also contribute it is called a "contributory" pension plan.

recognized as pension expense will equal the aggregate amount of employer contributions made to the plan. Under a defined benefit plan (DBP) the employee's periodic (e.g., monthly) entitlement upon retirement is stipulated in the pension agreement; whereas under a defined contribution plan (DCP) the required periodic (e.g., quarterly) employer contribution is stipulated and the pension benefits paid in retirement depend upon the return earned on the fund investments. The risk associated with pension fund investment return is borne by the employer in DBPs, whereas the risk is borne by the employee in DCPs. Since employees bear the risk of return in DCPs, they usually have some discretion regarding the nature of their particular fund investments.

Although most pensions were traditionally DBPs, recently most have become DCPs. Employers' accounting for DCPs is straightforward. Similar to employer's accounting for payroll, the required pension plan contribution is recognized as expense in the period the employee provides the service. For example, assume gross payroll for a particular month—December, 2011—is \$1 million and the DCP requires employer contribution in the amount of 3% of gross wages. Under the accrual basis, \$30,000 (\$1 million × 3%) of pension expense is recognized in December 2011 regardless of when the cash is paid into the trust fund. If the payment does not occur until early 2012, the year-end 12/31/11 balance sheet will simply include a \$30,000 current liability for the employer's contribution owed to the pension plan. The remainder of our discussion of employers' accounting for pension plans addresses the more complicated topic of DBPs.

Accounting for DBPs is more complex. The employer is obligated to provide future periodic retirement benefits to employees based upon some formula. The formula typically includes compensation level and years of service. For example, assume that Behrend's DBP formula stipulates an annual benefit equal to 2.5% of the employee's highest year's earnings for each year of employee service, with payments made monthly. An employee retiring after 24 years of service with a highest year's earnings of \$100,000 is entitled to \$60,000 per year (\$100,000 × 2.5% × 24), with monthly benefit payments of \$5,000 (\$60,000/12). Unlike DCPs the timing and dollar amounts of employer contributions are not typically stipulated for DBPs. However, the employer must make sufficient plan contributions so that combined with expected returns, the fair value of plan assets will be sufficient to make defined benefit payments to employees in retirement. Conceptually, the employer has both a liability and an asset related to DBPs. A liability exists because the employer is obligated to provide stipulated future retirement benefits. Since the employer provides contributions to a separate independent trust, they also have an asset—the pension trust fund. In such situations, GAAP typically requires that both the asset and the liability appear separately in the balance sheet. However, in accounting for DBPs, GAAP requires presentation of one net amount. If the plan is overfunded (plan assets > pension liability) a long-term asset appears in the balance sheet, whereas if the plan is underfunded (plan assets < pension liability) a long-term liability is included in the balance sheet.[5]

In gauging its funded status, the fair value of plan assets (including all unrealized gains and losses) is compared to the pension liability. Determining the fair value of plan assets is fairly straightforward with the information commonly provided by the pension plan trustee. However, estimating the pension liability is much more subjective. The liability is based upon estimates of benefits to be paid to employees in the distant future, with amounts and timing depending upon such things as employee turnover, retirement age, future salary levels, life expectancy, etc. Firms typically hire an "actuary" to assist in making required DBP estimates. Actuaries are certified professionals trained in the area of actuarial science. Actuaries are employed by insurance companies in setting policy premiums based upon the estimated likelihood, amounts, and timing of future loss payments to the policyholder. Regarding DBPs, actuaries estimate the probabilities of future outcomes that will affect the amounts and timing of retirement benefits. They also assist the firm in establishing requisite plan funding patterns given the estimated returns on investments. It is important to know that these actuarial estimates and assumptions relate to event outcomes of high uncertainty in the distant future. When actuarial assumptions and estimates are revised, they result in gain or loss. The term gain/loss

[5] In rare instances where the fund payments to employees occurring in the next 12 months exceed the fair value of plan assets, the excess is reported as a current liability.

is applied from the employer's perspective. For example, if a cure for cancer is discovered, a "loss" would result because from the employer's perspective the increased estimate of retiree life expectancy would increase the estimated pension liability.

Because retirement benefits are expected to be paid in the extended future, the pension liability is measured at a discounted present value amount. The discount rate applied is the "settlement" rate. The settlement rate should reflect the rate currently available on high quality annuity investments that could be used to "settle" the employer's pension liability. The actuary assists in estimating an appropriate settlement rate. The relationship between the settlement rate and the pension liability is negative—the higher the assumed settlement rate, the lower the estimated pension liability (and vice versa). The actuary can provide three different present value measures of the pension liability: vested benefit obligation, accumulated benefit obligation, and projected benefit obligation. The vested benefit obligation (VBO) includes only those pension benefits that are vested—those that require future payment regardless of the employees' continued service to the firm. The accumulated benefit obligation (ABO) includes vested benefits and all other estimated future pension benefits expected to be paid as a result of employee service rendered to date, with future benefit amounts estimated using **current** employee salary levels. The projected benefit obligation (PBO) is calculated the same way as the ABO but estimates of **future** salary levels are used in estimating future benefit payment amounts. Given that employees usually get raises and earn larger compensation in their later periods of service, the relative pension liability amounts are PBO > ABO > VBO. For purposes of the balance sheet presentation of a DBP's funded status, and determination of other financial statement amounts, GAAP consistently uses the PBO. A pension asset appears on the balance sheet if the PBO < FV plan assets, and a pension liability appears on the sheet if PBO > FV plan assets. This being the case, we will consistently refer to the pension liability as the PBO.

Prior to 2006, accounting for DBPs had an income statement focus. Consistent with current GAAP, the amount of pension expense was calculated by formula (discussed below). The difference between the expense recognized (per GAAP) versus the employer's plan contribution increased or decreased a pension asset or liability on the balance sheet. If a firm had cumulatively funded more than it cumulatively recognized as expense, it presented an asset on the balance sheet, whereas if cumulative funding was less than cumulative expense, a liability was presented.[6] It was possible for firms to present an asset "prepaid pension expense" on their balance sheet while the DBP was in fact underfunded (or to present a liability when it was overfunded). Although disclosed in the financial statement notes, prior to issuance of SFAS No. 158 in 2006, the funded status of a DBP was not recognized as an asset or liability on the balance sheet.

DBPs are treated somewhat like a separate entity with the net effect of its transactions included in the financial statements as single amounts, rather than being separately presented. As discussed previously, the funded status of the plan is included as either an asset or a liability in the balance sheet, and pension expense is recognized as one single amount in the income statement. Unlike DCPs, the amount of pension expense for DBPs is a compilation of several different pension plan elements merged into one amount that is recognized in net income (NI). The amount of pension expense recognized in NI is based upon five elements with the following +/– effects:

+ Service cost,
+ Interest cost,
– Expected return on plan assets,
+/– Amortization of loss or gain, and
+/– Amortization of prior service cost.

Service cost is estimated by the actuary and represents the increase in the PBO from employee services performed during the period. Service cost is recognized during each period of employee service to the

---

[6] There was a "minimum liability" requirement in cases where the fair value of plan assets < ABO. The minimum liability has been superseded and is not discussed further.

corporation. **Interest cost** is the "settlement" rate applied to the beginning of the period PBO.

Before discussing the remaining three components of pension expense, it is important to note that in accounting for DBPs the FASB takes a long-range view so that deviations from long-term expectations are not immediately recognized in determining NI. There is an intentional bias to smooth out the effects of short-term fluctuations in computing periodic pension expense. This being the case, the **expected return on plan assets** (not actual return) component reduces pension expense. Deviations between actual and expected plan asset returns becomes part of "gain or loss" (G/L) that is initially recognized in "other comprehensive income" (OCI) with possible subsequent **amortization of G/L** to pension expense. G/L includes not only the difference between actual and expected return on plan assets, but also includes the effects that changes in actuarial assumptions and estimates have on the PBO. For example, an increase in the assumed "settlement" rate would decrease the PBO and result in a gain, while an assumed increase in retiree life expectancy (discussed previously) would increase the PBO and result in a loss. Although these various gains and losses should offset, if the net amount becomes sufficiently large, amortization to pension expense is required. Gain amortization decreases pension expense and loss amortization increases pension expense. Amortization does not occur unless the cumulative net gain or loss at the beginning of the period exceeds a threshold or "corridor" amount. The corridor amount is arbitrarily defined as 10% of the beginning of the period PBO, or FV plan assets—whichever is larger. If the corridor is exceeded, the excess gain or loss is amortized to pension expense over the average remaining service period of employees in the plan.

The final component of pension expense is **amortization of prior service cost**. Prior service cost (PSC) is the amount of increase or decrease in the PBO that results from plan amendment. For example, assume that the defined benefit formula previously described is subsequently amended to entitle employees to 3% (instead of 2.5%) of their highest year's compensation for each year of service. The actuary's estimated increase in the PBO resulting from this plan amendment is not immediately recognized in NI, but instead is recognized as a loss in OCI. Subsequently the PSC amount is amortized by increasing pension expense (in NI) over the average remaining service period of employees in the plan.[7] Like G/L, the full amount of PSC is initially recognized in OCI, but unlike G/L, the full amount of PSC is subsequently amortized to pension expense—there is no corridor amount to trigger amortization.

Recall that comprehensive income (CI) has two components: NI and OCI, and items recognized in OCI are closed to "accumulated other comprehensive income" (AOCI), whereas items recognized in NI are closed to retained earnings. Both retained earnings and AOCI are components of stockholders' equity appearing in the balance sheet. Since G/L and plan amendments are initially recognized in OCI, subsequent amortization to pension expense (recognized in NI) requires a reclassification in order to avoid double counting (i.e., first in OCI and again in NI). With reclassification, neither CI or stockholders equity is affected by amortization of either G/L or PSC. For example, gains and plan amendments that decrease the PBO amount are initially recognized by increasing OCI and AOCI. Subsequent amortization reduces pension expense, increasing both NI and retained earnings. However, the necessary reclassification reduces OCI and AOCI by an equal offsetting amount.

To illustrate the income statement recognition of pension expense and the balance sheet presentation of the plan's funded status, assume the following for Behrend Corp. (in millions):

PBO at 12/31/11	$120
Fair Value Plan Assets at 12/31/11	$100
Settlement Rate	6%
Expected Return on Plan Assets	8%
Actual Return on Plan Assets 2012	$12
Behrend's Contribution to the Pension Plan during 2012	$6
Benefits Paid by Plan to Retirees during 2012	$2

[7] Plan amendments that decrease the PBO are also amortized but instead decrease pension expense over the average remaining service period of employees. Using our example, that would be the case if the employee was to receive annual benefit at the reduced amount of 2% per year of service.

Unamortized PSC at 12/31/11 (amendment increased PBO, and annual amortization = $2 million/yr)	$18
Unamortized Net Gain at 12/31/11	$5
Service Cost—2012	$10

Based upon the preceding information we can determine the following items that should have appeared in Behrend's 12/31/11 balance sheet:

Underfunded Pension Liability = $20 million (PBO > FV plan assets),
AOCI (unamortized net gain) = $5 million, and
AOCI (unamortized PSC) = $–18 million (a contra equity account).

We can also determine the components of 2012 pension expense (in millions):

Service Cost	$10.0
Interest cost (PBO 1/01/12 × settlement rate = 120 million × 6%)	$7.2
Expected Return on plan Assets (FV plan assets 1/01/12 × expected return rate = 100 million × 8%)	$–8.0
Amortization of net gain/loss	$0.0[8]
Amortization of PSC (previous period plan amend. amortized over avg. remain. service period)	$2.0
Total calculated 2012 Pension Expense	$11.2

Before considering the full impact on Behrend's financial statements additional information is required. Assume that there are no changes in actuarial assumptions or estimates, or any plan amendments during 2012.

---

[8] Note that no amortization occurs because the beginning of the period net gain of $5 million is less than the corridor amount (larger of **PBO** or FV plan assets × 10% = $120 million × 10%, or $12 million).

With the information provided, we can determine the 12/31/12 amounts of PBO and FV plan assets (in millions):

PBO 1/01/12	$120
+ Interest at 6%	$7.2
+ Service Cost	$10
+/– 2012 PSC (no plan amendment in 2012)	$0
+/– Change Actuarial Estimate or Assumption	$0
– Benefits Paid to Retirees	$–2.0
PBO 12/31/12	$135.2

FV Plan Assets 1/01/12	$100
+ Actual Return on Plan Assets	$12
+ Plan Contributions	$6
– Benefits Paid to Retirees	$–2.0
FV Plan Assets 12/31/12	$116.0

We now illustrate the pension related effects on Behrend's financial statements in accounting equation format (in millions):

ASSETS	=	LIABILITIES	+	SE	
		Record 2012 Pension related effects			
– Cash – 6		– Und. Fund. Pen. Liab. –.8		+ Pension Exp. (NI)	– 11.2
				+ OCI: **G**/L	+ 4.0
				+ OCI: PSC	+ 2.0

In addition to reducing cash by $6 million and reducing retained earnings by $11.2 million, after closing entries are made, the following pension related items should appear in Behrend's 12/31/12 balance sheet:

Underfunded Pension Liability = $19.2 million,
AOCI: **G**/L = $9 million ($5 million + $4 million 2012 "unexpected" return on plan assets), and
AOCI: PSC = $–16 million (a contra equity account).

Note that reported comprehensive income of $–5.2 million indicates the true cost of Behrend's pension plan in 2012. Although pension expense reduces NI by $11.2 million, Behrend recognizes $6 million in positive OCI ($4 million unexpected return on plan assets gain, and $2 million reclassification of PSC amortization from OCI to pension expense in NI). Behrend's 2012 comprehensive income of $–5.2 million equals the change in net assets ($6 million in cash paid minus the $.8 million reduction in the underfunded pension liability).

Disclosure

Much of the detailed information used in calculating the pension related amounts that are recognized in the financial statements is required to be disclosed in the notes to the financial statements. Required disclosures include:

1) The individual component amounts included in reported pension expense.
2) A schedule reconciling the change in the PBO and FV plan assets from the beginning to the end of the year.
3) The assumed interest rates used for settlement, expected return on plan assets, and future employee compensation increase.
4) Composition of FV plan assets (debt securities, equity securities, etc.),
5) Estimated benefit payments to plan participants in each of the next five years, and the aggregate amount of estimated payments in future years six through ten.
6) The amount of AOCI:PSC and AOCI:G/L that will be amortized to net income in the next year.

Other Postretirement Benefits

Employers frequently provide additional nonpension benefits to employees in retirement. Such benefits may include healthcare, life insurance, financial advisory services, etc. The accounting for all such benefits is similar. Our discussion will be limited to healthcare because other than pensions, it is the major postretirement benefit employers provide.

There are many similarities between DBPs and postretirement healthcare plans (PHPs). The actuary assists in making requisite assumptions and estimates of employee turnover, retirement age, life expectancies, the appropriate "discount" rate, etc. However, there is much more uncertainty in estimating the plan liability because there is no stipulated formula that determines future benefit amounts. Benefit amounts will depend upon future healthcare costs and the incidence of retiree illness (and typically illness of their spouse and dependents), which can vary significantly from individual to individual and year to year. Another important distinction is that the mandatory funding requirements and favorable tax treatment of DBPs do not apply to PHPs. As a result, many PHPs are unfunded, with employers applying a "pay-as-you-go" system, where plan contributions are delayed until benefits are paid on behalf of retirees. Also, in DBPs employees typically earn higher benefit amounts with continued service beyond the vesting date (e.g., 2.5% of highest year's compensation for each year worked thereafter). However, PHPs usually provide for full benefit upon vesting with no additional benefit resulting from an employee's continued service. For example the plan may entitle employees to full healthcare benefits by accumulating a minimum 15 years of service and reaching the age of 60. Any employee with 15 or more years of service and reaching age 60 earns no additional benefit with continued employment.

The accounting for PHPs is very similar to that for DBPs. Although PHP expense has the same five component parts previously discussed for DBPs, there are some differences. Whereas **service cost** is recognized over the entire period of employment for DBPs, it is recognized over a shorter "attribution" period in the case of PHPs. The attribution period begins when the employee starts earning credit for postretirement healthcare benefits (usually their hire date) and concludes on the date benefits vest. Since the vesting date precedes retirement, the attribution period is shorter than the entire term of employment. The FASB uses this shorter attribution period for recognizing the service cost component because the employer is liable for the full PHP amounts upon employee vesting. The **interest cost** component is determined by applying the settlement rate[9] to the beginning of the period "Accumulated Postretirement Benefit Obligation" (APBO). The APBO is the present value of estimated future postretirement healthcare benefits attributed to employee service to date. The APBO substitutes for the PBO not only for purposes of determining the interest cost component of expense recognized in net income, but also for purposes of presenting the funded status of the plan on the balance sheet. Since PHPs are significantly underfunded (if funded at all), usually the APBO > FV of plan assets, and an underfunded liability appears on the balance sheet. Like accounting for DBPs, the **expected return on plan assets** reduces benefit expense, and **amortization of G/L** in excess of the corridor[10] and **amortization of PSC** increases or decreases benefit expense over the average remaining attribution period of employees.[11]

Required disclosures regarding PHPs are very similar to those for DBPs, but some additional information must be provided. In addition to disclosing the assumed discount rate and assumed rate of return on plan assets, employers must also disclose the assumed rate of increase in healthcare cost and how a +/– 1% change in the assumed rate of healthcare cost increase would impact the APBO.

U.S. GAAP versus IFRS in Accounting for Postretirement Benefits

Accounting for postretirement (postemployment) benefits under IFRS is provided in International Accounting Standard No. 19, "Employee Benefits." Before discussing differences in reporting postretirement benefits under U.S. GAAP versus IFRS it is important to note that the FASB and IASB are currently working in an effort to revise accounting for postretirement benefits and eliminate differences in conflicting

[9] Although the FASB uses the term "settlement" rate in addressing accounting for DBPs, they actually use the term "discount" rate in addressing accounting by PHPs.

[10] The corridor is the larger of the FV of plan assets or the APBO at the beginning of the period.

[11] Under certain circumstances a different amortization period is used for PSC.

accounting standards. It is also important to note that many postretirement benefits that are the responsibility of U.S. employers may be the primary responsibility of governmental units in the case of foreign employers. That being said, although U.S. GAAP and IFRS are fairly consistent, differences currently exist when accounting for postretirement benefits. Recently the IASB significantly revised the required accounting for postretirement benefits under IAS No. 19 effective for fiscal periods beginning on or after 1/01/2013, with early adoption permitted. Current differences between U.S. GAAP and pre-2013 IFRS are discussed first, followed by a discussion of IFRS under the revised IAS No. 19.

IFRS —Current Requirements Under IAS No. 19

A major difference between U.S. GAAP and current IFRS relates to the treatment of gains and losses. IFRS allows G/L of the period to be:

1) Recognized in full in OCI (consistent with U.S. GAAP), but closed to retained earnings—not AOCI with no subsequent amortization to NI (inconsistent with U.S. GAAP), or
2) Recognized in full in NI and closed to retained earnings[12], or
3) Not initially recognized at all (inconsistent with U.S. GAAP), but may subsequently be amortized to benefit expense recognized in NI using the corridor approach (consistent with U.S. GAAP).

Note that by choosing the first IFRS alternative, gains and losses will not impact reported NI (or earnings per share) of the employer firm.

[12] This option is also permitted under US GAAP, FASB ASC 715-30-35-25; Original pronouncement: Financial Accounting Standards No. 87, "Employers' Accounting Pensions," FASB 1985, par. 33. Historically, few firms elected immediate recognition of gains and losses in net income. However, recently some US firms (e.g., Verizon and AT&T) have elected to change to this method of accounting. Such a change in accounting principle is accounted for retrospectively. Financial statement effects of accounting for changes retrospectively are discussed in the next chapter.

Another major difference under IFRS relates to treatment of PSC (called "past service costs" under IFRS) in the year of plan amendment. The PBO change related to benefits that are vested is immediately recognized through adjustment of benefits expense (NI). The remaining portion is not immediately recognized at all, but subsequently amortized to benefit expense (NI) on a straight line basis until vesting occurs.

Unrecognized G/L and unrecognized PSC that may exist under IFRS will affect the balance sheet presentation of the plan's funded status. Lacking financial statement recognition, they are excluded from the plan asset or plan liability amount that appears in the balance sheet. For example, consider an IFRS firm with a pension plan that is actually underfunded by $500 million (e.g., PBO = $900 million and FV plan assets = $400 million), but has an unrecognized loss of $50 million and unrecognized PSC of $100 million (plan amendment initially increased the PBO). The IFRS firm will present a pension liability of only $350 million in its balance sheet. The $150 million understatement of the pension liability is attributed to the unrecognized loss of $50 million and unrecognized PSC of $100 million.

IFRS also differs from U.S. GAAP concerning presentation of pension expense in the income statement. Although U.S. GAAP reports pension expense in its entirety as an operating item, IFRS allows separate presentation of the interest cost and expected return on assets components as financing and investing activities, respectively in the income statement.[13]

IFRS—Requirements Under Revised IAS No. 19

In June 2011, the IASB issued IAS No. 19 amendments that significantly change how employers account for postretirement benefits. As indicated previously, IAS No. 19 amendments are required to be implemented for fiscal periods starting on or after 1/01/2013, but early adoption is permitted. This being the case, some firms may initially apply Revised IAS No. 19 for fiscal years ended in 2012 (or 2011). At the time of writing

[13] This classification option is consistent with the statement of cash flows classification of interest paid/received allowed under IFRS as discussed previously.

this text, corresponding changes to U.S. GAAP have not been provided, but it is expected that the FASB will respond with similar changes sometime in the future.

Under revised IFRS, the full funded status of the benefit plan will be recognized and presented in the balance sheet as an asset if overfunded or as a liability if underfunded. Each period's full postretirement benefit cost will be recognized within three categories: 1) service cost, 2) net interest expense or net interest income, and 3) remeasurements. Each of these categories is discussed separately, followed by a summary of the financial statement implications.

Service cost is defined and accounted for consistent with previous IFRS. Service cost is recognized as employee compensation expense in NI and closed by reducing retained earnings presented in the balance sheet.

Expected return on plan assets will no longer be used in determining periodic benefit expense. Instead, the beginning of the period funded status of the plan will determine if net interest expense or net interest income is recognized. The discount rate used in determining the benefit obligation is consistently applied to the plan's beginning of the period funded status, with interest expense recognized in the case of underfunded plans or net interest income recognized in the case of overfunded plans. Investment income is recognized in NI for overfunded plans, whereas financing expense is recognized in NI for underfunded plans. The closing process increases or decreases retained earnings presented in the balance sheet.

Remeasurements are all other items that affect the funded status of the plan. Remeasurements are recognized immediately, in full in OCI and closed directly to retained earnings (not AOCI). Therefore, remeasurement items are never recognized in NI and never impact reported earnings per share. This default category includes gains and losses on plan assets, changes in the benefit obligation due to changes in actuarial estimates and assumptions, and changes in the benefit obligation due to plan amendments (PSC).

The amendments to IAS No. 19 can have substantial effects on the balance sheet and the statement of comprehensive income. Firms in an unrecognized loss position (significant amounts of unrecognized losses and/or unrecognized PSC from plan amendments that enhanced employee benefits) will be required to recognize large losses in OCI. Although this will not impact NI or earnings per share, decreases in net assets (stockholders' equity) will occur.[14] If such firms have debt covenants or other contractual/legal restrictions limiting their debt to equity ratios, they could be negatively impacted. Also, expected return on plan assets reduces the amount of benefit plan expense recognized in NI under current GAAP.[15] Since riskier assets have a higher expected rate of return, current GAAP may provide an incentive for risky investment strategies. Amended IAS No. 19 will no longer use expected return in determining benefit expense. Firms with relatively risky plan assets will recognize higher benefit related expense in NI, which will reduce reported earnings per share. It will be interesting to see if firms' investment strategies shift to lower risk assets as a result of the changes in IAS No. 19. Amended IAS No. 19 is another example of the economic consequences of GAAP.

Income Taxes[16]

As mentioned at the beginning of the chapter, the accrual basis of accounting is required when accounting for income taxes. The accrual basis must be used under both U.S. GAAP and IFRS. The amount of a period's GAAP-based "income before income tax" (IBIT) reported in the income statement may differ from the amount of "taxable income" (TI) reported in the same period's tax return. This is logically expected since the objective of the financial reporting differs from the objectives of taxing authorities.[17] The objective of financial reporting is to provide

[14] The opposite effects will occur for firms in a previously unrecognized gain position.

[15] This is the case under both current IFRS and current US GAAP.

[16] U.S. GAAP discussion is based upon FASB ASC 740; Original pronouncement: Statement of Financial Accounting Standards No. 109, "Accounting for Income Taxes," FASB 1992. IFRS discussion is based upon International Accounting Standard No. 12, "Income Taxes," IASB.

[17] State, local, and foreign governments as well as the federal government levy income taxes. Since the accounting for income taxes is consistent across taxing authorities, our discussion will be based upon federal income taxation.

external users with information useful for decision making; whereas the objectives of taxing authorities are to raise revenues and to influence taxpayer behavior.[18] Differences between reported IBIT and TI are of two types:

1) permanent differences, and
2) temporary differences.

Permanent differences are those revenue and expense items that are recognized in either IBIT or TI, but never recognized in the other. An example of a permanent difference is municipal bond interest. Because municipal bond interest is excludable for federal income tax purposes, it is never included in the investor firm's TI; however the interest revenue is appropriately included in IBIT in the period earned under the accrual basis of accounting. Temporary differences are those revenue and expense items that are recognized in both IBIT and TI but during different periods. Under the accrual basis of accounting the amount of income tax expense that appears for the particular period in the income statement is not necessarily the amount of taxes paid or payable for that period per the tax return. The income statement reports as expense the amount of tax that would have resulted if the firm used the same accounting methods for tax reporting as they used in the GAAP based income statement (excluding permanent differences).[19] The accounting for permanent differences is straightforward. The tax effects of permanent differences are reflected in the period's tax expense in the GAAP-based income statement consistent with the related tax effects per the tax return. In our example of municipal bond interest, although the interest revenue would be included in GAAP-based

[18] Tax laws are used to both encourage and discourage certain behavior. For example, to increase economic activity an investment tax credit may be enacted to encourage investment in certain types of productive assets by allowing taxpayers a tax credit equal to a portion of the asset's cost, whereas penalties and fines incurred in doing business are generally not tax deductible to discourage such illegal behavior.

[19] Adjustments to income tax expense involve changes in tax rates and other issues that will be discussed later.

income before income taxes, it does not affect the amount presented as the period's income tax expense because it will never be subject to income taxes.

To discuss the accounting for temporary differences we will consider a common situation where a firm uses straight line (SL) depreciation for book (financial reporting) purposes but uses accelerated depreciation for tax purposes. Assume that Behrend Corp. purchases a piece of equipment with a 4-year service life and zero residual value for $100,000 on 1/01/2010. For the sake of simplicity we assume consistency in all factors for tax versus book reporting purposes except that Behrend chooses the Sum-of-the-Years' Digits (SYD) method for tax reporting of depreciation.[20] Annual depreciation for book purposes is $25k per year ($100k – $0)/4). Depreciation for tax purposes is $40k in 2010, $30k in 2011, $20k in 2012, and $10k in 2013. This and other detailed information relating to our example is provided in Exhibit 8.1 Panels A and B. Note that regardless of the method used, the total income effect is equal; total depreciation recognized for both tax and book purposes = $100k. This is the nature of a "temporary difference." The amount of expense (or revenue) recognized is equal for tax and book purposes in the aggregate, but the amounts recognized on a period-by-period basis are different. With this information from Exhibit 8.1 Panels A and B, we derive the following:

Year	Tax Depr.	Book Depr.	Difference	Cumulative Dif.
2010	$40k	$25k	$15k	$15k
2011	$30k	$25k	$5k	$20k
2012	$20k	$25k	$–5k	$15k
2013	$10k	$25k	$–15k	$0k

[20] Depreciation for tax reporting is referred to as "cost recovery" with the periodic deductible amounts determined under the "Modified Accelerated Cost Recovery System" (MACRS). Schedules provided under MACRS indicate the percentage of an asset's cost that is deductible in each of a predetermined number of years (which is not necessarily equal to the asset's estimated service life). MACRS percentages are derived using the declining balance method—not the SYD method. Also, MACRS ignores residual value and generally applies the half-year convention.

Exhibit 8.1. Temporary Difference Example—SL Depr. for Financial Reporting and SYD Depr. for Tax Assuming: 4-Year Life, Zero Residual Value, 40% Tax Rate, and Taxable Income before Depreciation is Equal to Book Income before Depreciation and Income Tax of $125,000 each Year

Panel A—Financial Reporting Under Straight Line Depreciation					
Year	**Depreciable cost**		**SL rate**	**Depreciation expense**	**Book value 12/31**
2010	100,000		1/4	25,000	75,000
2011	100,000		1/4	25,000	50,000
2012	100,000		1/4	25,000	25,000
2013	100,000		1/4	25,000	0
Total				100,000	
Panel B—Tax reporting under sum-of-the-years' digits depreciation					
Year	**Depreciable cost**	**Remaining life 1/1**	**SYD rate**	**Depreciation expense**	**Tax basis 12/31**
2010	100,000	4 Years	4/10	40,000	60,000
2011	100,000	3 Years	3/10	30,000	30,000
2012	100,000	2 Years	2/10	20,000	10,000
2013	100,000	1 Year	1/10	10,000	0
Total				100,000	

Panel C—Income statement with interperiod income tax allocation—required by GAAP					
Year	Income before Depr. and Inc. tax	Depr. exp.	Income before income tax	Income tax expense	Net income
2010	125,000	25,000	100,000	40,000	60,000
2011	125,000	25,000	100,000	40,000	60,000
2012	125,000	25,000	100,000	40,000	60,000
2013	125,000	25,000	100,000	40,000	60,000
Total	500,000	100,000	400,000	160,000	240,000
Panel D—Income tax paid/currently payable from tax return					
Year	**Taxable Inc. before Depr.**	**Deductible depreciation**	**Taxable income**	**Inc. tax paid or currently payable**	
2010	125,000	40,000	85,000	34,000	
2011	125,000	30,000	95,000	38,000	
2012	125,000	20,000	105,000	42,000	
2013	125,000	10,000	115,000	46,000	
Total	500,000	100,000	400,000	160,000	

(*Continued*)

Exhibit 8.1. *Temporary Difference Example—SL Depr. for Financial Reporting and SYD Depr. for Tax Assuming: 4-Year Life, Zero Residual Value, 40% Tax Rate, and Taxable Income before Depreciation is Equal to Book Income before Depreciation and Income tax of $125,000 Each Year—(Continued)*

Panel E—Income Statement Without Interperiod Income Tax Allocation—Not Allowed by GAAP					
Year	Income before Depr. & Inc. Tax	Depr. exp.	Income Before Income Tax	Income Tax Expense	Net Income
2010	125,000	25,000	100,000	34,000	66,000
2011	125,000	25,000	100,000	38,000	62,000
2012	125,000	25,000	100,000	42,000	58,000
2013	125,000	25,000	100,000	46,000	54,000
Total	500,000	100,000	400,000	160,000	240,000

The temporary difference is said to "originate" in one or more earlier periods, and then "reverse" in one or more later periods. In our example, tax depreciation exceeds book depreciation in 2010 and 2011, whereas book depreciation exceeds tax depreciation in 2012 and 2013. The temporary difference originates in the amount of $15k in 2010 and an additional $5k in 2011, and then reverses in the amount of $5k in 2012 and $15k in 2013. Consistent with the pattern of temporary differences, note that the total originating difference of $20k ($15k in 2010 and $5k in 2011) is subsequently reversed in the equal total amount of $20k ($–5k in 2012 and $–15k in 2013).

Note also that the cumulative temporary difference equals the difference between the asset's tax "basis" and its book value. Basis is the term used for tax purposes to refer to an asset's unrecovered cost, which is also its future tax deductibility. Book value of an asset relates to the reduction of future periods income through expense recognition.[21] With the information from Panels A and B we illustrate that cumulative temporary difference amounts can be derived by comparing an asset's tax basis to its book value:

Year Ended	Book Value	Tax Basis	Difference (Future Taxable Amt.)
12/31/2010	$75k	$60k	$15k
12/31/2011	$50k	$30k	$20k
12/31/2012	$25k	$10k	$15k
12/31/2013	$0k	$0k	$0k

Temporary differences between book value and tax basis result in future taxable and future deductible amounts. If the future tax implications from tax basis are negative relative to book value amounts, they are considered "future taxable amounts" whereas if future tax implications are relatively positive they are considered "future deductible amounts." Our depreciation example creates future taxable amounts because the asset's lower tax basis relative to book value has negative future tax implications

[21] In our example, tax basis and book value result in future depreciation expense. If an asset is disposed of before its tax basis or book value is reduced to zero, the remaining amount reduces gain or increases loss on sale.

(we get to deduct less in the future and in doing so increase "future taxable amounts"). The specific future taxable amount is: \$15k on 12/31/10, \$20k on 12/31/11, and \$15k on 12/31/12. There is no future taxable amount on 12/31/13 because the asset's tax basis and book value are equal (\$0).[22] If book value = tax basis, the asset's book value in the balance sheet reflects the tax benefit that will occur in future periods through tax deductions. However, if an asset's book value > its tax basis, the amount that appears on the balance sheet exceeds its future tax benefits and the difference is the future taxable amount.

If we switched our depreciation example to instead assume that Behrend used SYD for financial reporting purposes and used SL for tax purposes, the asset's book value would be less than its tax basis at 12/31/10, 12/31/11, and 12/31/12 resulting in "future deductible amounts."[23] Typical temporary differences that create future deductible amounts are discussed later.

We continue our example to illustrate how temporary differences affect the determination of income tax expense and the related balance sheet implications. We assume that Behrend reports identical amounts of "income before depreciation and income tax" on its GAAP-based income statement as it reports in its tax return as "taxable income before depreciation" of \$125k in each year 2010, 2011, 2012, and 2013. We also assume that Behrend is consistently subject to a tax rate of 40%. Exhibit 8.1 Panel C indicates how the accrual basis is applied in determining income tax expense for each period's income statement. Behrend determines periodic income tax expense as if they used the straight line method for tax purposes, in which case taxes would have been \$40k each year (\$125k – \$25k = \$100k @ 40% = \$40k). Exhibit 8.1 Panel D indicates how much tax is actually payable in each of the four years based upon the tax returns that are filed using SYD depreciation. Note that tax expense on each period's income statement differs from the amount of taxes

[22] Note that this was also the case on 1/01/2010 because the asset's book value and tax basis were equal to its cost of \$100k.

[23] Instances of firms actually using accelerated depreciation for book purposes and SL for tax reporting would be rare.

paid/currently payable per the tax returns filed. This difference is called "interperiod income tax allocation" which is required under both U.S. GAAP and IFRS, and results in presentation of "deferred tax assets" and "deferred tax liabilities" in the balance sheet. Deferred tax assets are recognized in cases of future deductible amounts, whereas deferred tax liabilities are recognized in cases of future taxable amounts.

Panel E shows how the each year's income statement would appear without interperiod income tax allocation. It is important to note that such presentation is not permitted under U.S. GAAP or IFRS. Under the expense recognition principle, deferred tax accounting is required in order to properly associate income tax expense with the amount of IBIT presented in the period's income statement. As illustrated in panel E, reporting tax expense based upon the amount of tax payable per each year's tax return causes income tax expense (and net income) to differ each period even though each period's income before tax is $100k and the tax rate is consistently assumed at 40%. However, with interperiod income tax allocation (Panel C) the firm reports tax expense consistent with IBIT amounts reported in the income statement.

For purposes of simplification we assume that each period's income taxes paid/currently payable per the tax returns filed are paid in cash. The following illustrates the financial statement effects of interperiod income tax allocation for our depreciation example in accounting equation format (in 000s):

	ASSETS		=	LIABILITIES		+	SE	
2010	– Cash	– 34	+	Deferred Taxes	+ 6	+	Inc. Tax Exp.	– 40
2011	– Cash	– 38	+	Deferred Taxes	+ 2	+	Inc. Tax Exp.	– 40
2012	– Cash	– 42	–	Deferred Taxes	– 2	+	Inc. Tax Exp.	– 40
2013	– Cash	– 46	–	Deferred Taxes	– 6	+	Inc. Tax Exp.	– 40
Total	– Cash	– 160			0	+	Inc. Tax Exp.	– 160

Note that the total cash flow of $–160k equals the total accrual based income tax expense recognized over the entire 4-year period, but the amounts differ from period to period. Note also that at the end of each year, the cumulative difference between the cash basis and the accrual basis amounts is included in the balance sheet as a "deferred tax liability." The deferred tax liability included in the year-end 2010, 2011, 2012, and 2013 balance sheets is $6k, $8k ($6k + $2k), $6k ($6k+$2k-$2k), and $0 ($6k+$2k-$2k-$6k), respectively. The deferred tax liability appearing in the year-end balance sheets can be derived by applying the effective tax rate to the end of the year cumulative temporary difference or "future taxable amounts" as:

Year-Ended	Book Value	Tax Basis	Future Taxable Amt.	Tax Rate	Deferred Tax Liability
12/31/2010	$75k	$60k	$15k	40%	$6k
12/31/2011	$50k	$30k	$20k	40%	$8k
12/31/2012	$25k	$10k	$15k	40%	$6k
12/31/2013	$0k	$0k	$0k	40%	$0k

This knowledge is important to understand accounting for deferred taxes from a balance sheet (asset/liability) perspective.

Both the FASB and the IASB feel that temporary differences that create future taxable amounts result in liabilities that should be presented in the balance sheet. Recall that a liability is defined as a "probable future economic sacrifice as a result of past transactions or events." Both bodies contend that the need to make larger tax payments in the future constitutes a future economic sacrifice that results from previously using more conservative accounting methods for tax purposes than were used for financial reporting purposes.

Note that unlike other liabilities, deferred tax liabilities are not discounted to present value (neither are deferred tax assets). Deferred tax liabilities are presented at the full future amount regardless of when they are expected to reverse (and require higher tax payment). For example, even though the $6k deferred tax liability on 12/31/2010 is expected to increase an additional $2k during 2011, and not fully reverse until 2013, GAAP does not permit balance sheet presentation at a reduced (discounted) amount. Presentation at full future value is required under both U.S. GAAP and IFRS and is a common criticism of interperiod income tax allocation.

Deferred Tax Assets

In previous chapters we discussed temporary differences where expense recognition on the GAAP-based income statement precedes recognition on the tax return. These include accounting for bad debts and accounting for warranty costs. Under the expense recognition principle, these expenses are recognized with related revenue in the period of sale by estimating future uncollectible accounts receivable and estimating the future cost of performing under the warranty. For tax purposes, bad debts are only deductible later—when particular customers' accounts are written off, and warranty costs are not deductible until the period when defective products are repaired or replaced. These situations involve temporary differences that are the opposite of our depreciation example. Using straight line depreciation for book purposes while using accelerated depreciation for tax purposes creates future taxable amounts that result in reporting a deferred tax liability in the balance sheet. Temporary differences in accounting for bad debts and warranties are the opposite. Recognizing expense on the income statement before deduction on the tax return creates "future deductible amounts" because of the favorable future tax implications relative to the amounts recognized in the GAAP based income statement. While future taxable amounts result in deferred tax liabilities, future deductible amounts result in deferred tax assets. The future deductible amount is the difference in the cumulative difference in the amount of bad debts and warranty expense recognized for book versus tax purposes. The deferred tax assets associated with bad debts and warranties can be calculated by applying the current tax rate to the future taxable amounts. Like deferred tax liabilities, temporary differences associated with deferred tax assets originate in one or more early periods and subsequently reverse in one or more later periods.

For example, assume that on 12/31/2011 PSU sells goods to customers with a 2-year warranty and estimates that $50k of related future warranty costs will be incurred. Recall from chapter 5 that under GAAP, the full $50k is recognized as expense in the 2011 income statement under the expense recognition principle. We assume that actual warranty performance costs related to the 2011 sale are $50k, with $25k paid in 2012 and $25k paid in 2013. Although the full $50k was recognized as expense in the 2011 income statement, warranty costs only become deductible in 2012 and 2013 when $25k of actual warranty performance cost is paid each year. We also assume that PSU's effective tax rate is consistently 40%. This temporary difference originates in 2011, creating $50k of future deductible amount, and subsequently reverses in 2012 and 2013 by $25k/year. PSU's 2011 GAAP-based income statement will include income tax expense that is $20k less than the amount of income tax paid/payable per the tax return ($50k @ 40%). That $20k difference will appear as a deferred tax asset in the 12/31/2011 balance sheet. In each of the reversing years 2012 and 2013, income tax expense on the income statement will be $10k higher than the amount of taxes paid/payable per the tax return. The $25k reversing difference in 2012 reduces the future deductible amount to $25k and a deferred tax asset of $10k appears in the 12/31/12 balance sheet (($50k – $25k) @ 40%). A deferred tax asset will not appear in the 12/31/2013 balance sheet because the temporary difference will have completely reversed leaving $0 of future deductible amount at that time (($50k – $25k – $25k) @ 40%).

In summary, temporary differences that create future taxable amounts result in deferred tax liabilities being presented in the balance sheet, whereas temporary differences that create future deductible amounts result in reporting deferred tax assets. Although our examples were limited to income statement recognition of expense and the related tax deductibility, temporary differences also arise from differences in revenue recognition. Revenue recognition on the GAAP-based income statement before it is recognized in the tax return creates future taxable amounts and results in balance sheet presentation of deferred tax liabilities. An example of such a temporary difference occurs when goods are sold to a customer on a delayed payment plan and the selling firm uses the general revenue recognition principle for book purposes (reports gross profit in full in the year of sale), while using the installment sales method for tax purposes (delaying gross profit recognition until cash collection). Revenue recognized for tax purposes before it is recognized for book purposes creates future deductible amounts and deferred tax assets result. An example of such a temporary difference occurs when rent revenue is received in advance. Although GAAP requires that rent revenue received in advance be deferred until the period it is earned (recall that rent received in advance appears in the balance sheet as a liability "unearned rent"), it is required to be included in taxable income in the period the cash is received.

Accounting for Operating Losses

An operating loss occurs when a firm reports negative taxable income (the tax return includes deductible amounts from expenses and losses in excess of reported taxable revenues and gains of the period). Not only does the firm pay no tax in an operating loss year, they are permitted to offset taxable income of the two preceding years and the subsequent 20 years. An operating loss qualifies for "carryback" deduction by filing amended returns for the preceding two years and receiving a refund of taxes previously paid. If any operating loss remains after carryback to the two preceding years, it is deductible through "carryforward" deduction when filing returns for the next 20 years.[24] Any available operating loss carryback and carryforward must be deducted in successive periods until fully utilized. Under GAAP, the income statement presents a net loss that is reduced by the amount of tax benefit resulting from operating loss carryback and carryforward deductions.

For example, assume that Behrend Corp. has no temporary or permanent differences and reports a 2012 operating loss of $400k, but previously reported taxable income of $100k in 2010 and $200k in 2011. Assume further that Behrend has been and expects to continue being taxed at a 40% rate. With an assumed 40% tax rate, Behrend would have paid taxes of $40k for 2010 ($100k @ 40%) and $80k for 2011 ($200k @ 40%). The $400k operating loss experienced in

[24] Firms may elect to not carryback the operating loss to the preceding two periods and in doing so utilize the full operating loss deduction exclusively through carryforward. A firm may elect to carryforward the full operating loss, if, for example, they were subject to lower effective tax rates during the preceding two years than they anticipate in the future.

2012 can be deducted through carryback first to 2010 when taxable income of $100k was reported. The remaining 2012 operating loss carryback deduction of $300k is applied to $200k of taxable income of 2011. In utilizing the operating loss carryback, Behrend would receive a full refund of all $120k of taxes paid in 2010 and 2011. After carryback, the remaining 2012 operating loss of $100k ($400k – $100k – $200k) is deductible through "carryforward" to future years until fully utilized (2013–2032). The $100k of operating loss carryforward creates a future deductible amount that results in a deferred tax asset of $40k.

Behrend's 2012 income statement would include the following

Loss Before Income Tax	$400,000
Income Tax Benefit	160,000
Net Loss	$240,000

Note that with an assumed 40% tax rate, deductibility reduces the operating loss presented on the income statement to 60% of the pretax loss amount ($400k – ($400k × 40%)). The effects of accounting for operating loss on Behrend's financial statements in accounting equation format (in 000s) are:

ASSETS		=	LIABILITIES	+	SE	
Record tax effects of 2012's operating loss						
+Tax Refund Rec.	+ 120				– Income Tax Exp	+ 160
+Deferred Tax Asset	+ 40					

Deferred Tax Asset Valuation Allowance

Unlike deferred tax liabilities where reversal will create taxable income, ultimate benefit to be derived from deferred tax assets will occur only if there is sufficient taxable income in the years of reversal to provide a reduction in the amount of cash paid for income taxes. Recall that the definition of an asset is probable future economic benefit as a result of past transactions and events. Therefore, a deferred tax asset should appear in the balance sheet only if it is deemed "probable" that taxable income will be generated in future years to provide tax benefit from the future deductible amounts. Under U.S. GAAP, a valuation allowance (a contra account) is used to reduce the deferred tax asset to the amount deemed "more likely than not" to materialize. The valuation allowance is reviewed periodically with any change in estimate accounted for prospectively. Increase or decrease of the valuation allowance is offset in the accounting equation by decreasing or increasing the amount of income tax expense recognized in the year of change in estimate. IFRS has similar guidelines but does not permit recognition of the deferred tax asset at all unless it is deemed "probable" that future tax benefit will be derived. Although not specifically defined, the IFRS threshold of deferred asset recognition is higher than the "more likely than not" threshold prescribed under US GAAP. Therefore deferred tax assets (and stockholders' equity) might be presented at lower amounts for particular firms under IFRS.

To illustrate the valuation allowance, assume that in our previous operating loss example that Behrend estimates that it is more likely than not that only $25k of taxable income will be generated in the carryforward period.[25] With this estimate, the deferred tax asset should appear in Behrend's 12/31/12 balance sheet at only $10k ($25k @ 40%). Under U.S. GAAP, the deferred tax asset is recorded at the full $40k, but a $30k valuation allowance needs to be recorded so that the deferred tax asset appears in the balance sheet at the $10k net amount as follows:

Deferred Tax Asset	$40,000	
Less Valuation Allowance	30,000	$10,000

Behrend's 2012 income statement would include the following:

Loss Before Income Tax	$400,000
Income Tax Benefit	130,000
Net Loss	$270,000

[25] This assumption is intended for illustration purposes only. Given that Behrend generated taxable income of $300k in the last two years and that the carryforward period is 20 years, assuming that most of the tax benefit from the operating loss carryforward will not materialize is probably overly pessimistic.

The effects of accounting for operating loss on Behrend's financial statements in accounting equation format (in 000s) are:

ASSETS		=	LIABILITIES	+	SE	
Record 2012's operating loss assuming only that $10k of the $40k future tax benefit likely to occur						
+ Tax Refund Rec.	+ 120				– Income Tax Exp	+ 130
+ Deferred Tax Asset	+ 40					
+ Valuation Allowance	– 30					

Under IFRS since there is no "valuation allowance," the deferred tax asset would simply have been recorded at the amount of the estimated "probable" future tax benefit ($10,000).

Multiple Temporary Differences and Balance Sheet Presentation

Under U.S. GAAP, deferred tax assets and deferred tax liabilities are required to be presented in the balance sheet at one net current and one net long-term amount. The classification as current versus long term is determined by the classification of the related balance sheet item (if any). For example, the deferred tax liability resulting from using straight line depreciation for books while using accelerated depreciation for taxes is related to long-term operating assets presented in the balance sheet and as such is also classified as long term. The deferred tax asset resulting from using the allowance method of recognizing bad debts for book purposes but using the direct write-off method for tax purposes relates to a current asset account (accounts receivable) on the balance sheet, and as such should be classified as current. If a deferred tax asset or liability is not related to a particular balance sheet item, its classification as current versus long term is based upon when the temporary difference is expected to reverse. For example, a deferred tax asset from an operating loss carryforward is not related to any particular balance sheet item and should therefore be classified as current only to the extent it is expected to reverse by generating a tax deduction next year. There is a notable difference in balance sheet classification under IFRS, which simply requires that all deferred tax assets and liabilities be classified as long term. Therefore only one net amount will appear as either a long-term asset or liability.

Changes in Tax Rates

The amount of deferred tax assets and deferred tax liabilities is determined by multiplying the future deductible or taxable amounts by enacted tax rates. An accounting issue arises when there is a change in enacted tax rates. Throughout our discussion we have assumed a tax rate of 40%. What if taxing authorities increased the tax rate to 50% or decreased it to 30%? Recall that deferred tax asset and deferred tax liability amounts are determined by applying the enacted tax rates to future deductible or future taxable amounts, respectively. Any increase or decrease in tax rates will result in a corresponding increase or decrease in deferred tax assets or liabilities. Both U.S. GAAP and IFRS require that tax rate changes be accounted for prospectively by increasing or decreasing income tax expense reported in the income statement of the period in which tax rates are changed.

As an example, assume that Behrend has $100k of future taxable amounts resulting from differences in accounting for depreciation (use straight line method for books but accelerated method for tax) when in 2012 tax rates are increased from 40% to 50%. The increase in rates will cause an increase in the reported deferred tax liability from $40k ($100k @ 40%) to $50k ($100k @ 50%) = $10k. The effects of tax rate change are illustrated in accounting equation format (in 000s):

ASSETS	=	LIABILITIES		+	SE	
		Record the effect of 2012 tax rate increase from 40% to 50% on deferred tax liability				
		+ Def Tax Liab	+ 10		+ Inc Tax Exp	– 10

The increase in the deferred tax liability is offset in the accounting equation by decreasing owners' equity through an increase in the amount of tax expense recognized in the year of tax rate change.

If the tax rate was decreased from 40% to 30%, a decrease in the reported deferred tax liability will be offset in the accounting equation with an increase in owners' equity by decreasing income tax expense:

ASSETS	=	LIABILITIES		+	SE	
		Record the effect of 2012 tax rate decrease from 40% to 30% on deferred tax liability				
		– Def Tax Liab	– 10		– Inc Tax Exp	+ 10

Assume now that Behrend has $100k of future deductible amounts resulting from differences in accounting for bad debts (allowance method for books but direct write-off for tax) when in 2012 the tax rate is increased from 40% to 50%. The increase in rate will cause a $10k increase in the reported deferred tax asset from $40k ($100k @ 40%) to $50k ($100k @ 50%). The effects of tax rate change are illustrated in accounting equation format (in 000s):

ASSETS		=	LIABILITIES	+	SE	
			Record the effect of 2012 tax rate increase from 40% to 50% on deferred tax asset			
+ Def Tax Asset	+ 10				– Inc Tax Exp	+ 10

The increase in the deferred tax asset is offset in the accounting equation by increasing owners' equity through a reduction in the amount of tax expense recognized in the year of tax rate change.

If instead we assume that the tax rate was decreased from 40% to 30%, a decrease in the reported deferred tax asset will be offset in the accounting equation by decreasing owners' equity by increasing income tax expense:

ASSETS		=	LIABILITIES	+	SE	
			Record the effect of 2012 tax rate decrease from 40% to 30% on deferred tax asset			
– Def Tax Asset	– 10				+ Inc Tax Exp	– 10

In summary, changes in tax rates have a direct effect on individual deferred tax assets and liabilities with an offsetting effect on owners' equity. Owners' equity is increased or decreased respectively, by decreasing or increasing the amount of income tax expense recognized in the period of the rate change. If a firm has aggregate deferred tax assets equal in amount to its aggregate deferred tax liabilities immediately before a tax rate change, the increase or decrease in deferred tax assets and liabilities will exactly offset in the accounting equation, and owners' equity (income tax expense) will not be affected. If however a firm has aggregate deferred tax assets > aggregate deferred tax liabilities immediately before a tax rate change, a rate increase will increase owners' equity by decreasing the period's income tax expense, whereas a rate decrease will decrease owners' equity by increasing the period's income tax expense. If a firm is in the opposite deferred tax position (aggregate deferred tax liabilities > aggregate deferred tax assets) immediately before a tax rate change, the opposite effects will occur.

Intraperiod Income Tax Allocation and Presentation of Other Comprehensive Income Items

The income tax expense that appears on the income statement relates to the tax impact of all items effecting income from continuing operations before income tax. Any "below the line items"[26] are each shown separately, on a net of tax basis. Everything appearing above the line (the line is income from continuing operations) is shown at its gross (before tax) amount, whereas below the line items are shown net of tax effects. For example assume a firm subject to an income tax rate of 40% reports income from continuing operations before tax of $1 million, and also reports an extraordinary loss before tax of $100k. The total tax provision for the period is $360k (($1,000k – $100k) @ 40%). However, the period's income statement will provide the following presentation (in 000s):

Income from Continuing Operations before Income Tax		$1,000
Less Income Tax Expense		400
Income from Continuing Operations		$600
Extraordinary Loss	$100	
Less Tax Benefit	40	–60
Net Income		$540

This is referred to as intraperiod tax allocation because the period's total tax provision of $360k is allocated to continuing operations and to the extraordinary loss within the particular period's income statement. Income tax expense is presented as if there were no below the line items

[26] Under U.S. GAAP there are two below the line items: 1) discontinued operations, and 2) extraordinary items, whereas under IFRS discontinued operations is the only such item.

(40% tax on $1,000k of income from continuing operations would have been $400k) and the tax benefit provided by the extraordinary loss deduction ($100k @ 40% = $40k) reduces the extraordinary loss amount reported below the line.

Like below the line items, components of the period's "other comprehensive income" (OCI) are also shown net of tax.[27] All OCI items are considered temporary differences that create future deductible or taxable amounts resulting in deferred tax asset or deferred tax liability recognition, respectively. Since OCI items are recognized net of tax, when they are closed to "accumulated other comprehensive income" (AOCI), they also appear on a net of tax basis in the stockholders' equity section of the balance sheet. For example, assume that during Behrend's **first year of operations** they have an unrealized holding gain of $5k on their "available for sale" (AFS) securities portfolio. Recall that the mark to market process utilizes a "fair value adjustment" (FVA) account to write up or write down the portfolio to market value for balance sheet presentation. The following financial statement effects would occur (in 000s):

ASSETS	=	LIABILITIES	+	SE
Year-end adjustment to mark-to-market AFS sec. portfolio				
+ FVA AFS Sec. + 5		+ Def Tax Liab + 2		+ Unreal Gain AFS (OCI) + 3
Close OCI temporary accounts to AOCI				
				– Unreal Gain AFS (OCI) – 3
				+ AOCI: AFS Sec. + 3

Note that similar to "below-the-line" income statement items, both OCI and AOCI appear in the financial statements on a net of tax basis.

[27] There are four OCI items under U.S. GAAP: 1) unrealized holding gain/loss on available for sale securities, 2) unrealized gain/loss on derivatives designated as cash flow hedges, 3) changes in funded status of post retirement plans not recognized in net income, and 4) the foreign currency translation adjustment when consolidating a foreign subsidiary.

The gross unrealized gain of $5k is reduced by the 40% tax effect to $3k with recognition of a $2k deferred tax liability. Subsequent changes in income tax rates or changes in the deferred tax asset valuation allowance related to OCI items are accounted for with recognition of gain or loss in OCI (not by adjusting the amount of income tax expense recognized in the net income).

CHAPTER 9

Stockholders' Equity and Earnings Per Share

Introduction

Recall that owners' equity (stockholders' equity in the case of corporations) is defined as the residual interest in assets of the entity after deducting liabilities. Stockholders' equity (SE) is not defined in itself other than being the net assets (assets – liabilities) of a business entity. There are five main sections of SE: Paid-In Capital,[1] Retained Earnings, Accumulated Other Comprehensive Income, Noncontrolling Interest, and Treasury Stock. Noncontrolling interest arises in consolidated financial statements where the parent corporation controls a subsidiary but does not own 100% of its voting stock. An introduction to the accounting for noncontrolling interests was introduced in chapter 7, and will not be repeated here. Accumulated other comprehensive income (AOCI) is the balance sheet presentation of the four items[2] initially recognized in "other comprehensive income." Three of these AOCI components were discussed in previous chapters: unrealized gains and losses from "available for sale securities" and derivatives classified as "cash flow hedges" were discussed in chapter 7; and the unamortized gain or loss and/or past service cost associated with pensions and other postretirement benefits was discussed in chapter 8. The remaining AOCI component is the cumulative "foreign currency translation adjustment" (FCTA) that results from the consolidation process when a parent corporation has one or more foreign subsidiaries. Foreign subsidiaries maintain their books not in US$, but in units of the local currency.

[1] In practice, "Paid-In Capital" is frequently referred to as "Contributed Capital." The discussion here consistently refers to "Paid-In capital."

[2] As discussed in chapter 4, IFRS has a fifth AOCI item—"remeasurement gain" recognized in applying the revaluation option when accounting for operational assets.

In consolidation, the foreign subsidiary's accounts are restated into US$ by applying foreign currency exchange rates. However, different exchange rates are applied to different financial statement items. Although the subsidiary's accounts are in balance when presented in foreign currency units, they likely do not balance when restated into US$. The "plug" amount necessary to balance the accounts is usually presented in AOCI with the necessary change in that amount recognized in OCI.[3] Detailed discussion of the exchange rates used to restate a foreign subsidiary's local currency into US$ is not provided, and AOCI will not be discussed further. Each of the remaining three components of SE will be examined including discussion of: stock-based compensation, and accounting for error corrections and changes in accounting principle. The chapter concludes with a discussion of earnings per share.

Stockholders' Equity

Paid-in Capital

Corporations are separate legal entities created under the incorporation laws of one of the 50 states. Since corporations are separate legal entities, owners (stockholders) enjoy "limited liability." With limited liability, the most an owner can lose is the amount paid for their investment because the owners' personal assets are generally protected from creditor claims in bankruptcy. This being the case, state laws have been enacted in an attempt to (among other things) protect creditor interests by constraining corporate distributions to stockholders that are detrimental to creditor claims. This is why corporations distinguish paid-in capital from retained earnings.[4] Although there has been movement toward

---

[3] Under certain circumstances (the foreign subsidiary's "functional" currency is not the local currency), the required change is recognized in net income and closed to retained earnings.
[4] Only corporations and other forms of business entities that enjoy limited liability provide such distinction. Limited liability partnerships and limited liability companies also enjoy limited liability and therefore distinguish paid-in capital from retained earnings. Proprietorships and partnerships do not distinguish paid-in capital from retained earnings because they are not legal entities separate from their owners and as such do not enjoy limited liability.

uniformity,[5] incorporation laws differ from state to state. It is noteworthy that many large businesses are incorporated in the state of Delaware because of its "business friendly" governance laws including lax limitations on corporations' dividend paying ability. Unless contractually constrained by debt covenants, a corporation's retained earnings is generally available for legal distribution to stockholders. However, in order to keep track of a corporation's legal ability to make shareholder distributions (which differs from state to state), detailed records are maintained in multiple paid-in capital accounts. For financial reporting purposes however, there are two primary classifications of paid-in capital reported in the balance sheet: a stock's par value, and additional paid in capital (APIC). We will forego discussion of the detailed information kept in multiple paid-in capital accounts and concentrate instead on the financial statement impact of the issuance of equity type securities and related subsequent transactions by assuming direct recognition in general APIC that is reported in the balance sheet.

Common Stock

When a corporation obtains permission to form, it receives from the state of incorporation its charter (also called articles of incorporation) that indicates the nature of business to be conducted and the authorization to issue a certain number of shares of different types (classes) of stock. Initially corporations generally issue just one class of stock—common stock.[6] These common stockholders are the ultimate risk takers and true residual owners of the firm's assets. Unless specifically indicated otherwise, a stockholder has the following rights:

1) To vote in matters concerning the corporation including electing its board of directors,
2) To share proportionately in dividends if declared by the board of directors, and
3) To share proportionately in assets remaining after satisfaction of all creditor claims (liabilities) in the case of corporate liquidation.

---

[5] Revised Model Business Corporations Act, American Bar Association, 1994.

[6] When only one class of stock is issued, it is sometimes referred to as "capital" stock.

By electing its board of directors, common stockholders indirectly control the corporation because the board hires and fires management who make decisions regarding the day-to-day operations of the firm.

Common stock usually has a nominal "par value" amount.[7] Traditionally, par value was approximately equal to a stock's issuance price and therefore represented "paid-in capital." Currently however, the majority of publicly traded common stocks have a par value of $1/share or less while having fair value in excess of $20/share. This being the case, it is important to note that **the par value of a corporation's common stock is meaningless** and has nothing to do with its fair value and little if anything to do with its issuance price. There is no theoretical rationale for separately reporting the par value of common stock in the balance sheet and it is useless in financial analysis. Nonetheless, accounting convention has resulted in separately presenting a stock's par value from additional paid in capital (APIC) on the balance sheet. For example, if Behrend Corp. issues 1 million shares of common stock with a par value of $1 per share for $30 per share, it will account for the issuance as follows (using the accounting equation format (in millions)):

ASSETS	=	LIABILITIES	+	SE
Issue 1 million shares of common stock with a par value of $1/share for $30/share				
+ Cash + 30				+ Common Stk. + 1
				+ APIC + 29

If this is the original issuance of stock the balance sheet immediately afterward will consist entirely of the asset cash in the amount of $30 million and two items within stockholders' equity: common stock at its par value of $1 million and APIC of $29 million. The common stock account (or any stock account) will have a balance equal to the number of shares issued times the par value/share. Cash received from the issuance of common (or any type of stock or debt security) is classified as a financing activity in the statement of cash flows. Stock may be issued

[7] Some stock has a "stated" value rather than a par value. Stated value common stock is accounted for the same way as par value common stock. Stated value simply substitutes for par value in the accounting.

in exchange for assets other than cash or in exchange for services. Under these circumstances, either the fair value of the stock issued or the fair value of the noncash assets or services received, whichever is more clearly determinable, is used to value the transaction.

Preferred Stock

In addition to common stock, firms may issue "preferred" stock. Preferred stock is traditionally termed such because its owners are provided certain preferred rights relative to common stockholders. Preferred stockholders usually have a preference in receiving dividends when (and if) declared by the board of directors and sharing in assets upon liquidation. In exchange for these preferences, preferred shareholders usually give up the right to vote. Unlike interest that is a contractual obligation that requires periodic payment, dividends on preferred stock are only paid if declared by the board of directors. The periodic preferred dividend "requirement" can be stated as a specific dollar amount per share, or like debt can be expressed as a percentage of the stock's par value. For example $100 par value preferred stock can have its $5 annual dividend requirement expressed directly as $5/share, or as 5% of par (5% × $100 par value = $5/share).

Almost all preferred stock is "cumulative," which means that the preferred stockholders must receive the unpaid dividends of all previous periods plus the current period's dividend before the common shareholders receive any dividend.[8] If the board of directors fails to declare and pay the period's preferred dividend, it is said to be "passed." At any point in time the amount of accumulated unpaid dividends on cumulative preferred stock is referred to as "dividends in arrears," and although not reported as a liability in the balance sheet, must be disclosed in the financial statements. To illustrate the dividend preference, assume that 5 years ago, Behrend Corp. issued cumulative preferred stock with a total annual dividend requirement of $50,000. Assume also that Behrend has not paid a dividend in the previous 2 years or the current year. In this example common stockholders will not receive a dividend unless Behrend declares

[8] If a preferred stock issue is not specifically identified as "noncumulative," it is generally held to be cumulative.

and pays dividends in the current year in excess of $150,000. Preferred shareholders have priority claim to 3 years of dividends (2 years in arrears and the current year).

Currently, firms issue different types of stock with diverse restrictions and preferences. Such issuances have blurred the distinction between preferred and common stock. This being the case, both U.S. GAAP and IFRS require disclosure of detailed information concerning the pertinent rights and privileges of each class of a corporation's stock.[9] Differences currently exist between U.S. GAAP and IFRS regarding balance sheet classification of "preferred" stock.[10] Under U.S. GAAP, "preferred" stock is classified as stockholders' equity unless it is "mandatorily redeemable." Mandatorily redeemable preferred stock is stock that must be bought back in the future at a specified date or upon the occurrence of an event that is certain to occur. Whereas only mandatorily redeemable preferred stock is classified as debt under U.S. GAAP, IFRS requires most preferred stock to be classified as debt. Classification as debt not only increases the debt ratio, but also requires that periodic "dividend" payments be reported as interest expense on the income statement.

Given the similarity of preferred stock to debt, its fair value tends to change primarily from changes in interest rates. Like callable bonds discussed in chapter 5, callable preferred stock is callable at the option of the issuing corporation. This being the case, firms that issue "callable" preferred stock can benefit from interest rate decreases that occur after issuance. If interest rates decline, the call feature enables the firm to call-in and retire the preferred stock at a price lower than would otherwise exist in the market (absent the call feature). However, unlike retirement of debt, no income statement effect (gain or loss) is ever recognized from a firm's dealings in its own stock. A more detailed discussion of a firm's

---

[9] FASB ASC 505-10-50; Original pronouncement Statement of Financial Accounting Standards No. 129, "Disclosure of Information about Capital Structure," FASB 1997, par. 4. International Accounting Standard No. 1, "Presentation of Financial Statements," IASB, par. 79.

[10] FASB ASC 480-10-5; Original pronouncement: Statement of Financial Accounting Standards No. 150, "Accounting for Certain Financial Instruments with Characteristics of Both Liabilities and Equity," FASB 2003 par. 3. International Accounting Standard No. 32, "Financial Instruments: Presentation," IASB, par. 16.

accounting for dealings in its own stock (acquisition and subsequent reissuance or retirement) is provided later in the chapter.

Convertible Preferred Stock and Convertible Debt

Convertible preferred stock and convertible debt securities are typically convertible into a predetermined number of common shares at the option of the investor. If the issuing corporation prospers and its common stock increases in value, convertible preferred shareholders and convertible bond holders can benefit beyond their periodic dividend/interest claims by exercising their conversion option. Convertible preferred stock and convertible debt may change in value with changes in interest rates or with changes in market value of the common stock, depending upon the likelihood of conversion. Under IFRS, the proceeds from issuance of convertible debt must be allocated between debt and the conversion feature (equity) on the balance sheet; whereas under U.S. GAAP, the conversion feature is ignored and the full issuance proceeds are accounted for as debt. For example, assume that Behrend issues 8% convertible bonds for $1,050,000 and estimates the fair value of the conversion feature at $50,000 and also estimates that the bonds would have been issued at face value if they weren't convertible. Behrend would account for the issuance under U.S. GAAP versus IFRS as follows (using the accounting equation format (in millions)):

ASSETS		=	LIABILITIES		+	SE	
U.S. GAAP accounting for convertible bonds issued for $1.05 million							
+ Cash	+ 1.05		+ Bonds Pay.	+ 1.00			
			+ Bond Prem.	+ .05			
IFRS accounting for convertible bonds issued for $1.05 million							
+ Cash	+ 1.05		+ Bonds Pay.	+ 1.00		+ APIC	+ .05

Debt Issued with Detachable Stock Purchase Warrants

Firms may also issue debt with separately detachable stock purchase warrants. A stock purchase warrant entitles the holder to purchase a certain number of shares of stock at a predetermined price. U.S. GAAP is consistent with the IFRS accounting (illustrated in previous example) and requires that the issuance proceeds be allocated between the debt and the stock purchase warrants (APIC).[11] The reason for different accounting treatment of convertible debt versus debt with detachable stock purchase warrants under U.S. GAAP is the ability to separately determine fair value of the debt and equity components only in the case of detachable stock purchase warrants. Convertible bonds do not allow the separate trading of the debt component (the bonds) from the equity component (the conversion feature).

Retirement of Stock

Firms may choose to acquire and retire shares of stock. The acquisition may be the result of: an open market purchase, shareholders exercising their redemption option, or the corporation exercising a call option. Formal retirement results in shares reverting to "authorized" but unissued status. This contrasts with shares purchased as "treasury stock" which is discussed next. As indicated previously (and most importantly), no gain or loss is recognized by a corporation from dealings in its own stock. If the amount paid to acquire the shares exceeds the original proceeds from their issuance, retained earnings (RE) is usually reduced for the difference.[12] A corporation's retained earnings-may be decreased, but will never be increased as a result of dealings in their own stock. To illustrate, we return to our initial example where Behrend originally issued 1 million shares of $1 par value common stock for $30/share. Assume that Behrend acquires and formally retires 100,000 of these shares paying $40/share. The following illustrates the acquisition and retirement using the accounting equation format (in millions):

---

[11] If the sum of the fair values of the equity and debt components does not equal the issuance proceeds, an allocation is made based upon relative fair values.

[12] Depending upon the circumstances, state law may allow specific detailed additional paid-in capital accounts to be reduced in addition to, or instead of retained earnings.

ASSETS		=	LIABILITIES	+	SE	
Acquire and retire 100k shares of common stock at $40/share that were originally issued at $30/share						
– Cash	– 4.0				– Common Stk.	– .1
					– APIC	– 2.9
					– RE	– 1.0

Treasury Stock

Firms may acquire shares of their own stock with the intention to reissue the shares in the future. Such shares are called "treasury stock." Treasury stock may be used for: satisfying exercise of options by convertible security holders (discussed previously), stock based employee compensation plans (discussed later), avoiding a hostile takeover, signaling that its stock is undervalued,[13] etc. Shares held in the "treasury" are considered to be "issued" but not "outstanding." Outstanding shares are those held by the true owners of the corporation—its stockholders. A corporation cannot own itself. For this reason treasury stock is not considered an asset of the corporation but is instead classified as a contra stockholders' equity item on the balance sheet.[14] Treasury shares do not vote, do not receive dividends, and do not share in assets upon liquidation. The cost of the treasury shares is recognized in the treasury stock account without regard to the amount of original issue proceeds.[15] To illustrate the accounting for treasury stock, we reconsider the previous example (Behrend acquires 100,000 of its shares for $40/share) but we now assume the shares are not formally retired, but instead are held in the treasury. The following

[13] Announcements of stock buy-back programs related to managements' belief that the stock is undervalued generally result in an increase in the market price of the firm's stock.

[14] Under rare circumstances treasury stock may be presented among assets.

[15] This is called the "cost" method of accounting for treasury stock. An alternative method is called the "par value" method. The par value method is similar to the accounting for formal stock retirement but instead of reducing the common (or preferred) stock at par value, treasury stock is recognized at the stock's par value. Since the par value method has all but disappeared from practice, it is not presented or discussed further.

illustrates the acquisition of the treasury stock using the accounting equation format (in millions):

ASSETS	=	LIABILITIES	+	SE

Acquire 100k shares of common stock for $40/share to be held as treasury stock

ASSETS		LIABILITIES	SE	
– Cash	– 4.0		+ Treasury Stk.	– 4.0

If the treasury shares are subsequently reissued for more or less than cost, no gain or loss is recognized, and although retained earnings may be decreased, it will never be increased as a result of treasury stock transactions. Let's assume that all 100,000 treasury shares are subsequently reissued for $35/share. The following illustrates the reissuance of the treasury stock using the accounting equation format (in millions):

Reissue 100k shares of treasury stock for $35/share that were previously acquired for $40/share

ASSETS		LIABILITIES	SE	
+ Cash	+ 3.5		– Treasury Stk.	+ 4.0
			– RE	– .5

If the 100,000 treasury shares were instead reissued for $45/share, the following financial statement effects would result (using the accounting equation format (in millions)):

Reissue 100k shares of treasury stock for $45/share that were previously acquired for $40/share

ASSETS		LIABILITIES	SE	
+ Cash	+ 4.5		– Treasury Stk.	+ 4.0
			+ APIC	+ .5

All cash flows associated with a firm's dealings in its own stock are classified among financing activities in the statement of cash flows.

Retained Earnings

Retained earnings represent the cumulative net income of a firm since its inception that has been retained in the business (i.e., has not been distributed to its stockholders). As illustrated previously, distributions to stockholder can occur through stock acquisition. By far however, the most common form of distribution to stockholders is cash dividends.

Cash Dividends

Cash dividends are declared at the discretion of the board of directors. Although the amount legally available is a consideration in the cash dividend declaration decision, availability of sufficient cash is usually the key factor. High growth corporations tend to pay little if any dividends because earnings (equal to cash flow in the long-run) need to be reinvested in the firm. Stockholders of high growth firms are primarily interested in the market value of their investment rather than the receipt of periodic dividends. However, some corporations have a long track record of paying regular cash dividends at periodic intervals (e.g., a quarterly dividend of $.25 per share). Corporations that pay regular periodic dividends would be hesitant to reduce or cease dividend distributions because it is likely that their shareholders initially purchased the stock and continue to hold it because they expect to receive periodic cash dividends.

Certain dividend related dates are important from an accounting or investment perspective. In chronological order these are: 1) the date of declaration, 2) the ex-dividend date, and 3) the date of payment. Although dividends are at the discretion of the board of directors, once declared they become a legal liability of the corporation. On the declaration date retained earnings is reduced and the liability dividends payable is recognized. The ex-dividend date determines who will receive a dividend that has been declared, but not yet paid. If a stock that is trading "ex-dividend' is purchased, the purchaser will not receive the forthcoming dividend. The holder of the stock immediately preceding the ex-dividend date will receive the dividend. This being the case, a stock's market value generally declines on its ex-dividend date. There is no financial statement impact recognized on the ex-dividend date. On the date of payment, the liability dividends payable and cash are reduced. To illustrate, assume that Behrend has 1 million shares of common stock outstanding on 12/15/2012 when its board of directors declares a cash dividend of $.25/share, payable on 1/15/2013. The following illustrates the financial statement effects using the accounting equation format (in millions):

ASSETS	=	LIABILITIES	+	SE
12/15/12 Behrend declares a cash dividend of $.25/share on its 1 million outstanding common shares				
		+ Dividends Pay. + .25		– RE – .25

Recall from previous discussion that dividends have no income statement effect.

ASSETS	=	LIABILITIES	+	SE
1/15/13 Behrend pays the cash dividend declared on 12/15/12				
– Cash – .25		– Dividends Pay. – .25		

Property Dividends

Although rare, firms may pay their shareholders a "property dividend." For example a corporation may distribute to its stockholders shares of stock in an unaffiliated firm previously held for investment. The dividend reduces retained earnings at the fair value of the property to be distributed. In writing the property up or down to its fair value, a realized gain or loss is recognized in the income statement. Again, dividends are not recognized as an expense in the income statement. Any income statement effect associated with a property dividend is attributed to the disposal of the property—not the dividend distribution.

Stock "Dividends" and Stock Splits

Stock dividends and stock splits are similar in that they both result in a distribution of a firm's stock to existing shareholders proportionate to their ownership interest. This distribution increases the number of shares outstanding. The relative increase in shares outstanding (distribution size) reflects management intent in making the distribution. Large distributions are intended to reduce the share price, bringing it within a desired trading range, and in doing so increase the stock's marketability. Small distributions are intended to substitute for cash dividends. Small distributions provide the shareholder with something (additional shares) while conserving the firm's cash. This difference in management intent regarding the distribution is reflected in the accounting for stock dividends and stock splits.

Stock dividends by a corporation involve a firm's distribution of its own shares to existing shareholders proportionate to their ownership interest. For example, assume that a firm has 10,000 shares of $1 common stock issued and outstanding on which the firm distributes a 10% stock "dividend." The firm will issue an additional 1,000 shares (10,000 × 10%) of common stock to its existing shareholders, and after the stock dividend the firm will have 11,000 shares outstanding. An investor owning 1,000 shares of stock before the stock dividend will receive an additional 100 shares and own 1,100 shares after the stock dividend. Note that there is no change in the firm's assets or its liabilities as a result of stock "dividends," and an investor's proportionate ownership interest in the net assets of the firm does not change either. Before the stock "dividend" our investor owned 1,000 of the firm's 10,000 outstanding shares (10%) and afterward owns 1,100 of the 11,000 outstanding shares (10%). Stock dividends are not really dividends at all because nothing of worth (e.g., cash or property) is transferred from the corporation to its stockholders.

An accounting standard was issued in 1941 to discourage firms from issuing misleading stock "dividends" by requiring a reduction in retained earnings (like a cash dividend) and in doing so decrease the corporation's future dividend paying ability. GAAP distinguishes "small" from "large" stock dividends. Small stock dividends are defined as less than 25%, while those 25% or larger are defined as large. In the case of small stock dividends, retained earnings is reduced by the fair value of the shares distributed (like a cash dividend). Large stock dividends require reduction of retained earnings at the minimum amount required by state law (usually par value).[16] It is important to note that there is no theoretical support for the required accounting for stock "dividends" under GAAP. To illustrate the accounting for a small

[16] FASB ASC 505-20-25 & 30; Original pronouncement Accounting Research Bulletin No. 43, "Restatement and Revision of Accounting Research Bulletins," AICPA 1961, chapter 7 par. 10–13.

stock dividend, consider the previously discussed 10% stock dividend. Assume that the fair value of 1,000 shares distributed was $20/share = $20,000. Since this is a small stock dividend, retained earnings is reduced (capitalized) in the full fair value of the shares with an increase in paid-in capital. Although total stockholders' equity is unchanged, components of stockholders' equity are changed as follows using the accounting equation format (in 000s):

ASSETS	=	LIABILITIES	+	SE	
Distribute a small stock dividend, 1,000 shares with fair value = $20/share and par value = $1/share					
				– RE	– 20
				+ Common Stock	+ 1
				+ APIC	+ 19

If we now instead assume the stock dividend was 30% (a large stock dividend), 3,000 shares will be distributed but retained earnings will be capitalized only to the extent of the stock's par value. The stockholders' equity accounts will be affected as follows (in 000s):

Distribute a large stock dividend, 3,000 shares with par value = $1/share	
– RE	– 3
+ Common Stock	+ 3

The common stock account is increased so that its balance is equal to the number of shares issued times the par value per share (3k additional shares issued @ $1 par/share = $3k increase).

A stock split is similar to a stock dividend, but the stock's par value is reduced in proportion with the share increase so that no formal accounting entry is necessary. For example, in our previous discussion the firm had 10,000 common shares issued and outstanding with a par value of $1/share. The balance in the common stock account would be 10,000 shares @ $1 par value/share = $10,000. If the firm distributes a 2 for 1 stock split, the number of shares will double to 20,000 shares, and the par value will be cut in half to $.50/share. The balance in the common stock account remains at $10,000, which is equal to the postsplit number of shares issued times their par value/share (20,000 shares

@ $.50/share = $10,000). No accounting entry is made and all account balances are unchanged.[17]

An investor receiving shares from a stock dividend or stock split simply reduces their cost per share upon receipt of the additional shares. If the investor we previously discussed in our 10% stock dividend example had originally purchased the 1,000 shares for $22,000 = $22/share sometime prior to the stock distribution, their new cost per share is computed as $22,000/1,100 shares = $20/share.

Does the shareholder receive anything as a result of a stock dividend or stock split? Technically the answer is no, but research shows that typically stock dividends and stock splits announcements are interpreted as good news, evidenced by increased market value.[18] Regardless of whether the distribution is termed a "stock dividend" or a "stock split," if as a result the stock's market value increases, the investor does receive something of worth.

Stock-Based Employee Compensation Plans

Stock related employee compensation may include stock option plans, stock award plans, stock purchase plans, and stock appreciation rights. All of these stock-based compensation plans are considered forms of employee compensation that require determination of two factors:

- Factor 1) The amount of employee compensation to be recognized as expense (in net income (NI)), and
- Factor 2) The allocation of compensation expense to the periods during which the employee provides the service being compensated through the plan.

---

[17] Reverse splits are the opposite. The number of shares is reduced and the par value per share is proportionately increased. Again there is no effect on account balances.

[18] For example, an increase in the stock's market value occurs for a two for one split (or 100% stock dividend) when the postdistribution share price is greater than 50% of the predistribution share price.

Stock-based employee compensation plans are intended to create "goal congruent" compensation schemes. A goal congruent compensation scheme attempts to align the employee's goals congruent with those of the firm. Goal congruence exists if the firm's goals are being achieved when the employee acts in a manner that achieves their personal goals. Individuals are generally motivated to behave in ways that maximize their personal wealth. Employees who own stock or hold options to purchase stock at a fixed price in the future have a personal incentive to maximize the market price of the firm's stock, which is a shared objective with the firm's stockholders. In addition to the formal recognition in the financial statements (discussed below), extensive information relating to employee stock-based compensation plans is required to be disclosed in the financial statement notes.

Stock Option Plans

Stock options awarded (granted) to key employees enable them to purchase the firm's stock at a predetermined price. It is important to note that there is no downside risk to the employee associated with stock options, only up-side potential return. Stock options are similar to stock purchase warrants discussed previously, but unlike warrants are generally not immediately exercisable at the grant date. Instead, stock options become exercisable at some future point in time. The time period from the grant date until it becomes exercisable is called the vesting period. The vesting period is usually assumed to be the compensation period (factor 2 above) during which the employee provides services to the firm. The amount of compensation expense to be recognized (factor 1 above) is based upon the estimated fair value of the stock options at the grant date.

There are two components in the fair value of an option: intrinsic value, and time value. Intrinsic value exists only if an option is "in the money." An option is in the money if the market price exceeds its exercise or "strike" price. Options will only be exercised when they are "in the money." Because the strike price is usually set at the market price on the date of grant, the options have no intrinsic value at that time.[19] However, the options have time value at the date of grant, which is a function of estimated amounts and likelihood of the stock's price exceeding the strike price when the options become exercisable in the future. The fair value of a stock option is estimated using an option pricing model. Option pricing models consider a number of variables (e.g., vesting period, exercise period, expected volatility in stock's price, etc.). It is important to note that the total amount of compensation expense (factor 1 above) recognized is based upon the option's estimated fair value at the date of grant and is not adjusted for subsequent increases or decreases in fair value of the firm's stock. However, vesting estimates do affect the total amount of compensation expense recognized (factor 1), with subsequent changes in vesting estimates accounted for prospectively.[20] Vesting will not occur for example if the employee leaves the firm before the vesting date.

The following example is used to illustrate a firm's accounting for an employee stock option plan. Assume that on 1/01/11 when Behrend's stock was trading for $20/share, they issued 10 employees options to each purchase 10,000 shares of Behrend's common stock for $20/share anytime during 2014, provided they are still employed by Behrend on 12/31/13. Assume also that on 1/01/11 (the grant date) an option pricing model estimates that each share option is worth $1.50, and that 70% of the options

---

[19] For tax purposes, such plans are called "qualified" stock option plans, which are most commonly used in practice. The firm gets no tax deduction in association with qualified employee stock option plans. Therefore the difference between taxable income per the tax return and income before tax under GAAP is attributed to a "permanent difference" without deferred tax consequences (chapter 8). Unqualified plans include those where the strike price is set less than the market price at the grant date. Unqualified plans provide the firm with a tax deduction at the time of exercise equal to the market value of the shares issued in excess of the amount received from employees. Unqualified employee stock option plans require deferred tax asset recognition. Unqualified plans are not discussed further.

[20] Some stock option plans (and stock award plans discussed below) may vest only if certain performance targets are met (e.g., 10% sales growth, 15% growth in earnings, etc.). These performance conditioned stock compensation plans require estimates regarding whether or not it is probable that the performance target will be met (and vesting will or will not occur). Any such change in estimate is also accounted for with a catch-up adjustment in the amount of compensation expense recognized in the period of estimate change.

will vest (i.e., 7 of the 10 employees will still be employed by Behrend at 12/31/13). Based upon this information, total compensation expense (factor 1) is estimated at $105,000 (100,000 shares @ $1.50/share × 70%). The period of employee service (factor 2) is the 3-year vesting period 2011, 2012, and 2013. Based upon the original vesting estimate, the yearly compensation expense is $35,000 ($105,000/3 years). Assuming that the 70% vesting estimate is unchanged at 12/31/11 and 12/31/12, the following financial statement effects will occur (in accounting equation format (in 000s)):

ASSETS	=	LIABILITIES	+	SE	
12/31/11 Recognize employee stock option plan compensation expense for 2011					
				+ Comp. Exp.	– 35
				+ APIC	+ 35
12/31/12 Recognize employee stock option plan compensation expense for 2012					
				+ Comp. Exp.	– 35
				+ APIC	+ 35

We continue the example but assume that 9 of the 10 employees are still employed by Behrend at 12/31/13 and therefore the vesting rate estimate is changed from 70% to 90%, which increases total compensation expense (factor 1) from $105,000 to $135,000 (100,000 shares @ $1.50/share × 90%). The change in estimate is accounted for prospectively through a catch-up adjustment to the amount of compensation expense recognized in the year of the changed estimate. Compensation expense for 2013 is $65,000 determined as follows:

Compensation expense to date	$135,000	($135,000 × 3/3)
Compensation recognized previously	70,000	($35,000 in each year 2011 and 2012)
Compensation expense for 2013	$65,000	

The financial statement effects for 2013 are as follows (in 000s):

12/31/13 Recognize employee stock option plan compensation expense for 2013	
+ Comp. Exp.	– 65
+ APIC	+ 65

Assume that the market price of Behrend's stock exceeds the $20 strike price during 2014 and all 90,000 optioned shares are purchased by the employees paying $1,800,000 (90,000 optioned shares @ $20/share). The financial statement effects for 2014 are as follows (in millions):

Employees exercise their options and purchase 90,000 shares @ $20/share

+ Cash	+ 1.8	+ Common Stk.	+ .09
		+ APIC	+ 1.71

Note that any changes in the market price of Behrend's stock that may have occurred during the entire 4-year option period are ignored. The stock is assumed to be issued for $1,935,000, which is partially received in cash ($1,800,000), and partially received through employee services ($135,000). The cash received is classified as a financing activity in the statement of cash flows. If the stock's price was less than the $20 strike price throughout 2014, the options would have expired unexercised. Nonetheless, the $135,000 of compensation expense still would have been recognized during 2011, 2012, and 2013 and offset in the accounting equation with the increase in APIC as was presented previously. No financial statement effects are recognized as a result of stock options expiring unexercised.[21]

Prior to 2006, firms were not required to recognize expense related to stock options provided that the strike price was set at an amount at least equal to the stock's fair value at the grant date. This was referred to as the "intrinsic method" because employee compensation expense was recognized only if a stock option had intrinsic value (was in the money) at the date of grant. Since most firms set the strike price equal to the stock's grant date fair value, no compensation expense was recognized under prior GAAP. In 2004 the FASB issued a standard mandating use of the "fair value method."[22] The fair value method requires estimating and expensing the full grant date fair value of stock options. This is the

---

[21] The detailed accounting records would require a reclassification between specific APIC accounts.

[22] Financial statements for periods preceding 2006 were not required to be restated under the fair value method, Statement of Financial Accounting Standards No. 123 (revised 2004), "Share Based Payments," FASB 2004, par. 74.

method illustrated previously, where compensation expense includes both an option's intrinsic value and its time value. Usage of stock options as a form of employee compensation has recently been on the decline. This decline may be partially caused by the requirement to expense stock options' full fair value that became effective in 2006.

Stock Award Plans

As indicated previously, stock option plans have declined in use. Nevertheless, it seems that firms continue their desire to use stock-based compensation with the intention to achieve goal congruent employee behavior. This is evidenced by the growth in popularity of stock award plans. Stock award plans are sometimes referred to as "restricted" stock. These plans simply transfer shares of a firm's stock to key employees at some future point in time. Unlike stock option plans, employees pay nothing for the stock. Stock award plans are accounted for similar to stock option plans. The total amount of compensation to be recognized (factor 1) is based upon the fair value of the stock on the grant date, and the expense is usually recognized over the vesting period (factor 2). The vesting period begins on the grant date and ends on the date the stock is transferred to the employee. Like stock options, the amount of compensation expense is affected by the estimate of the awards that will vest, but not by changes in the stock price that may occur after the grant date. Also like stock option accounting, any change in estimate of the portion of stock awards that will vest is accounted for prospectively, with a catch-up adjustment reflected in compensation expense recognized in the period of the change in estimate.

As an example, assume that on 1/01/11 when Behrend's common stock was trading for $40/share, they grant a stock award to the CEO that entitles her to receive 10,000 shares of Behrend's common stock with a par value of $1/share on 12/31/12 provided she is still employed by Behrend at that time. Behrend initially anticipates (estimates) that the stock award will vest. The amount of total compensation expense is the fair value of the shares on the grant date (10,000 shares @ $40/share = $400,000) and the period of employee service is the two year vesting period 1/01/11–12/31/12. Assuming the anticipated vesting is unchanged on 12/31/11, and vesting actually occurs resulting in the stock transfer on 12/31/12, the following financial statement effects will occur[23] (in accounting equation format (in 000s)):

ASSETS	=	LIABILITIES	+	SE	
12/31/11 Recognize employee stock award compensation expense for 2011					
				+ Comp. Exp.	– 200
				+ APIC	+ 200
12/31/12 Recognize employee stock award compensation expense for 2012 and transfer the stock					
				+ Comp. Exp.	– 200
				+ Common Stk.	+ 10
				+ APIC	+ 190

The entire assumed proceeds from the issuance of stock awards is attributed to employee services.

Assume instead that in July 2012 the CEO leaves Behrend. The previously anticipated vesting does not occur and therefore the stock is not transferred to the CEO on 12/31/12. This change in estimate requires a catch-up adjustment that results in a negative amount of compensation expense recognized in 2012. The following financial statement effects would result (in 000s):

Recognize change in estimate concerning employee stock award plan that occurred in 2012	
– Comp. Exp.	+ 200
– APIC	– 200

This is simply a reversal of the accounting entry made during 2011. Negative expense recognition increases reported net income or decreases reported net loss (like revenue and gain recognition).

[23] The employer firm receives a tax deduction from stock award plans equal to the market price of the stock in the year the stock is transferred to the employee. Until the stock is transferred, the future deductible amount associated with the temporary difference would result in a reduction of tax expense and recognition of a deferred tax asset. The temporary difference reverses in the year of stock transfer to the employee. To concentrate on the accounting for stock award plans, the related deferred tax complications are not presented.

Stock Purchase Plans

Stock purchase plans are made available to essentially all of a corporation's employees and allow purchase of the employer's stock at a price somewhat below its fair value. Employee compensation is ignored if the discount is 5% or less. If the discount exceeds 5%, the stock issuance is accounted for at their full fair value and the entire discount is recognized as employee compensation expense.[24] For example, assume Behrend's employee stock purchase plan allows employees to purchase its $1 par value common stock at a 5% discount when its stock is trading at $40/share. Assume 10,000 shares are purchased by plan employees paying $38/share ($40 × 95% = $38/share), or $380,000. Behrend will account for the issuance as follows (using the accounting equation format (in 000s)):

ASSETS		=	LIABILITIES	+	SE	
Issue 10,000 $1 par value common shares with fair value of $40/share at a 5% discount to employees						
+ Cash	+ 380				+ Common Stk.	+ 10
					+ APIC	+ 370

If instead, Behrend's stock purchase plan allowed employees to purchase shares at a 15% discount, and we again assume 10,000 shares are issued under the plan, the total proceeds are $340,000 ($40 × 85% = $34/share × 10,000 shares). Behrend will account for the stock issuance as follows (using the accounting equation format (in 000s)):

Issue 10,000 $1 par value common shares with fair value of $40/share at a 15% discount to employees			
+ Cash	+ 340	+ Common Stk.	+ 10
		+ APIC	+ 390
		+ Comp. Exp.	– 60

[24] FASB ASC 718-50-25-1; Original pronouncement: Statement of Financial Accounting Standards No. 123 (revised 2004), "Share Based Payments," FASB 2004, par. 12.

Note that the entire 15% discount ($40/share × 15% = $6/share × 10k shares = $60k) is recognized as compensation expense.

Stock Appreciation Rights

Stock appreciation rights (SARs) are awarded to key employees as an incentive compensation scheme intended to achieve goal congruence by motivating the employee to maximize market value of the firm's stock. However, unlike stock options, stock award plans, and stock purchase plans, wherein the employee receives stock, SARs require future cash payment to employees based upon the appreciation in the firm's stock value that occurs over a period of time. For any compensation scheme where the employee is entitled to future cash payment, compensation expense recognition is offset in the accounting equation with recognition of a liability. The amount of total compensation expense recognized (factor 1) equals the amount that is ultimately paid to the employee. The period of expense recognition (factor 2) is typically the vesting period. Since the amount of total compensation isn't known with certainty until the employee "cashes in," estimates need to be made in order to formulate financial statements at the end of each period. Changes in estimate are accounted for with a catch-up adjustment to the amount of compensation expense recognized in the year of estimate change.

To illustrate, assume that on 1/01/11 five key employees of Behrend Corp. are granted SARs to receive a cash payment on 12/31/12 in an amount equal to the market value appreciation on 10,000 firm shares during the 2-year period 1/01/11 to 12/31/12. In order to qualify (vest), the employee must remain employed with Behrend until 12/31/12. We assume the market price of Behrend's stock was $25/share on 1/01/11, $29/share on 12/31/11, and $28/share on 12/31/12. Behrend estimates that all five employees' SARs will vest. Total compensation is estimated at the end of each year based upon the year-end market value of Behrend's stock. Expense is allocated to the 2-year vesting period 2011 and 2012. Compensation expense of $100,000 is recognized in 2011 through a year-end adjustment (50,000 shares @ $4/share × ½). The $4/share estimated compensation equals the market price at 12/31/11 ($29/share) minus the base price established on 1/01/11, the date of grant ($25/share).

Behrend's 12/31/11 adjustment will affect the financial statements as follows (using the accounting equation format (in 000s)):

ASSETS	=	LIABILITIES		+	SE	
		12/31/11: Year-end adjustment to recognize SARs compensation expense				
		+ Est. SARs Payable	+ 100		+ Comp. Exp.	– 100

The $100,000 estimated SARs payable liability will be classified as current on the 12/31/2011 balance sheet because payment is due within one year.

At 12/31/12 we assume all five participating employees are still employed by Behrend, so that the total actual amount of SARs compensation (and actual cash payment required) is $150,000 (50,000 shares @ $3/share ($3/share = $28/share – $25/share)). The 2012 catch-up adjustment for the change-in estimate results in recognition of only $50,000 of SARs compensation expense in 2012 ($150,000 total compensation expense minus the $100,000 recognized in 2011). The 12/31/12 cash payment will have the following financial statement affects (using the accounting equation format (in 000s)):

		12/31/12: Record SARs cash payment to employees				
Cash	– 150	– Est. SARs Payable	– 100		+ Comp. Exp.	– 50

Since the SARs related cash payment is a form of employee compensation, it is classified as an operating activity in the statement of cash flows.

Accounting for Correction of Errors and Changes in Accounting Principle[25]

The required accounting in cases of error correction and changes in accounting principle is one and the same. They are accounted for retrospectively. Unlike changes in estimate that are accounted for prospectively,

[25] Discussion in this section based upon FASB ASC 250; Original pronouncement: Statement of Financial Accounting Standards No. 154, "Accounting Changes and Error Corrections," FASB 2005, and International Accounting Standard No. 8, "Accounting Policies, Changes in Accounting Estimate and Errors," IASB.

retrospective treatment requires restatement of previously issued financial statements. The cumulative income statement effect for all prior periods requires an adjustment to beginning retained earnings.

Errors include the failure to apply GAAP as well as computational mistakes, omissions, etc. As an example, assume that in 2012 Behrend Corp. discovers that an error was made in its physical inventory count taken for the year ended 12/31/11. Merchandise owned by Behrend with a cost of $1,000,000 that was held on consignment with a vendor was erroneously excluded from the year-end inventory count. As a result of the error, 2011's year-end balance sheet understated inventory by $1,000,000 and their income statement for the year-ended 12/31/11 overstated cost of goods sold by $1,000,000. We will also assume that Behrend is subject to income taxes at a 40% rate, and that the inventory error resulted in a $1,000,000 understatement of 2011's taxable income. Behrend intends to file an amended tax return for 2011 and pay an additional $400,000 in income taxes. During 2012 Behrend will correct the 2011 error as follows (in accounting equation format (in millions)):

ASSETS		=	LIABILITIES		+	SE	
2012—Correct 12/31/11 $1 million inventory understatement (40% tax rate)							
+ Inventory	+ 1.00		+ Inc. Tax Payable	+ .40		+ RE, 1/01/12	+ .60

Note that no income statement effect is recognized in 2012. The 2011 error overstated cost of goods sold by $1,000,000 and understated income tax expense by $400,000. The error's net of tax effect on 2011's net income was an understatement of $600,000. Recall that all income statement accounts are "temporary" accounts that are closed to retained earnings at the end of the year. The closing process caused retained earnings at year-end 12/31/11 (and on 1/01/12) to be understated by $600,000.

Firms present comparative financial statements, which include balance sheets, and income statements for the current year-end and the previous year-end. When issuing its 2012 financial statements, the 2011 comparative amounts must be retrospectively changed to the correct amounts. That is, relative to the amounts included in the originally issued 2011 financial statements, inventory will be increased by $1,000,000 and cost of goods sold will be decreased $1,000,000, and both income tax expense and income tax payable will be increased $400,000. Also, ending retained earnings in the 12/31/11 balance sheet will be increased $600,000 (the increase in 2011 reported net income).

Changes in accounting principle also generally require retrospective accounting treatment.[26] If we assume that in 2012 Behrend changed its method of inventory costing from LIFO to FIFO, they would need to restate all previous period's financial statements. Behrend's 12/31/11 balance sheet will be restated to include the FIFO inventory amount, and 2011's cost of goods sold would be restated based upon the combined effects of beginning and ending inventory restatement from LIFO to FIFO.[27] Retained earnings on 12/31/2011 will be restated for the cumulative income effect (net of tax). Recall that LIFO is not permitted under IFRS. Unless changes in GAAP occur, U.S. firms using LIFO that adopt IFRS in the future will be required to change to another inventory method (e.g., FIFO) and restate previously issued financial statements. IAS No. 1 requires presentation of three balance sheets (for the current year-end and for the two previous year-ends) and two of each of the other statements (e.g., current year-end and previous year-end income statements).[28] Therefore, a calendar year firm changing to IFRS in 2015 will need to provide restated comparative balance sheets on 12/31/15, 12/31/14, and 12/31/13, and two of each of the other financial statements for the years-ended 12/31/15 and 12/31/14.

Prior to 2006, U.S. GAAP required most changes in accounting principle be recognized through presentation in the income statement "below the line" and net of tax in the year of the accounting principle change. This is the same presentation format discussed previously in accounting

---

[26] Particular exceptions to retrospective treatment may be required by GAAP or it may be impractical to determine prior period financial statement amounts. For example, GAAP requires that depreciation method changes be accounted for as changes estimate—prospectively. Also, since it is impractical to determine prior period financial statements amounts, changing to the LIFO inventory method is usually accounted for prospectively.

[27] Recall from chapter 3 that the difference in cost of goods sold equals the change in the LIFO reserve.

[28] International Accounting Standard No. 1, "Presentation of Financial Statements," IASB, par. 39.

for extraordinary items and discontinued operations. In an effort to harmonize GAAP, the FASB issued Statement No. 154 in 2005 (ASC Topic No. 250). U.S. GAAP now requires retrospective treatment of changes in accounting principle, which is consistent with the accounting required under IFRS.

Earnings Per Share[29]

Earnings per share (EPS) is the most common measure of a firm performance cited in the financial press. To accommodate trend analysis, a firm's earnings performance must be stated in standardized terms. Increases/decreases in aggregate reported income (earnings) of a firm from period to period may or may not indicate better/worse earnings performance. For example, assume a firm reported aggregate earnings of $1 million for the previous year, and this year reports earnings of $1.6 million. Looking at the aggregate earnings amounts seems to indicate current year performance better than last year (a 60% increase in earnings). Assume however that on the first day of the current year, the firm doubled the number of shares of stock outstanding from 200,000 to 400,000 (through a large stock issuance). From a stockholder's perspective, the firm's aggregate earnings should have doubled to match last year's performance. EPS provides a standardized measure of earnings performance over time (not only in the past but also forecasted for the future). A simplified measure of EPS indicates the actual decrease in earnings performance from $5/share last year ($1 million/200k shares) to $4/share this year ($1.6 million/400k shares). EPS can also be used in calculating ratios that are useful in making comparisons across firms. Examples of such commonly used ratios include the price to earnings ratio (market price of firm's stock/EPS) and dividend payout ratio (dividends per share/EPS).

Both U.S. GAAP and IFRS require all firms to present "basic" EPS amounts. Depending upon the circumstances, firms may also be required

[29] Discussion of earnings per share is based upon: FASB ASC 260; Original pronouncement: Statement of Financial Accounting Standards No. 128, "Earnings per Share," FASB 1997; and International Accounting Standard No. 33, "Earnings per Share," IASB.

to present "diluted" EPS. Since diluted EPS is computed by using basic EPS as the starting point, basic EPS is discussed first.

Basic EPS

EPS is more appropriately termed earnings per **common** share for firms that have preferred stock in their capital structure. Basic EPS is calculated based upon actual transactions and events that occurred during the period. The formula for computing basic EPS is as follows:

$$\frac{\text{Income Available to Common Stockholders}}{\text{Weighted Average Number of Common Shares Outstanding}}$$

If a firm has preferred stock outstanding, not all of the period's reported income is "available to the common stockholders." Recall that dividends are not recognized as expense on the income statement. Since preferred shareholders have a priority claim to dividends, their claim must be deducted to determine the residual claim of the common stockholders. The numerator (income available to common stockholders (IATCS)) is calculated as:

IATCS = Period's Reported Net Income – Period's Preferred Dividend Requirement

Assuming the preferred stock is cumulative, the preferred dividend requirement is deducted in computing each period's EPS regardless of whether or not declared by the board of directors. The denominator (weighted average number of common shares outstanding (WA#CSO)) is calculated by taking into account changes in the number of common shares outstanding that occurred during the period (e.g., from the purchase and reissuance of treasury stock, etc.).

Consider the following example: Behrend Corp has 10,000 shares of $100 par value cumulative preferred stock outstanding throughout 2012. The annual preferred dividend requirement is $5/share (10,000 shares @ $5/share = $50k) and Behrend reports 2012 net income of $2,100k. Based upon this information we determine the numerator (IATCS) is $2,050k ($2,100k – $50k). Note that dividends declared/paid on common stock (if any) do not enter into the EPS calculation. Regarding the denominator (WA#CSO), assume that Behrend had 1 million shares of common stock outstanding on 1/01/12, issued an additional 100k shares on 4/01/12, and purchased 200k shares of treasury stock on 10/01/12. Based upon this information Behrend had 1,000k shares outstanding for three months (January–March), 1,100k shares outstanding for 6 months (April–September) and had 900k shares outstanding for 3 months (October–December). The denominator (WA#CSO) = 1,025k shares ((1,000k × 3/12) + (1,100k × 6/12) + (900k × 3/12)). Basic EPS is computed as:

Basic EPS = $2,050k/1,025k shares = $2/share

Note that in practice, all reported EPS amounts are rounded to the nearest cent.

In the case of firms reporting below the line items,[30] per share amounts are provided for income from continuing operations, each below the line item, and net income.[31] For example assume from the previous example that Behrend reported net income of $2,100k but actually included income from continuing operations of $3,125k and an extraordinary loss of $1,025k. The following would be reported by Behrend:

		Per Share
Income from Continuing Operations	$3,125K	$3.00
Extraordinary loss	–1,025k	–1.00
Net Income	$2,100k	$2.00

Note that "income from continuing operations" is reduced by the preferred dividend requirement ($50k) for purposes of determining the reported per share amount (($3,125k – $50k)/1,025k shares = $3.00/share). EPS amounts for below the line items are simply the aggregate

[30] Recall that under U.S. GAAP both discontinued operations and extraordinary items are presented on the income statement below the line, whereas only discontinued operations is presented below the line under IFRS.

[31] Only per share amounts for income from continuing operations and net income are required to be presented on the face of the income statement. Per share amounts for below the line items can be disclosed in the notes to the financial statements. However, most firms present separate per share amounts for below the line items directly on the face of the income statement.

amounts presented in the income statement divided by the number of shares per the denominator. Net income per share is the sum of the per share amounts from continuing operations and below the line items ($3/share – $1/share = $2/share).

Stock dividends and stock splits increase in the number of shares outstanding. For EPS amounts to be comparable over time, percentage change in shares outstanding from stock splits/dividends is accounted for retrospectively. Recall that retrospective treatment requires restatement of amounts presented in previously issued financial statements. For example, assume that Behrend issued a two for one stock split in July of 2013. The 100% increase in shares outstanding as a result of the stock split requires restatement of the 2012 EPS amounts initially reported.[32] The following restated 2012 EPS amounts will be provided:

		Per Share
Income from Continuing Operations	$3,125K	$1.50
Extraordinary loss	–1,025k	– .50
Net Income	$2,100k	$1.00

Restated 2012 per share amounts are one half those initially reported. This is the result of retroactively doubling the number of shares in the EPS denominator from 1,025k shares to 2,050k shares. The 2012 numerator amounts initially used for EPS calculations are not changed. If instead of a two for one stock split, Behrend had issued a 25% stock dividend, the denominator would be retroactively increased by 25% from 1,025,000 shares to 1,281,250 shares, and reported EPS from continuing operations would be decreased to $2.40 and an $.80 extraordinary loss per share would be presented. Stock splits and dividends of other sizes would retroactively increase the denominator (number of shares outstanding) the same way as presented for the two for one stock split and the 25% stock dividend.

[32] EPS amounts reported for all periods prior to 2012 would also be retroactively reduced for the 2013 stock split. The 2013 weighted average number of shares calculation would also require doubling the number of shares outstanding for the portion of the year preceding the actual issuance of shares per the stock split.

Diluted EPS

The starting point for determining "diluted" EPS is basic EPS. Unlike basic EPS where only actual transactions and events are used in computations, diluted EPS assumes the issuance of additional shares of common stock that were not actually issued. These are shares of common stock that may be issued in the future in association with "potentially dilutive securities." Issuance of the common shares is assumed for purposes of the diluted EPS calculation only if the effect is a reduction or "dilution" of EPS. Potentially dilutive securities include convertible bonds and convertible preferred stocks that through "conversion" may become common stock in the future, as well as options, warrants, etc., that through "exercise" may become common stock in the future. Through conversion/exercise such securities have the potential to become common stock and in doing so, share in corporate earnings in the future. Therefore diluted EPS is viewed as a forward looking standardized measure of the firm's earnings performance. Although all firms report basic EPS, not all firms report diluted EPS. If a firm has no potentially dilutive securities, or if their assumed conversion/exercise does not reduce EPS, diluted EPS will not be presented.

For purposes of determining if the potentially dilutive security's assumed conversion/exercise has a dilutive effect, the critical measure is "EPS from continuing operations." If assumed conversion/exercise decreases "EPS from continuing operations" it is included in calculating diluted EPS. Therefore, "diluted EPS from continuing operations" (if reported) will always be less than the firm's reported "basic EPS from continuing operations" amount. In situations where the firm has multiple potentially dilutive securities, they are ranked from most dilutive to least dilutive. Each security is incrementally introduced in recalculating "diluted EPS from continuing operations" starting with the one that has the most dilutive effect. The recalculating process continues for each potentially dilutive security unless its assumed conversion/exercise has the effect of increasing "diluted EPS from continuing operations". At that point, the security's assumed conversion/exercise has an "antidilutive" effect. Additional shares of common stock are not assumed to have been issued from conversion/exercise of securities if the effect is antidilutive; so the income statement reports "diluted EPS from continuing operations" calculated in the immediately preceding iteration. Using these calculation procedures, the amount reported as "diluted EPS from continuing operations" provides a worst case scenario.

To illustrate the diluted EPS procedures, we continue from our Behrend basic EPS example. To concentrate on diluted EPS calculations we return to a previous example (before the stock dividend/split complication was introduced). Recall that Behrend reported the following in its 2012 income statement:

		Basic Per Share
Income from Continuing Operations	$3,125K	$3.00
Extraordinary loss	–1,025	–1.00
Net Income	$2,100k	$2.00

Recall that "income from continuing operations" was reduced by the preferred dividend requirement ($50k) to get IATCS and the actual WA#SO during 2012 was 1,025k shares. Basic EPS from continuing operations is calculated as $3.00/share (($3,125k – $50k)/1,025k shares = $3.00/share). We now introduce four potentially dilutive securities: convertible preferred stock, convertible bonds, stock options, and restricted stock. Each will be described in detail with the related EPS implications discussed.

Convertible Preferred Stock

We now assume that the previously discussed preferred stock with the $50k annual dividend requirement was convertible into 100k shares of Behrend Corp. stock at the option of the preferred shareholder. In determining the potential impact of an assumed conversion on EPS, we consider the effects on both the numerator and denominator. Since the preferred stock was outstanding throughout 2012, we assume conversion of the preferred stock and the related assumed issuance of the common stock occurred at the beginning of the year.[33] If conversion occurred

[33] In the case of all potentially dilutive securities, common stock is assumed to be issued at the beginning of the period or the date of issuance or grant of the potentially dilutive security, whichever occurs later. For purposes of our illustration, we assume none of the potentially dilutive securities were issued during 2012, so that all related common stock issuances are assumed to have occurred on 1/01/2012.

on 1/01/2012 the numerator would increase by $50k and denominator would increase by 100k shares. The "incremental effect" on the EPS calculation is calculated by dividing the change in the numerator by the change in the denominator: $50k/100k = $.50/share. Since the incremental effect is less than basic EPS (from continuing operations) $.50/share < $3.00/share, an assumed conversion of the preferred stock will decrease EPS. This can be demonstrated by re-computing EPS with the assumed conversion of the preferred stock: ($3,075k + $50k)/(1,025k + 100k) = $2.78/share. If the preferred stock was the only potentially dilutive security reported diluted EPS from continuing operations would be $2.78.

Convertible Bonds

We assume that Behrend has $2,000k of 8% bonds issued at face value, outstanding all of 2012 and are convertible into 33k shares of common stock. Unlike dividends on preferred stock, interest is tax deductible. Therefore, the after tax impact of assumed conversion is used to adjust the numerator. For purposes of the calculation, we assume that Behrend is subject to income taxes at a 40% rate. If the bonds were converted on 1/01/2012 interest expense would be reduced by $2,000k @ 8% = $160k, but income tax expense would increase by $160k @ 40% = $64k. The change in the numerator, net of tax, is an increase of $96k. The change in the denominator is an increase of 33k common shares. The incremental effect is calculated at $96k/33k = $2.91/share.

Treasury Stock Method

For options, rights, warrants, restricted stock, etc. the impact of assumed exercise on EPS is computed using the treasury stock method. Under the treasury stock method, it is assumed that the firm uses the assumed proceeds from issuance of the stock to simultaneously purchase treasury stock. The assumed proceeds from exercise include the option price (if any), and the employee compensation to be recognized in future periods.[34]

[34] In the case of unqualified plans, there is an additional element of "excess tax benefit." The excess tax benefit component is not discussed.

Recall that employee compensation from stock based-compensation is generally recognized over the vesting period. The assumed proceeds from the exercise of granted but not yet vested plans will include the future compensation expense component.[35] It is assumed the firm purchases the treasury shares at the stock's average market price for the period. Exercise is assumed only if the number of shares to be issued exceeds the number of shares to be purchased for the treasury. In such cases the EPS denominator will increase (the number shares issued exceeds the number of treasury shares acquired). Note, however, that there is no assumed effect upon the EPS numerator. Provided a firm reports positive income from continuing operations, increasing the denominator without changing the numerator will dilute EPS.[36]

Stock Options

We assume that prior to 2012 Behrend had granted qualified stock options to employees to purchase 100k shares of its common stock at $20/share. Assume further that the options are vested and exercisable at 12/31/2012 (no related employee compensation expense will be recognized in future periods), and the average market price of Behrend's stock was $40/share during 2012. Under the treasury stock method we determine that 50k incremental shares are assumed to be issued:

Proceeds from issuance:	$2,000k (100k shares issued @ $20 option price/share)
Number of shares purchased for the treasury	50k ($2,000k/$40 cost/share)
Incremental number of shares	50k (100k issued – 50k purchased for treasury)

The incremental effect of the stock options is $0/share (change in numerator = $0/change in denominator = 50k shares).

[35] IFRS does not include the future compensation expense component in the assumed proceeds from issuance of shares under the treasury stock method. Lower assumed proceeds reduces the number of shares assumed purchased for the treasury by IFRS compliant firms, likely resulting in lower reported diluted EPS amounts.

[36] Note that if the firm reported a loss from continuing operations, exercise would not be assumed because the result would be antidilutive (the loss per share would be reduced).

Restricted Stock

Assume that on 1/01/2012 Behrend granted stock awards to employees to receive 80k shares of Behrend stock at 12/31/14 provided they are still employed by Behrend at 12/31/14. The market value of the stock at 1/01/2012 was $30/share and Behrend estimates all restricted stock will vest. The compensation cost under the plan is $2,400k (80k shares @ $30/share) of which 2/3 will be expensed in 2013 and 2014. Although the option price is $0, there is still $1,600k of assumed proceeds from issuance equal to the employee service to be provided in future periods (the future compensation expense component). Under the treasury stock method we determine that 40k incremental shares are assumed to be issued:

Proceeds from issuance:	$1,600k (compensation expense of future periods)
Number of shares purchased for the treasury	40k ($1,600k/$40 cost/share)
Incremental number of shares	40k (80k issued – 40k purchased for treasury)

The incremental effect of the stock options is $0/share (change in numerator = $0/change in denominator = 40k shares).

Comprehensive Diluted EPS Example

With the incremental effects of each potentially dilutive security calculated we rank them in the order of most dilutive to least dilutive. Since both stock options and restricted stock have an incremental effect of $0/share (change in numerator = $0, change in denominator = 50k shares and 40k shares, respectively) we classify them together and rank them #1. The convertible preferred stock is ranked #2 with the incremental effect of $.50/share, and the convertible bonds are ranked #3 with an incremental effect of 2.91/share. We start with basic EPS (from continuing operations) and adjust the numerator and denominator and re-compute EPS.

First Iteration—assume exercise of stock options and issuance of restricted shares:

($3,075 + $0)/(1,025k + 90k) shares = $3,075/1,115k shares
= $2.76/share

Note that the re-computed EPS exceeds the incremental effect of the next ranked potentially dilutive security—the convertible preferred stock ($2.76/share > $.50/share). Therefore we proceed with the second iteration because the assumed conversion of the preferred stock will dilute EPS.

Second Iteration—assume conversion of the preferred stock:

($3,075 + $50k)/(1,115k + 100k) shares = $3,125k/1,215k shares
= $2.57/share

Note that recomputed EPS is less than the next ranked potentially dilutive security—the convertible bonds ($2.57/share < $2.91/share). Therefore we do not proceed to the third iteration because doing so will increase EPS. Diluted EPS from continuing operations is presented on the income statement at the minimal amount of $2.57/share.[37]

Behrend's 2012 income statement would include the following information:

		EPS Basic	EPS Diluted
Income from Continuing Operations	$3,125k	$3.00	$2.57
Extraordinary loss	−1,025k	−1.00	−.84
Net Income	$2,100k	$2.00	$1.73

Note that the diluted extraordinary loss per share is calculated using the 1,215 weighted average shares assumed outstanding for purposes of calculating diluted EPS from continuing operations. The same 1,215 shares are used to compute net income on a per share basis. Note also that the preferred dividend is not subtracted from net income in computing diluted EPS because the preferred stock was assumed to be converted for diluted EPS computations.

[37] To show this is the case, the third iteration would have assumed conversion of the bonds and EPS would have increased EPS to $2.58: ($3,125k + $96k)/(1,215k + 33k) shares = $3,221/1,248 shares = $2.58/share.

CHAPTER 10

Statement of Cash Flows

Like the income statement and the statement of stockholders' equity, the statement of cash flows (SCF) is for a period of time that concludes at the end of the period balance sheet date. The purpose of the SCF is not to indicate the amount of change in cash,[1] but instead to explain how changes in cash occurred. The presentation in this chapter will concentrate on U.S. GAAP, with relevant differences under IFRS provided as needed.[2]

The SCF presents changes in cash that occurred during the period in three activity categories: 1) operating, 2) investing, and 3) financing. Users place primary emphasis on cash flows from operating activities because a firm's long-term viability is dependent upon its ability to generate sufficient positive net cash flow from its ongoing central operations. Ironically, GAAP does not provide an all-inclusive list of cash flows that are classified as operating activities. Instead GAAP specifically identifies cash flows that constitute investing or financing activities, and any remaining cash flows not specifically identified as investing or financing are by default considered operating activities.

---

[1] The statement of cash flows actually shows changes in cash and "cash equivalents" (discussed in chapter 2). FASB and IASB have tentatively agreed to eliminate the financial statement presentation of "cash equivalents." For this reason and in order to concentrate on the fundamentals of the statement of cash flows, our discussion will be limited exclusively to "cash" flows.

[2] Chapter material is based upon: FASB ASC Topic 230; Original pronouncement: Financial Accounting Standard No. 95, "Statement of Cash Flows," FASB, 1987, and International Accounting Standard No. 7, "Statement of Cash Flows'" IASB.

Investing activities include cash inflows and cash outflows from:

1) purchase and sale of operating assets,
2) purchase and sale of securities of other entities[3] or other investments (e.g., real estate), and
3) loans made to other entities and the collection of principal on those loans.

Financing activities include cash inflows and cash outflows from:

1) issuance and reacquisition of the firm's own stock,
2) issuance of debt and the retirement of debt, and
3) payment of dividends.

Although an all-inclusive list is not provided for operating activities its main cash flow components generally include:

1) collections of cash from sale of goods and services to customers,
2) payments to suppliers,
3) payments to employees and others for operating expenses,
4) payment of income taxes,
5) payment of interest, and
6) dividends and interest received from investment securities.

Theoretically, dividends and interest received on investment securities are considered investing activities, while interest paid on debt is considered a financing activity. However, since U.S. GAAP does not specifically identify these cash flows as investing or financing, they are classified as operating activities in the SCF. Recall from previous discussion that IFRS differs from U.S. GAAP by allowing, but not requiring dividends or interest received and interest paid to be classified as operating activities. IFRS permits firms to present dividends or interest received as investing activities and interest

[3] Recall from chapter 7 that in situations where purchase and sale of trading securities is part of normal ongoing business operations, related cash inflows and outflows are considered operating activities.

paid as a financing activity. IFRS also allows firms to present dividends paid as either an operating or financing activity, whereas U.S. GAAP mandates presentation of dividends paid to be classified as a financing activity.

Recall from chapter 1 that the initial step in formulating the SCF was classifying each transaction affecting cash as an investing, financing, or operating activity. We then formulated the SCF by presenting the major cash inflows and outflows by category (operating, investing, and financing). Investing and financing activities are consistently reported in the SCF by showing the gross amounts of their major cash inflows and outflows. For example, if during the period a firm pays \$250 million to purchase operating assets and receives \$50 million from the sale of operating assets, each should be presented separately, with the purchase shown as an investing cash outflow of \$250 million and the sale shown as an investing cash inflow of \$50 million. The two gross amounts should not be netted to show one \$200 million net cash outflow amount. Although GAAP is consistent in the required format for presenting investing and financing cash flows, two different formats are permitted for presenting operating cash flows. Firms can choose to present operating cash flows under either the "direct" method or the "indirect" method. The direct method is consistent with the presentation format for investing and financing cash flows—the direct method shows all major operating cash inflows and outflows at their gross amounts. We assumed that Behrend used the "direct" method in presenting operating cash flows in our chapter 1 discussion.

Exhibits 10.1 and 10.2 are duplications of Behrend's SCF and income statement for the year ended 12/31/12 from chapter 1 (Exhibits 1.4 and 1.2, respectively). Note that the direct method shows operating cash inflow and outflow amounts that are directly comparable to related income statement amounts. Revenues are associated with cash inflows while expenses are associated with cash outflows. Accrual basis revenues and expenses are presented in the income statement, whereas the related gross operating cash inflow and outflow amounts are presented under the direct method. For example, Behrend reports "cash collected from customers" and "cash paid to suppliers for inventory" amounts in the SCF under the direct method (Exhibit 10.1), that can be compared with the related "net sales revenue" and "cost of goods sold" amounts that appear in the income statement (Exhibit 1.2).

Exhibit 10.1. Behrend Corp. Statement of Cash Flows—Direct Method Year Ended 12/31/2012

Cash Flow from Operating Activities:			
Collected from Customers		$1,890,000	
Paid to Suppliers for Inventory	$1,120,000		
Paid to Employees for Salaries and Wages	600,000		
Paid for Research and Development	55,000		
Interest Paid	50,000		
Income Tax Paid	20,000	<1,845,000>	$45,000
Cash Flow from Investing Activities:			
Cash Paid for Truck			<50,000>
Cash Flow from Financing Activities:			
Cash Received from Stock Issuance		$50,000	
Cash Paid for Dividends	$25,000		
Cash Paid for Debt Principal	100,000	<125,000>	<75,000>
Change in Cash 2012			$ <80,000>
Cash on 1/01/2012			150,000
Cash on 12/31/2012			$70,000

Although both IASB and FASB express a preference for presenting operating cash flows under the direct method, in practice most firms choose the indirect method presentation format.[4] Under both U.S. GAAP and IFRS, firms choosing to apply the direct method must provide supplemental disclosure that reconciles reported net income to the period's cash flow from operations. This mandated disclosure is the same information presented within the operating cash flows section under the indirect method. However, firms that choose to apply the indirect method are not required to provide supplemental disclosure of major gross operating cash inflow and outflow amounts similar to what would have been presented under the direct method. In other

[4] A recent survey indicates that 99% of surveyed firms choose to present operating cash flows under the indirect format; "Accounting Trends and Techniques 2010," AICPA, pg. 533.

Exhibit 10.2. Behrend Corp. Income Statement Year Ended 12/31/2012

Net Sales Revenue		$1,900,000
Cost of Goods Sold		1,000,000
Gross Profit		$900,000
Operating Expenses:		
Selling & General Administrative Expenses:		
Salary and Wage Expense	$610,000	
Research and Development Expense	55,000	
Depreciation Expense	40,000	705,000
Operating Income:		$195,000
Other Revenue, Expense, Gain, and Loss:		
Interest Expense		45,000
Income From Continuing Operations Before Tax		$150,000
Income Tax Expense		30,000
Income From Continuing Operations		$120,000
Extraordinary Loss	$50,000	
Less Tax Benefit	10,000	40,000
Net Income		$ 80,000
Earnings Per Share:		
Income From Continuing Operations		$1.20
Extraordinary Loss		$.40
Net Income		$.80

words, firms choosing the direct method must also apply the indirect method, but firms applying the indirect method do not also have to apply the direct method. This may be the reason why the indirect method is overwhelmingly used in practice—cash flow from operations only needs to be provided once (indirectly, through reconciliation with net income).

Behrend's 2012 SCF under the indirect method format is provided in Exhibit 10.3. Note that the only difference between Exhibits 10.1 and 10.3 is the presentation format used in presenting "Cash Flow from Operating

Exhibit 10.3. Behrend Corp. Statement of Cash Flows—Indirect Method Year Ended 12/31/2012

Cash Flow from Operating Activities:			
Net Income		$80,000	
Addition Adjustments:			
Depreciation Expense	$40,000		
Extraordinary Loss (Gross)	50,000		
Increase in Salaries and Wages Payable	10,000	100,000	
Subtraction Adjustments:			
Increase in Accounts Receivable (Net)	10,000		
Increase in Inventory	100,000		
Decrease in Accounts Payable	20,000		
Decrease in Interest Payable	5,000	<135,000>	$45,000
Cash Flow from Investing Activities:			
Cash Paid for Truck			<50,000>
Cash Flow from Financing Activities:			
Cash Received from Stock Issuance		$50,000	
Cash Paid for Dividends	$25,000		
Cash Paid for Debt Principal	100,000	<125,000>	<75,000>
Change in Cash 2012			$ <80,000>
Cash on 1/01/2012			150,000
Cash on 12/31/2012			$70,000

Activities," which is consistently $45,000. However, the indirect method does not show the particular major gross operating cash inflow and outflow amounts. Instead, net operating cash flow is derived through a reconciliation starting with net income and making addition and subtraction adjustments to arrive at net operating cash flow amount. It is important to note that net cash flow from operations is the same amount regardless of the presentation format used (direct method or indirect method).

Users generally find operating cash flows information provided under the direct method to be more useful for decision making because it allows direct comparisons of income statement amounts with the related gross amounts of operating cash inflow and outflow.[5] Since most firms do not provide operating cash flow information under the direct method, users commonly try to approximate the major gross operating cash inflow and outflow amounts by using information provided elsewhere in the financial statements (including the information provided under indirect method). The concepts and procedures applied in approximating gross cash inflow and outflow amounts are similar across all three cash flow categories. Because of this similarity, we initially discuss how financial statement information is used to derive gross financing and investing cash flow amounts (even though they are presented as such in the SCF). With this background knowledge, we then discuss concepts and procedures actually applied in practice to approximate gross operating cash inflow and outflow amounts.

Throughout our analysis we apply the accounting equation in noting the offsetting effects that must be associated with inflows and outflows of cash. Consider the following derivation from the accounting equation:

ASSETS = LIABILITIES + OWNERS' EQUITY,

And since cash is an asset:

CASH + NONCASH ASSETS = LIABILITIES + OWNERS' EQUITY,

And since every transaction or event affects two or more accounts in double entry accounting:

CHANGE IN CASH + CHANGE IN NONCASH ASSETS = CHANGE IN LIABILITIES + CHANGE IN EQUITY

With this derived balance sheet equation, we consider the effects that changes in noncash assets, liabilities, and owners' equity accounts may have upon cash (i.e., cash inflows and outflows).[6] Cash inflows are associated with increases in liabilities or equity, and decreases in noncash assets.

[5] Both FASB and IASB agree that the direct method provides more useful information. Although not current GAAP, they have tentatively agreed to require operating cash flow presentation exclusively under the direct method sometime in the future.

[6] Changes in noncash balance sheet items can be offset by changes in other noncash items rather than affecting cash. Noncash investing/financing activities are discussed later.

Cash outflows are associated with decreases in liabilities or equity, and increases in noncash assets.

Financing Activities

Note that cash flows from financing activities are generally related to changes in liability and equity accounts as indicated in the following examples:

a) The firm increases equity through the issuance of stock for cash: the increase in equity on the right side of the equation is offset with the increase in cash on the left side (cash inflow),
b) The firm issues debt for cash: the increase in liabilities on the right side of the equation is offset by the increase in cash on the left side (cash inflow),
c) The firm declares and pays a cash dividend: the decrease in equity on the right side of the equation is offset with the decrease in cash on the left side (cash outflow).

Investing Activities

Note that cash flows from investing activities are generally related to changes in noncash asset accounts as indicated in the following examples:

a) The firm purchases equipment for cash: the increase in noncash assets on the left side of the equation is offset by the decrease in cash, also on the left side,
b) The firm collects principal due on a maturing bond investment: the decrease in noncash assets on the left side of the equation is offset by the increase in cash, also on the left side.
c) The firm sells investments or operating assets at a gain or loss: The decrease in noncash assets on the left side of the equation plus gain or minus loss recognized[7] equals the increase in cash, on the left side.

[7] Gain or loss on sale increases or decreases owners' equity, respectively, on the right side of the accounting equation.

Operating Activities

Because of its common use in practice, we initially discuss the indirect method and the common reconciling items needed when reconciling net income to cash flow from operations. We then discuss procedures commonly applied in formulating an approximation of major gross operating cash inflows and outflows that would be provided under the direct method. An understanding of the indirect method is useful to comprehending these procedures. To accommodate discussion, we assume that Behrend experienced the same 2012 transactions and events as were discussed in chapter 1. Exhibit 10.4 provides comparable balance sheet information for Behrend on 12/31/11 and 12/31/12 with the amount of change in each item that occurred during 2012,

Exhibit 10.4. Behrend Corp. Comparative Balance Sheet Information 12/31/2011 and 12/31/2012

Assets:	12/31/2011	12/31/2012	Change
Current Assets:			
Cash and Cash Equivalents	$150,000	$70,000	$–80,000
Accounts Receivable	140,000	150,000	+10,000
Inventory	250,000	350,000	+100,000
Long-Term Assets:			
Operating Assets (Net)	400,000	360,000	–40,000
Total Assets	$940,000	$930,000	$–10,000
Liabilities			
Current Liabilities:			
Accounts Payable	$100,000	$80,000	$–20,000
Debt Currently Due	100,000	-0-	–100,000
Salaries and Wages Payable	50,000	60,000	+10,000
Interest Payable	25,000	20,000	–5,000
Long-Term Liabilities:			
Long-Term Debt	400,000	400,000	-0-
Stockholders' Equity:			
Paid-in Capital	100,000	150,000	+50,000
Retained Earnings	165,000	220,000	+55,000
Total Liabilities and Stockholders' Equity	$940,000	$930,000	$–10,000

Exhibit 10.5. Behrend Corp. Statement of Stockholders' Equity Year Ended 12/31/2012

	Paid-in capital	Retained earnings	Total stockholders' equity
Beginning of Year 12/31/2011	$100,000	$165,000	$265,000
Issued Stock	50,000		50,000
Net Income 2012		80,000	80,000
Dividends	______	<25,000>	<25,000>
End of Year 12/31/2012	$150,000	$220,000	$370,000

and Exhibit 10.5 is Behrend's 2012 statement of stockholders' equity.[8] All information contained in Exhibits 10.1–10.5 was derived from the chapter 1 exhibits.

Operating Cash Flows—The Indirect Method

As we discussed many times previously, a firm's income and net cash flow (excluding contributions from and distributions to owners) are equal in the long run. The period of income statement recognition of revenue or expense under the accrual basis of accounting may differ from the period of related cash receipt or cash payment, but they are equal in the long run. These concepts are the underpinnings of the indirect method. Under the indirect method we start with a firm's net income under the assumption that revenues and expenses recognized in the period's income statement were also collected or paid in cash during the period. Stated differently, we initially assume that revenues = cash inflows and expenses = cash outflows of the period. If information indicates that assumption is incorrect, an addition or subtraction adjustment is made in order to reconcile

[8] Although we do not directly refer to Exhibit 10.5 in the text, it is provided to illustrate the source of financing cash flow information ($50k inflow from the issuance of common stock, and $25k outflow for the payment of dividends).

net income to the amount of net operating cash flow of the period. The following reconciliation schedule provides typical reconciling items when applying the indirect method:

Net Income (Starting Point)

Addition adjustments:

1) depreciation, amortization and depletion expense;
2) increases in liabilities from operating activities;
3) decreases in noncash assets from operating activities; and
4) losses on sale of operating assets or investment securities, or from retirement of debt.

Subtraction adjustments:

5) decreases in liabilities from operating activities;
6) Increases in noncash assets from operating activities; and
7) gains on sale of operating assets or investment securities, or from retirement of debt.

Net Operating Cash Flow (End Point)

Keep in mind that under the indirect method we start at net income with the intention to eventually arrive at net operating cash flow. If a particular reconciling item causes net operating cash flow to be larger than net income, it requires an addition adjustment, whereas items that cause net operating cash flow to be less than net income require subtraction adjustments.

Depreciation, amortization, and depletion (items included in 1), above) require no cash outflow. Expense recognition may be required for these items under the accrual basis of accounting (reducing reported net income), but there was no associated cash outflow. Recognition of depreciation, amortization, or depletion expense causes net operating cash flow to exceed reported net income. Therefore, these expense items require addition adjustments in determining net operating cash flow under the indirect method.

Items 2), 3), 5), and 6) all relate to changes in noncash assets and liabilities that occurred during the period from operating activities. Recall that operating activities include all activities not specifically defined as investing or financing activities. Because of their conceptual similarity, these four items are discussed as one. These items relate directly to differences between the accrual basis and the cash basis of accounting. Consider the following operating activity examples:

a) Accounts receivable at the end of the period is less than accounts receivable at the beginning of the period: the decrease in the noncash asset on the left side of the equation is offset by an increase in cash, also on the left side. Recall that under the accrual basis, sales on account are recognized by increasing both sales revenue and accounts receivable in the period when goods or services are provided to the customer regardless of when the cash is received. Recall also that cash collections from customers decrease accounts receivable. A decrease in accounts receivable indicates that cash collected from customers exceeds the amount of sales revenue recognized in the income statement. Holding all else constant, net operating cash flow exceeds reported net income, so an addition reconciliation adjustment is needed,
b) Salaries and wages payable at the end of the period are higher than salaries and wages payable at the beginning of the period: the liability increase on the right side of the equation is offset by an increase in cash on the left side. Recall that under the accrual basis, salaries and wages expense is recognized in the period employees provide service regardless of when they are paid. An increase in salaries and wages payable indicates that the amount of cash paid for salaries and wages during the period is less than the amount of salaries and wages expense that was recognized in the income statement. Holding all else constant net operating cash flow exceeds reported net income, so an addition reconciliation adjustment is needed, and
c) Interest payable is less at the end of the period than it was at the beginning of the period: the decrease in the liability on the right side of the equation is offset by a decrease in cash on the left side. Recall that under the accrual basis, interest expense is recognized in the period incurred regardless of when the cash is paid. A decrease in interest payable indicates that the amount of cash paid for interest during the period exceeds the amount of interest expense recognized in the income statement. Holding all else constant, net operating

cash flow is less than reported net income, so a subtraction reconciliation adjustment is needed.

Items 4) and 7) involve investing and financing activities that are reported in net income as gain or loss. When the sale of an asset is considered to be an investing activity, the entire proceeds from the sale should be included exclusively within the investing activities section. When the retirement of debt is considered to be a financing activity, the entire amount paid to retire the debt should be included exclusively within the financing activity section. These reconciliation adjustments simply add back such losses and subtract such gains that are recognized in net income but are not properly classified as operating cash flows.

The following summarizes the indirect method. Net operating cash flow is presented through a reconciliation schedule that starts with net income or net loss under the assumption that revenues and expenses recognized in net income under the accrual basis are equal to their related cash inflows and outflows, respectively. In terms of the accounting equation analysis, net income or net loss increases or decreases equity (retained earnings) on the right side of the equation, which is offset by the assumed increase or decrease in cash on the left side. If there are no changes in noncash assets or liability accounts relating to operating activities, and no gains or losses requiring reclassification as investing or financing activities, reported net income or net loss will be equal to net operating cash flow. If that is not the case, addition and subtraction reconciliation adjustments are required. Addition adjustments indicate that net operating cash flow > net income. This is explained by the following three reasons:

A) cash inflow > related revenue,
B) cash outflow < related expense, or
C) losses are recognized in net income, that are appropriately considered investing or financing activities (item 4 above) and should be classified as such.

Subtraction adjustments under the indirect method indicate that net operating cash flow < net income. This is due to one of the following reasons:

A) cash inflow < related revenue,
B) cash outflow > related expense, or

C) gains are recognized in net income, that are appropriately considered investing or financing activities (item 7 above) and should be reclassified as such.

Using the Behrend Corp. information from chapter 1 we derive net operating cash flow under the indirect method that is illustrated in Exhibit 10.3. Each of the following addition reconciliation adjustments is made because it causes net operating cash flow to exceed net income. Addition reconciliation adjustments are made as follows:

1) Depreciation expense of $40k (Exhibit 10.2) is added back because there is no related cash outflow;
2) The gross extraordinary loss of $50k (Exhibit 10.2) is added back to determine net operating cash flow because disposals of long-term operating assets are considered investing activities (normally resulting in an investing cash inflow; however, recall that this loss was uninsured, so that no related investing cash flow appears in the SCF); and
3) The $10k increase in salaries payable (Exhibit 10.4) indicates net operating cash flow exceeds net income because less cash was paid for salaries and wages during the period than was recognized as expense in the income statement.

Subtraction reconciliation adjustments are made because net operating cash flow is less than reported net income for the following reasons:

1) The $10k increase in accounts receivable (Exhibit 10.4) indicates that cash collected from customers was less than sales revenue recognized in the income statement.
2) Both the $100k increase in inventory and the $20k decrease in accounts payable (Exhibit 10.4) indicate that the amount of cash paid to suppliers for inventory exceeds cost of goods sold expense recognized under the accrual basis by a combined $120k (this is discussed more fully below under the direct method).
3) The $5k decrease in interest payable (Exhibit 10.4) indicates that the amount of cash paid for interest exceeds the amount of interest expense recognized under the accrual basis.

Operating Cash Flows—The Direct Method

As indicated previously, most firms do not provide gross operating cash inflow and outflow amounts in the SCF because they choose the indirect presentation format. However, since this information is useful for financial analysis, users typically estimate the direct method amounts by using information provided elsewhere in the financial statements. In estimating each item, the starting point is the amount of revenue or expense reported in the income statement. Next, by analyzing changes in related balance sheet accounts and other financial statement information, addition and subtraction adjustments are made in an attempt to approximate the related gross operating cash inflow or outflow amount. Much of the underlying rationale for this adjustment process was discussed previously. Using the Behrend Corp. example from chapter 1, the accrual-based revenue and expense items versus their direct cash flow equivalents are as follows:

Income Statement Item	Operating Cash Flow Item
Net Sales revenue	Cash collected from customers
Cost of goods sold	Cash paid to suppliers for purchases
Salary and wage expense	Cash paid to employees for services
Research and development expense	Cash paid for research and development
Depreciation expense	Zero—Depreciation requires no cash outflow
Interest expense	Cash paid for interest
Income tax expense	Cash paid for income taxes
Extraordinary loss	Reclassified—Not an operating cash flow item

Note that since the extraordinary loss is appropriately classified as an investing activity, it is not included among the individual component amounts of operating cash inflow or outflow.[9]

[9] However, the tax benefit that reduces the reported extraordinary loss is relevant for purposes of determining cash paid for income taxes (discussed below).

As an illustrative example of how the individual gross amounts of operating cash inflows and outflows are derived, we start with each accrual based income statement amount provided in Exhibit 10.2. Through analysis of related information provided elsewhere in the financial statements (primarily changes in related balance sheet accounts from Exhibit 10.4), we derive the gross operating cash inflow and outflow amounts presented under the direct method in Exhibit 10.1. Note that this exercise is intended to familiarize you with the common procedures used in deriving gross operating cash flow amounts. This is not intended as an all-inclusive prescriptive reference to be used to calculate gross operating cash inflow and outflow amounts under any and all circumstances. With a basic understanding of the underlying concepts and procedures, you should be able to make the appropriate adjustments when the circumstances are not identical to the Behrend example used here.

Sales revenue reported in the income statement is $1,900k.[10] The related balance sheet account in our example is accounts receivable. Holding all else constant, if there was no change in accounts receivable during the year, the amount of cash collected from customers would equal the amount of sales revenue recognized in the income statement. An increase/decrease in accounts receivable indicates less/more cash was collected from customers during the period than was recognized as sales revenue in the income statement.[11] Since accounts receivable increased by $10k during 2012, cash collected from customers is $10k less than the $1,900k of sales revenue reported in the income statement. Cash collected from customers equals $1,890K. The following schedule reconciles sales revenue with cash collected from customers:

Sales revenue	$1,900k
Subtract increase in accounts receivable	10k
Cash collected from customers	$1,890k

[10] In the case of sales returns, allowances, and/or discounts, net sales would be reported in the income statement and used for purposes of determining cash collections from customers.

[11] Our simplified example does not include complications related to accounting for bad debts. In practice, cash collected from customers is calculated as: (net sales revenue – bad debt expense) + decrease, or – increase in accounts receivable (net).

Note that in addition to accounts receivable, "unearned sales revenue" is another balance sheet account related to differences in sales revenue recognized under the accrual versus cash basis. Any change in the balance sheet liability "unearned sales revenue" needs to be considered in reconciling sales revenue reported in the income statement with cash collected from customers. Any increase/decrease in unearned sales revenue would require an addition/subtraction adjustment in determining cash collected from customers. Since Behrend has no unearned sales revenue in its comparative balance sheets, no adjustment is required in our example.

Before discussing individual expense items, it is important to note that for expenses under the direct method we are reconciling to the gross cash **outflow** amounts, whereas under the indirect method, we were reconciling to the overall net (positive) operating cash flow amount. Since higher or lower individual gross cash outflows have the opposite effect upon net cash flow (i.e., the larger the gross cash outflow, the lower the net cash flow, and vice versa), the expense related adjustments made under the direct method are the opposite of those made under the indirect method. That is, for expense items and related cash flows, addition/subtraction adjustments made under the indirect method will be the opposite under the direct method (subtraction/addition adjustments, respectively). Adjustments for revenues and their related cash inflows are consistent under the direct and indirect methods because the higher or lower the individual cash inflow amount, the higher or lower the net operating cash flow amount. Therefore, in the case of revenues and their related cash inflows, the addition and subtraction adjustments under the direct method are consistent with adjustments under the indirect method.

Cost of goods sold reported in the income statement is $1,000k. There are two balance sheet accounts related to cost of goods sold: inventory (a noncash asset account), and accounts payable (a liability account).[12] Determining cash paid to suppliers for inventory involves a two-step process. The first step starts with cost of goods sold and adds/subtracts

[12] For manufacturers, recall that cost of goods sold includes three components: direct material, direct labor, and manufacturing overhead (including depreciation), so there are numerous other related balance sheet accounts. Consistent with previous chapters, our discussion here is simplified by exclusively considering merchandisers.

any change in inventory to determine the amount of purchases made during the period. The second step determines cash paid to suppliers for inventory by adding/subtracting any decrease/increase in accounts payable that occurred during the period from the amount of purchases determined in the first step. The following schedule reconciles cost of goods sold to cash paid to suppliers for inventory:

Cost of goods sold	$1,000k
Add increase in inventory	100k
Purchases	$1,100k
Add decrease in accounts payable	20k
Cash paid to suppliers for inventory	$1,120k

To determine cash paid to employees for salaries and wages, any increase/decrease in the liability account "salaries and wages payable" must be subtracted/added in determining the related cash outflow amount. Since salaries and wages payable increased $10k during 2012, cash paid for salaries and wages is $10k less than the accrual-based $610k of salaries and wage expense from the income statement. Cash paid for salaries and wages is $600k as provided in the following schedule:

Salary and Wage expense	$610k
Subtract increase in Salaries and Wages Payable	10k
Cash paid for salaries and wages	$600k

In cases of employees being paid in advance of providing services, a related balance sheet asset account "prepaid salaries and wages" would need to be considered in reconciling the income statement expense amount to the cash outflow amount. Any increase or decrease in prepaid salaries and wages must be added or subtracted, respectively in determining the amount of cash paid for salaries and wages.

Research and development (R&D) expense of $55k is recognized in the income statement. Since there aren't any balance sheet accounts specifically related R&D, we assume that accrual basis R&D expense equals the amount of cash paid for R&D during 2012. However, note that there could be immaterial amounts included in accounts payable, salaries and wages payable, etc. that are related to research and development rather than being related to cost of goods sold, etc. Without more detailed specific information, only approximations of the actual gross operating cash inflow and outflow amounts that would be presented under the direct method can be derived from this process.

As discussed previously, depreciation requires no cash outflow. As such, depreciation (or amortization or depletion) does not appear at all in the operating section of the SCF under the direct method presentation format.[13]

The income statement includes $45k of interest expense recognized under the accrual basis. However, the $5k reduction in the related balance sheet account "interest payable" indicates that more than $45k was paid for interest during 2012. In determining cash paid for interest, the $5k reduction in interest payable is added to interest expense of $45k to arrive at cash paid for interest in the amount of $50k. The following schedule reconciles interest expense with cash paid for interest:

Interest expense	$45k
Add decrease in interest payable	5k
Cash paid for interest	$50k

Recall from chapter 5 that debt issued with an effective rate that differs from its stated rate results in recognizing more or less interest expense than the amount of interest paid, with the difference resulting in discount or premium amortization. Interest expense is computed under the effective interest method, whereas the amounts and timing of interest payments are based upon the stated rate, face value, and interest payment dates as specified on the debt instrument. Amortization of bond discount requires a subtraction adjustment, whereas amortization of bond premium requires an addition adjustment in calculating the amount of cash interest paid.[14]

[13] Likewise, bad debt expense has no related cash outflow, and as such does not appear under the direct presentation format.

[14] Similar adjustments would be required for the investor when determining cash received from interest relative to the amount of interest revenue recognized in the income statement. Changes in the interest receivable account and changes in the debt security investment account from amortization of premium or discount under the effective interest method would both require reconciliation adjustments.

The income statement recognizes income tax expense of $30k. However, intraperiod income tax allocation requires that all "below the line" items be presented net of tax. Therefore, Behrend's gross extraordinary loss of $50k is presented at $40k in the income statement (net of the associated tax benefit of $10k). This indicates that the amount of cash Behrend paid for taxes in 2012 is actually $10k less than the $30k income tax expense reported in the income statement. Cash paid for income taxes under the direct method is estimated at $20k. The following schedule reconciles income tax expense with cash paid for income taxes:

Income tax expense	$30k
Subtract tax benefit from extraordinary loss	10k
Cash paid for income taxes	$20k

Additional adjustments would be required in cases of changes in related balance sheet items such as income taxes currently payable and deferred income taxes. Increases or decreases in income taxes payable would be subtraction or addition adjustments, respectively in estimating the amount of cash paid for income taxes during the period. Also recall from our discussion of deferred income taxes in chapter 8 that income tax expense on the income statement includes the effects of changes in deferred tax assets and deferred tax liabilities. Changes in the net deferred tax position (deferred tax assets net of deferred tax liabilities) affecting the period's income tax expense would require an addition or subtraction adjustment in estimating the amount of cash paid during the period for income tax. For example, an increase/decrease in the net deferred tax asset position would require an addition/subtraction adjustment, whereas an increase/decrease in a deferred tax liability position would require a subtraction/addition adjustment in approximating the amount of cash paid for income taxes during the period. Since Behrend doesn't report any income taxes payable or deferred tax assets or liabilities on its balance sheet, these adjustments are not required in our example.

Additional SCF Issues

As discussed previously, more flexibility is permitted under IFRS regarding the classification of interest and dividends within the SCF. Another difference between U.S. GAAP and IFRS relates to the reporting income taxes paid within the SCF. Whereas U.S. GAAP requires all income taxes paid to be presented as an operating activity, IFRS requires any significant tax effects associated with investing and financing activities to be presented within these SCF categories. For example, assume that a firm subject to a tax rate of 40% sells an investment with a cost of $20 million for $30 million cash. Assume also that the gain increased the amount of income taxes paid during the period by $4 mil ((30 million – 20 million) × 40%). U.S. GAAP requires the gross receipt of $30 million from the sale of the investment to be classified as an investing cash inflow, and the $4 million of taxes paid be classified as an operating cash outflow. IFRS instead requires that the tax effects from this investing activity be excluded from operating cash flows, and that the SCF include an investing cash inflow of $26 million, the net of tax proceeds from sale.

Changes in noncash balance sheet items may be offset by changes in other noncash balance sheet items without affecting cash. Any such items that constitute noncash financing and/or investing activities are not presented in the SCF because there is no resulting cash inflow or cash outflow. However, significant noncash transactions must be disclosed in the notes or elsewhere in the financial statements. Examples of noncash investing and/or financing activities include acquisition of operating assets by issuing debt, a lessee entering into a capital lease (recall that the lessee recognizes equal amounts for the leased asset and the lease related obligation at the inception of a capital lease), and convertible bondholders exchanging their debt instruments for shares of the firm's common stock.

As mentioned previously, most firms apply the indirect method in presenting operating cash flows and therefore do not provide gross operating cash inflow and outflow amounts on the face of the SCF. However, all firms must disclose the amount of cash paid for interest and the amount of cash paid for income taxes either in the financial statement notes or elsewhere in the financial statements.

Index

OTHER TITLES IN OUR FINANCIAL ACCOUNTING AND AUDITING COLLECTION

Collection Editors: **Scott Showalter and Jan Williams**

- *An Executive's Guide for Moving From U.S. GAAP to IFRS* by Peter Walton
- *Effective Financial Management: The Cornerstone for Success* by Geoff Turner

And

MANAGERIAL ACCOUNTING COLLECTION

Collection Editor: **Kenneth A. Merchant**

- *Breakeven Analysis: The Definitive Guide to Cost-Volume Profit Analysis* by Michael Cafferky and Jon Wentworth
- *Corporate Investment Decisions: Principles and Practice* by Michael Pogue
- *Drivers of Successful Controllership: Activities, People and Connecting with Management* by Juergen Weber and Pascal Nevries
- *Revenue Management: A Path to Increased Profits* by Ronald J. Huefner
- *Working Capital Management: Principles and Practices* by Michael Pogue